Multivariate Analysis
In Educational Research

Multivariate Analysis
In Educational Research

**Applications of the
MULTIVARIANCE Program**

Jeremy D. Finn

Ingrid Mattsson

National Educational Resources
Chicago

Front cover: Public School No. 1, Dunkirk, New York, 1860
Back cover: Seating plan for Dunkirk School

International Standard Book Number: 0-89498-001-7
Library of Congress Catalog Card Number: 1028.F46

Distributed exclusively by:

International Educational Services
1525 East 53rd Street, Room 829
Chicago, Illinois 60615

This book has been typeset entirely by computer by TEXET of Chicago.

Contents

PREFACE

In this monograph we present four actual data sets from ongoing research, and discuss in detail how each might be analyzed. There are the inevitable problems of the unreliability of measures, of incomplete data, and of the uncertainty about which variables represent "causes" and which the "effects." We attempt to deal with these problems realistically.

We first describe the research problem that gave rise to each data set. We then discuss in turn the analysis problem presented by the data set, the statistical model that might be employed to solve the problem, the computer set-up based on the model, and the interpretation of the results of the computer run. Because these are real data sets, the analyses are not oversimplified. They demonstrate, in their full complexity, a variety of analysis models that are, or should be, widely employed in educational research. In sections of each chapter entitled "Special Considerations Required by the Data Set," we concentrate on problems such as unequal N's and empty cells in analysis-of-variance designs, ordered dependent variables, trend analysis in longitudinal data, and others.

This is not a statistical text on multivariate analysis and readers may refer for theory and the formulas to Finn (1974), Bock (1975), Tatsuoka (1971), Morrison (1967), or Anderson (1958). It is instead a compendium of studies which systematically demonstrates the application of the general multivariate model to educational data. Employing the general model releases us from many of the restrictions of the specific forms (for example, the restriction of equal N's in analysis-of-variance designs) or the artificial assumptions of the mixed-model analysis of repeated-measures problems ("within- and between-subjects analysis"). In particular, through application of the general model, the repeated-measures analysis is more correct and more efficient than common analysis procedures. This topic has received little attention in the literature and is given two chapters here for that reason.

All of the analyses have been executed using the MULTIVARIANCE computer program (Finn, 1976), and the input data and output listings, edited slightly, are reproduced in the manuscript. We hope that this will make the discussions concrete by relating any abstractions to the ultimate in practicality: the question of how to do the analysis (or, in this case, how to make the computer do it for us!). It also enables us to discuss the actual printed results for their statistical and interpretive meaning. The discussion here may be compared with those of Bettman (1971), Finn (1972), Harrison (1969), and Purves (1973) as examples of how multivariate results may be succinctly communicated.

This monograph represents the substance of a lecture series on applications of the MULTIVARIANCE program given at the University of Stockholm in the autumn of 1973 and sponsored by the Swedish Council for Social Science Research. The help of Mrs. Diane Setchell and Mrs. Zenia Hellström in the preparation of the manuscript is gratefully acknowledged. Leon Gross assisted in preparing the computer runs of the sample problems.

This document would not have been completed or even begun, however, without the support of the Spencer Foundation, which provided the research fellowship and thus the time for the first of us to participate in the project. Ingrid Mattsson's participation was supported by the Swedish Council for Social Science Research.

At many points the discussion assumes familiarity with the MULTIVARIANCE program and *User's Guide*. They may be obtained from International Educational Services, 1525 East 53rd Street, Chicago, Illinois 60615, the nonprofit organization which distributes the program.

JEREMY D. FINN

INGRID MATTSSON

1

INTRODUCTION

In this text we are concerned with the analysis of data that arise when the outcome of an experiment or comparative study is described by one or more quantitative measures. This is a common characteristic of most research in education, and much of behavioral research generally, and requires the use of statistical models that assume multiple dependent variables. We refer to such data and models as *multivariate*.

1.1 MULTIVARIATE DATA

At times we are uncertain of the definition of a construct and need multiple measures to assure that we have captured its meaning—to assure "referent generality" (Snow, 1974). At other times we are certain of the multiple aspects of an outcome that we wish to study jointly—for example, speed *and* power on an achievement test, cognitive *and* affective outcomes of a school course, or even cognitive processes at multiple levels of complexity (Bloom, 1956). In either case, it may not be appropriate to use a sum or weighted sum of the scores as a single "total" score. Important variation in the individual scales might be lost as a result. Neither would it be appropriate to analyze each scale separately. To do so would maximize statistical errors of the first kind and would minimize the replicability of the findings. The use of multivariate statistical analysis which treats the data as a whole, with appropriate consideration of the correlations among measures, avoids these difficulties.

A special type of multivariate data arises in the so-called "repeated-measures" situation, which occurs when we measure the same subjects *on the same scale* at more than one point in time. Repeated measures data are exemplified by pre- and post-test studies, and by experiments with "each subject as his own control." In this situation we not only have multiple observations of each subject, but we are also interested in trends among the measures—i.e., differences over time, or differences from one experimental condition to another. Multivariate methods enable us to analyze these trends and differences without the restrictive and often unrealistic assumptions of univariate analysis of variance.

Because the techniques of multivariate analysis treat the data as related aspects of a single response, it is desirable that the measures form a set that is conceptually meaningful. This desideratum can only be evaluated by the researcher. Does the set of measures "hang together?" Does it make sense to talk about individuals or groups being different with respect to the set of outcomes? Are the outcomes closely related, logically and theoretically? These questions become especially important when the time comes to interpret the output of multivariate programs.

The question of a "meaningful set" is conceptual and not a statistical question. To be meaningful, it is not sufficient that the set of variables be positively intercorrelated. Virtually all behavioral measures are so correlated. Thus, a finding that attitudes toward mathematics and reading speed are positively correlated is not a rationale for applying multivariate models to the two outcomes. The question is instead whether the two are logically part of the same response being studied, irrespective of whether the correlation is positive, zero, or negative. The advantage of multivariate models is that if conceptually-related measures are intercorrelated or

1

have different variances, the statistical analysis is not invalidated. Indeed, multivariate analysis of variance and regression assumes that there will be some (any) arbitrary set of variances and intercorrelations of the dependent variables. These are assumed in the model, estimated from the data, and used as an important part of the computation and inference.

1.2 MULTIVARIATE MODELS

The statistical analyses discussed in this monograph, and those performed by the MULTIVARIANCE program, may be classified by the number of *dependent* (criterion) variables. When there is a single dependent variable, the model and analysis are *univariate*. When there is more than one dependent variable, they are *multivariate*.

The number and type of *independent* variables, or antecedents, provide a further classification. In general, the independent variables are either scores on some behavioral measures (e.g., intelligence, age, or attitude) or else nominal (qualitative) variables defining a distinct group of subjects to which each person belongs (e.g., grade level, treatment group).

When the independent variables are measured (quantitative) scores, the analysis is termed *regression analysis* and the independent variables called *predictors*. A regression model with one predictor variable is the simple regression model; more than one predictor variable comprises the multiple regression model.

If the independent variables are defined by subjects belonging to distinct groups, the analysis is termed *analysis of variance*, and each independent variable is a *factor*. If there is one variable distinguishing groups, the model is a one-way or one-factor analysis-of-variance model. When there is more than one design factor, the model is the two-way or multi-way analysis-of-variance model. Each factor has two or more *levels* or values (e.g., sex has 2 levels, while grade may have anywhere between 2 and 13 levels).

When we have both quantitative independent variables, as well as qualitative group-membership independent variables, the model is that of *analysis of covariance*. In this case, the quantitative independent variables are usually termed *covariates* rather than predictor variables. With computer programs for analysis-of-covariance computations we have no need to categorize subjects on well-measured variables, e.g., no need to classify IQ scores into high, medium, or low. Instead we may perform the analysis on the data as we have collected them.

2

PREDICTING SCIENCE ACHIEVEMENT: UNIVARIATE AND MULTIVARIATE MULTIPLE REGRESSION ANALYSIS

Recent studies such as the Coleman report (Coleman et al., 1966), the studies of the International Association for the Evaluation of Educational Achievement (IEA) (Comber and Keeves, 1973; Purves, 1973; Thorndike, 1973), and the Jencks report (Jencks et al., 1972) have raised questions as to whether schools have any effect upon pupil achievement or on later occupational status and income. Research that distinguishes between various types of school achievement (of which the IEA studies are perhaps the best example) has shown that the effects of schooling depend on the *type of outcome* being studied. School achievement that is highly dependent on verbal ability and verbal skills, formed primarily in the home and primarily in the early years, is not easily influenced by teacher, classroom, and school factors. On the other hand, subject areas that are not introduced in the home, or not introduced as often, are more likely to be affected by the school and its curriculum. Among these areas are science and mathematics. The present study is an attempt to discover some of the antecedents of science achievement.

Concepts taught in science, to a greater extent than in mathematics, have a large verbal component, but are at the same time dependent upon mathematical and spatial skills. Thus, in focusing on science achievement as an outcome variable, our first consideration is to control for verbal abilities developed outside of school. Only then are we willing to attribute variation in science achievement to school and school-related factors.

2.1 THE VARIABLES

The dependent variables of this study are scores on the science achievement test developed by the IEA. Although this test was administered to 14-year-old children in a number of countries, we focus here only upon the Swedish sample. For purposes of comparison, the data will be analyzed by both univariate and multivariate methods. In the first analysis, the *total* science test score is employed as the single dependent variable. In the second analysis, four *subtest* scores of the science achievement test (biology, chemistry, physics, practical) are treated as four simultaneous dependent variables.

The independent variables in the analysis include, first, a measure of verbal ability (primarily a control variable) and, second, a measure of the effort that the child spends in learning science concepts, namely the amount of homework that he does, primarily in response to teacher assignments. The third and fourth independent variables, and the ones of greatest concern to us, measure the pupil's interest in science. We wish to investigate the extent to which motivational factors such as interest affect the pupil's science performance above and beyond his basic verbal skills and the effort he expends. The two measures of interest in the IEA data are (1) a score measuring "interest in science" and (2) a score assessing the student's view of the "importance of science" in the world.

3

To summarize, in both analyses the four independent variables are

$x_1 = $ Verbal ability or word knowledge

$x_2 = $ The amount of homework performed by the child

$x_3 = $ Interest in science

$x_4 = $ The importance of science in the world

In the first analysis, the dependent variable is y, the total science achievement score. In the second analysis, the dependent variables are achievement subtest scores:

$y_1 = $ Biology

$y_2 = $ Chemistry

$y_3 = $ Physics

$y_4 = $ Practical

We wish to test and to estimate, first, the effect of homework on science achievement above and beyond verbal ability, then the effects of interest in science above and beyond verbal ability and the amount of effort spent.

2.2   THE MODEL: UNIVARIATE

All of the independent variables are measured variables or scores on broadly graded scales. The linear model to be used in relating the independent variables to the criterion is the multiple regression model. If we assume first that there is only one dependent variable (the total score), then the model may be written as:

$$y_i = \alpha + \beta_1 x_{i1} + \beta_2 x_{i2} + \beta_3 x_{i3} + \beta_4 x_{i4} + \epsilon_i \tag{1}$$

On the left, y_i is the score on the achievement variable for subject i. On the right, x_{i1}, x_{i2}, x_{i3}, and x_{i4} are scores on the four independent variables for observation i. In a regression model, the independent variables, or antecedents, are referred to as *predictor* variables. β_1, β_2, β_3, and β_4 are partial regression weights, or weights applied to the predictor variables in order optimally to predict the outcome measure. The quantity α is the intercept constant in the model. The weights and the intercept absorb scaling factors and origin of measurement of the y and the x variables; thus there is no restriction on the mean or the standard deviation of any of the measures. Finally ϵ_i is the *residual*, or the discrepancy between the outcome y and some best linear combination of the predictor variables x. We shall assume that the ϵ's are independent and normally distributed with mean zero and common variance σ.

There are two restrictions upon the analysis under the model represented by (1). The first restriction is that the predictor variables x must not be exact linear functions of one another. We could not, for example, have as predictor variables three subtest scores and have also the total of the three subtest scores as a fourth predictor. Nor could we have as predictors percentage scores which sum to 100 percent for every subject. In each of these cases, it would be necessary to eliminate one of the interdependent measures from the set in order to proceed with the analysis. In the present data, we do not have this problem—there is no probability that the four variables will have an exact linear dependency because each has been measured by separate items on the student questionnaire.

The second restriction in regression analysis is that there must be at least as many subjects as the number of parameters in the model (α and β's). If an estimate of error variation is desired, additional observations beyond this minimum are required. In the present example there are scores for 119 subjects, well over the number required to estimate the parameters and the error variance.

Statistically speaking we may say that the analysis has two purposes—first, to test the fit of the model and, second, to obtain best estimates of the parameters we wish to maintain in the model. That is, at the first stage of analysis we decide which predictor variables contribute significantly to criterion variation; in the second stage we obtain "best" estimates of the regression weights for these predictor variables and discard the rest. At the same time, we may estimate other useful statistics, such as the correlation of the predictors with each other and with the criterion, and we may compute predicted outcome scores for individual subjects.

Thus, we may distinguish the *rank of the model for significance testing* from the *rank of the model for estimation*. The former is the total number of parameters in the complete model before we decide which do, or which do not, contribute to prediction of criterion variation. In the present example, the rank of model for significance testing is five, counting one for the α and four for the β's. The latter, the rank of the model for estimation, may have any value from one through five; it will be chosen after we inspect the results of the significance tests.

In testing the fit of alternative models of increasing rank, we shall test the contributions of the predictors in a fixed order. Only regression procedures having a fixed order of entering predictor variables have exact tests of significance and probability statements. We may represent the tests of significance to be conducted in an analysis-of-variance table such as Table 2.1.

We test the contribution of Word Knowledge x_1 to criterion variation; then we shall test the additional contribution of the amount of homework x_2, after eliminating variation that can be attributed to Word Knowledge. Interest is represented by two variables, x_3 and x_4. We shall test the contribution of the two predictors simultaneously to criterion variation, holding constant all other variables in the model. A source table like Table 2.1, including the degrees of freedom and the order of the independent variables, is invaluable in setting up any computer regression or analysis-of-variance run.

Table 2.1   Analysis-of-variance Source Table for
Univariate Regression Analysis

Source of Variation	Degrees of Freedom
Constant α	1
x_1, eliminating constant	1
x_2, eliminating x_1 and constant	1
x_3 and x_4, eliminating all above	2
Entire model	5
Residual	$N - 5$
Total	N

2.3 THE MODEL: MULTIVARIATE

The multivariate form of the model is similar to (1) except that y, α, the β's, and ϵ are all vectors having four elements. If we represent vectors by bold Roman or underscored Greek letters, then the multivariate form is represented by (2).

$$\mathbf{y}_i = \underset{\sim}{\alpha} + \underset{\sim}{\beta}_1 x_{i1} + \underset{\sim}{\beta}_2 x_{i2} + \underset{\sim}{\beta}_3 x_{i3} + \underset{\sim}{\beta}_4 x_{i4} + \underset{\sim}{\epsilon}_i \qquad\qquad\qquad (2)$$

Each vector has an element corresponding to each of the criterion variables. For example, $\mathbf{y}_i$ is a four-element response vector having subject i's score on the four science subtests. This may be depicted as in (3a), in which the superscript is used to indicate the particular criterion variable.

$$\mathbf{y}_i = \begin{bmatrix} y_i^{(1)} \\ y_i^{(2)} \\ y_i^{(3)} \\ y_i^{(4)} \end{bmatrix} \qquad\qquad\qquad (3a)$$

Likewise, $\underset{\sim}{\alpha}$ is a vector having a constant for each criterion variable; the constants for the different outcomes usually have different values. Each $\underset{\sim}{\beta}$ is also a vector. For example, $\underset{\sim}{\beta}_1$ may be depicted as in (3b).

$$\underset{\sim}{\beta}_1 = \begin{bmatrix} \beta_1^{(1)} \\ \beta_1^{(2)} \\ \beta_1^{(3)} \\ \beta_1^{(4)} \end{bmatrix} \qquad\qquad\qquad (3b)$$

Again the superscript is used to indicate the respective criterion measure. Since $\underset{\sim}{\beta}_1$ is a vector having four distinct elements, the model allows the score on predictor x_1 (Word Knowledge) to have a different direction and magnitude of effect on each of the four science achievement scores. That is, even though there is only a single Word Knowledge variable, that variable may have a different quantitative relationship with each of the outcome measures. Similarly, $\underset{\sim}{\beta}_2$, $\underset{\sim}{\beta}_3$, and $\underset{\sim}{\beta}_4$ each have four elements, as has $\underset{\sim}{\epsilon}$, indicating a possibly different degree of error for each outcome measure.

The purpose of the analysis is the same as the univariate case. That is, we wish to test the contribution of each predictor to criterion variation, and then we wish to estimate the regression weights and related functions for those predictors that are significant. Testing the multivariate contribution of a single predictor, however, requires a test of whether an entire vector of regression weights is null. For example, to test the contribution of Word Knowledge to the criterion variation, we test that all of the elements of $\underset{\sim}{\beta}_1$ are simultaneously zero. Likewise, testing the contribution of the two interest predictor variables requires testing the nullity of two vectors of regression weights. That is, we test whether the eight regression weights of the (four) science achievements on the (two) interest scores are all simultaneously zero. This is in contrast to the univariate model analysis where only a single weight is tested for each predictor.

The order of predictors and "ranks" of the multivariate model are the same as shown in Table 2.1. We test that x_1 is related to one or more of the *four* outcomes, then test x_2 eliminating x_1, then x_3 and x_4, eliminating those preceding.

The distributional assumption in the multivariate model is that the elements of vector $\underset{\sim}{\epsilon}_i$ are drawn from a multivariate normal population with mean zero, and that the errors for one observation are independent of those for any other. In other words, we assume that the scores of any one subject are not influenced by those of another. This does not mean the errors on different outcome measures are independent. On the contrary, the dependent variables may have *any* pattern admissible for variance and intercorrelations. In the present example, the four science achievement tests are closely related conceptually and probably have high intercorrelations.

This is *not* a restriction on the multivariate analysis and is additional reason for using multivariate methods instead of analyzing each outcome separately. In addition, the variances of the four science tests may be unequal, but again this does not restrict the multivariate model; the variances of the separate outcome measures may take on any finite values.

In multivariate analysis, we display the variances and correlations (or covariances) in a matrix having a row and a column for each dependent variable. Let S_j^2 be the variance of test y_j, and let S_{jk} be the covariance of test y_j with test y_k. Then the correlation of the two tests is $r_{jk} = S_{jk}/(S_j S_k)$. The *variance-covariance matrix* of the four science tests is:[1]

$$\mathbf{V} = \begin{bmatrix} S_1^2 & & & \\ S_{21} & S_2^2 & & \\ S_{31} & S_{32} & S_3^3 & \\ S_{41} & S_{42} & S_{43} & S_4^4 \end{bmatrix} \tag{4}$$

Since the multivariate model does not restrict either the diagonal or off-diagonal elements of $\mathbf{V}$, we say that it operates with an *arbitrary* error variance-covariance matrix. The matrix is assumed to be the same for all observations. (The error correlation matrix is obtained from $\mathbf{V}$ by dividing each element by the square root of the diagonal element in its row and column.)

The restrictions on the multivariate model are similar to those on the univariate. Again, the predictor variables cannot be exact linear combinations of one another; and in this case there must be more subjects than the number of parameters in the model *plus* the number of criterion variables. That is, if we let N be the number of subjects, q the number of predictor variables, and p the number of dependent variables, then N must be greater than $p + q + 1$. An additional restriction on the multivariate model is that the dependent variables also may not be linear combinations of one another. We cannot, therefore, include the total score and the four subtest scores in one multivariate analysis. This is why we are performing a separate univariate analysis on the total score.

2.4 ADDITIONAL CONSIDERATIONS REQUIRED BY THE DATA SET

In regression models there are two important considerations concerning the nature of the independent variables: the first is the order in which predictors are added to the regression equation; the second is the identification of the subgroup structure of the sample data set.

2.4.1 Predictor Order

The MULTIVARIANCE program requires that the order of predictor variables be fixed by the user prior to run time. This is in contrast to programs which use automatic unrestricted stepwise procedures, and allow the data to dictate the order of the predictor variables. The latter procedures seek a subtest of predictors that yields maximal prediction by a given number of antecedents.

Although there is a difference of opinion between the proponents of the two approaches, the methods must be seen as serving separate purposes. Unrestricted stepwise procedures assume that the researcher is ignorant of the processes which give rise to the measured outcomes. Thus, a researcher may sample the largest possible number of antecedents variables and allow the empirical relationships among them and with the criteria to dictate which are most important, which are of secondary importance, and so on. Research using this method

---

[1] Elements above the diagonal in (4) are the "mirror images" of the terms shown, i.e., $S_{jk} = S_{kj}$; similarly, $r_{jk} = r_{kj}$.

must be regarded as exploratory and requiring confirmation with a second data set. Often the second data set is a second random half of an original large file.

Problems inherent in unrestricted stepwise regression procedures may, however, be so great as to undermine their utility. First and foremost, these procedures ignore any information at the disposal of the investigator that *can* and *should* be used in formulating the statistical model and, if so used, would increase the power of the analysis. Second, a variable may appear unimportant not because it has a low correlation with the criterion, but because it is highly intercorrelated with other predictors already in the model. Third, tests of significance based on regression weights from stepwise procedures lack statistical validity; by seeking the variables with the highest correlations with y, the procedure will indiscriminantly select variables that are significant by chance along with those which truly belong in the equation. Finally, stepwise regression methods do not allow the researcher to locate *sets* of variables that contribute to criterion variation. In the present study, for example, the two interest measures are considered as a *set* in which each measures a different aspect of the same global trait.

The term "stepwise," although commonly associated with regression methods that attempt all possible orders of predictor variables, does not exclusively designate this situation. In fact, the term may be applied also to fixed-order analyses in which the effects of certain variables are tested, holding constant other variables in the set. Table 2.1, for example, indicates that we wish to test the predictor variables in a "stepwise" fashion in the study under discussion. This means simply that we test one predictor variable, the additional contribution of the second, and the additional contribution of the two others, after earlier variables are accounted for. Similarly, nonorthogonal analysis-of-variance models that test main effects and interactions in a particular order, at each stage holding constant the other effects, are also stepwise methods.

Step-down analysis, which utilizes an ordering of dependent variables, is also a stepwise procedure. Step-down analysis yields a test of significance for the first dependent variable, for the second dependent variable holding constant the first, for the third dependent variable holding constant the first two, and so on. Although in every case the order of variables is fixed, the procedure is still termed a stepwise procedure, or "stepwise elimination." Roy and Bargmann (1958) coined the term "step-down" to indicate that the dependent variables are being operated upon, as opposed to the independent variables.

In fixed-order regression analysis, we face the problem of which order to choose for the predictor variables. Although this is a complex question requiring some knowledge of the process under study, there are several general rules which may be followed. Most importantly, simple predictors are usually ordered first in the model, while complex predictors, including interactions, are ordered last. The rules of parsimony dictate that if the outcomes can be explained through a simple rationale, then more complex explanations are rejected. Thus, we test whether the complex explanations or predictors contribute to criterion variation above and beyond the simpler ones.

A second consideration is the extent to which the predictor variables are well-understood antecedents and not new. In the science achievement study, for example, we know that verbal ability is related to the criterion variables and is important in their prediction. Verbal ability is included in the regression model as the first predictor, but we have little interest in testing the significance of its contribution to regression, which is a foregone conclusion. Instead, it is more of a control factor such that we test the prediction of other variables, given that verbal ability is accounted for. Of the latter, the effect of amount of homework or effort represents an important hypothesis. Because we would like to establish that, among students of the same verbal skills, more homework will be reflected in science achievement, we place the amount-of-effort variable in a position following verbal ability and test its unique contribution. Finally, we place interest last in the prediction equation, thus testing the contribution of the interest measures to regression, above and beyond ability and effort. We would not like to attribute variation to so vague a variable as interest if it can be explained by more well-understood manipulable influences.

A third consideration that may be used in ordering regression predictors is time sequence: that is, events that occur early in a person's life can be ordered ahead of those that come at later times. For example, events which occur at school are usually ordered after events that occur at home. For, to be conservative, we should not consider school effective unless the results of instruction cannot be attributed to previous learning outside of school. Ultimately, the order of predictors in regression models, as well as their grouping in joint tests of significance, must be decided on their substantive role in the study.

2.4.2 Subgroup Structure

The main results in a regression analysis depend on the matrix of variances and covariances, or the matrix of correlations, among the y and x variables. The estimated regression weights are a function of the sample covariances between the y and x measures and of the variances and covariances of the x variables; simple, multiple, and canonical correlations are computed from the matrix of variable correlations as are the partial variances and standard deviations. It is essential, therefore, that the variance-covariance matrix computed be free of bias from extraneous sources of variation.

In particular, when there are subgroups within the data set that have different means on one or more variables, variation due to these means must be removed when computing the sample variance-covariance matrix. Failure to do so will result in variances that are systematically too large, and covariances and correlations that are systematically biased depending on the size and direction of the between-group mean differences. This issue is discussed at length in Finn (1974, pp. 80 ff.). In the data shown in Figure 2.1, there are two groups of subjects—males and females—which are likely to have different means on at least some of the independent and dependent variables.

Consider a simple example of how different means for boys and girls may bias a variance. Suppose that we first ignore group differences and treat all subjects as having arisen from one population. Then the variance of scores on any variable, e.g., test y, is given by (5).

$$S^2 = \frac{\sum (y_i - y_.)^2}{N - 1} \tag{5}$$

The variance is the average squared deviation of the scores from the mean of all N scores, $y_.$.

Suppose, however, that within the data set the mean of all N_1 boys is $y_{.1}$ and the mean of all N_2 girls is $y_{.2}$, so that the two means are not equal. Then the $y_.$ used in (5), in terms of the separate means, is given by (6).

$$y_. = \frac{N_1 y_{.1} + N_2 y_{.2}}{N_1 + N_2} \tag{6}$$

Suppose we now compute the variance for boys only by (7a).

$$S_1^2 = \frac{\sum (y_{i1} - y_{.1})^2}{N_1 - 1} \tag{7a}$$

Likewise, the variance for girls only is given by (7b).

$$S_2^2 = \frac{\sum (y_{i2} - y_{.2})^2}{N_2 - 1} \tag{7b}$$

It is likely that either result is smaller than the overall variance given by (5), because the mean deviations of the scores within one group are probably smaller than the deviations from the common mean. That is, the scores of the boys tend to be closer to the mean of the boys, and the scores of the girls tend to be closer to the mean of the girls, than to a common mean $y_.$. The further apart the mean for boys and the mean for girls are, the further they will be from the common $y_.$, and the more inflated will be S^2. The variance estimate computed without taking sex into consideration is biased upward.

Because of these considerations, subgroups within a data set having different means on one or more variables should be identified. The variance estimate, unbiased by differences in subgroup means, is the *pooled within-group variance* shown in (8).

$$S_w^2 = \frac{(N_1 - 1)S_1^2 + (N_2 - 1)S_2^2}{N_1 - N_2 - 2}$$

$$= \frac{\sum(N_j - 1)S_j^2}{\sum(N_j - 1)}$$

$$= \frac{\sum\sum(y_{ij} - y_j)^2}{N - J} \tag{8}$$

The variances for boys and girls separately are weighted by the number of subjects in the groups and averaged. As the last line of (8) shows, this is the same as computing the squared mean deviation of every score from its own *subgroup* mean. In this equation, J is the total number of subgroups (2 in the example).

Covariances, which are either positive or negative, may be biased in either direction—that is, they may be too large or too small. The correlations, which are a function of both covariances and variances, may also fluctuate in both directions in a more complex manner. Therefore, once the subgroups within the data are identified, equation (8) should be applied to each covariance of a pair of variables as well as to each variance.

The adjustment for different means of subgroups can be made to all variances and covariances simultaneously. Let V_j be the matrix of variances and covariances of all p criterion measures and all q predictors, in one subgroup j. That is, V_j is a $(p + q) \times (p + q)$ symmetric variance-covariance matrix for the group. Then the pooled within-group variance-covariance matrix is V_w, as given by (9).

$$\mathbf{V}_w = \frac{\sum(N_j - 1)\mathbf{V}_j}{N - J} \tag{9}$$

The parallelism of (8) and (9) is readily seen.

In terms of the model, the identifying of separate subgroups with different means is equivalent to having a distinct α constant for each group within the data. This requires adding a subscript for the group number to α, to the dependent variables y, and to all the predictor variables x. It means also that additional degrees of freedom in the analysis-of-variance table are used for estimating constants. There are J constants in the model instead of one constant, as shown in Table 2.1.

The MULTIVARIANCE program allows the user to identify subgroups of subjects from which the pooled within-group variance-covariance matrix of all measures is obtained. Subgroups are identified as in an analysis-of-variance design with one, two, or more dimensions of classification. Corrections to all subclass means are made simultaneously in computing the common within-group matrix. Other regression and correlation programs may not have this feature, and caution should be exercised in interpreting their results.

2.5 PUNCHING THE DATA CARDS

Before displaying the data for this example, we offer a few remarks on how data cards should be punched. Consider, for example, the Science Achievement data listed in Figure 2.1 in the following card columns:

Columns	Variables
8	Sex, 1 = male, 2 = female
13-16	Science Biology Achievement score
17-20	Science Chemistry Achievement score
21-24	Science Physics Achievement score
25-28	Science Practical Achievement score
29-33	Word Knowledge score
34-37	Interest in Science score
38-41	Science in the World score
42-45	Hours of Homework score

Subjects are 119 eighth-grade pupils in Swedish public schools. These are a random sample of the eighth-grade children from the IEA data bank. The analysis consists of two runs within the same job—the first using one subtest for predicting total Science Achievement score as the dependent variable, and the second using the four subtests jointly in this role. It may be noted that the subtest scores sum to the total score.

Both of the Interest-in-science scores and the Science-in-the-world score are scaled in the opposite direction from most common scales; i.e., a high score indicates a negative attitude, and a low score a more positive attitude. Hours of homework has five possible response values: 1 = 0-2 hours of homework per week; 2 = 2-5 hours; 3 = 5-10 hours; 4 = 10-20 hours; 5 = more than 20 hours a week on homework. Other scores on the data cards are not used in this analysis.

2.6 MULTIVARIANCE SETUP

The input to the MULTIVARIANCE program, exclusive of the data deck, is listed in Figure 2.2. Because none of the control cards required by MULTIVARIANCE for analysis-of-variance problems is needed in regression problems, input in this example is particularly simple. Page 81 of the MULTIVARIANCE *User's Guide* indicates which of the control cards are simplified or eliminated.

2.6.1 Control Cards

PHASE I.   The **Title** cards which begin the input phase need no particular explanation, except that there must be two such cards. The immediately following **Input Description** card describes the input data deck and the group structure within the data set. Two classes of variables are listed on the Input Description card: the number of *variables* in columns 1-4, and the number of *factors* in columns 7-8.

The number of variables includes all measured scales. These include all of the dependent variables, all of the predictors for regression analysis (or covariates for analysis of covariance), and other measured variables that the data cards may contain and the user desires to enter. The latter may include variables that are not necessary to the analysis but for which means and summary statistics are desired, or they may be variables used in transforming other measures.

```
                1         2         3         4         5         6         7         8
        1234567890123456789012345678901234567890123456789012345678901234567890123456789 0

101 17 1 238  78   65   58   38  160   6   -2   1  213   99  37   21   3   2
102 27 1 175  15   28  120   13   60   6   -3   3  160   13  39   -1   5   4
105  1 1 113   3   40   58   13   40   5   -2   1  280   67  26   13   4   1
105  7 1 575 115  115  195  150  240  -3   -7   2  373  267  40   13   5   2
107 10 1 300  90   28  133   50  220  -1   -4   2  227   72  40    9   5   2
107 13 1 343  68   55  133   88  220   4   -6   2  307  168  33   21   3   3
116 14 1 325  90   78  108   50  200   7    1   1  360  221  32   13   5   5
122  1 1 588 103  128  195  163  320   0   -5   2  453  267  40    1   4   5
122 11 1 388  78   65  145  100  300   5   -3   2  413  240  40    9   5   4
122 13 1   3  28  -32  -17   25  180   2    0   1   80   27  14   -7   2   3
123 15 1 163  15   53   58   38  240   1   -6   2  373  227  40   23   5   2
124 17 1 388 103  103   95   88   20   7    0   2  280  183  35   13   5   2
127 19 1 275  53   90  108   25  100  -3   -3   2   80   99  27   23   5   1
131 14 1 325  53  103   83   88  100   6   -3   1  273  187  40    9   5   3
132 11 1 313  40  103  108   63  140   8    1   2  213  187  39   11   5   3
139 14 1 550 103  128  195  125  300   4   -6   2  417  250  34    9   4   4
144  9 1 438 140   65  158   75  180   8   -7   1  373  200  35    9   5   1
145  5 1 155  53   15   50   38  120   4   -1   1  200    7  40   -1   4   1
145 10 1  13   3   15   33  -37  -39  11    3   1   67  110  40   11   5   1
147  4 1  38 -22    3   33   25  180   7    1   2  200   57  38    9   5   4
147  5 1 150  78   15    8   50  180  -4  -10   3  160  187  37   -5   5   5
147  9 1 180  53   40   60   28   20   0    5   2   70   17  40    3   3   5
148 15 1 400  65   90  170   75  220  -2   -1   2  307  267  40   13   5   2
150 20 1 225  90   65   70    0  200   4    0   1  160   67  31   27   1   3
150 22 1 263  90    3   95   75   30   4   10   5  240  156  40   11   5   5
151 11 1 325  65   53  145   63  160   3    1   2  333  173  30    5   4   5
152 23 1 300  78   65  120   38  180   2   -7   2  333  160  40    3   5   3
154 27 1 488  78  115  170  125  160  -2    2   2  360  240  40    1   5   1
156 16 1 138  53   28   33   25   40   2   -1   2  107  -24  40   17   2   3
156 19 1 250  78   53  108   13   40   1   -3   1  133  143  32   17   1   3
161 28 1 288  40  103  145    0  120  -2   -6   3  280  240  40   -1   5   2
163 27 1 450  65  103  183  100  220  -4   -5   1  373  293  40   -5   5   5
165  9 1 250  78   53   58   63  260   6   -6   2  373  240  40   21   5   5
175 16 1 288  90   28  145   25  220   4   -1   2  160  153  30   13   5   3
178 19 1 325  53   78  108   88  120   0   -7   2  307  213  30    9   5   3
178 21 1 200  53   15   45   88  160   2   -5   1  267  187  38    9   5   5
180 16 1 338 128   40   95   75  160   1   -7   3  240  139  40    3   5   2
181 14 1 375  90   78  133   75  240  -1   -2   2  267  200  40    3   5   3
181 16 1 513 103  153  158  100  260  -4  -12   2  400  187  34    3   5   5
183 18 1 385  83   63  135  105  260   6   -7   2  443  273  40    3   5   3
184 19 1 250  28   78   95   50  130   0   -1   1  293  187  30   19   5   1
184 23 1 308  68   70   95   75  140   2   -7   1  243  147  40   17   5   2
186 15 1 425 103  103  133   88   80   4   -6   3  267  107  25   21   4   5
188 20 1 463  78  115  170  100  240   0   -1   2  267  114  40   21   5   2
191 14 1 288  43   45  145   55  320   0   -5   2  333  173  29   -1   3   5
191 17 1 175  53   15   95   13  160  -2   -2   3  213  133  40    1   5   5
193 18 1 350  90   65  120   75  180   6    0   1  333  225  33   -1   5   4
193 21 1 175  40   40   70   25   40   7   -5   3  147  126  36    5   5   1
194  2 1  88  15   40   33    0   60   7    1   4  -52   29  40   23   5   4
194  6 1 413 140   90  133   50  140   7   -6   2  400  107  30    1   4   4
101 29 2 278  65   80   70   63  200   8    1   3  360  291  40    3   5   2
102 18 2  75  -9  -22   70   38   60   6   -4   2   93  147  36    1   4   5
106 17 2 325  90   53  108   75  210   3    0   2  427  265  35   -9   5   5
106 18 2 450 115  115  158   63  300   7    0   3  467  267  40  -11   5   5
110 15 2 338  78   90  108   63  180   8    0   3  293  213  32   11   5   4
111 15 2 125  15   65   58  -12  200   9   -5   1  280  227  37    1   5   5
111 23 2 303  90   90   83   40  160   4   -3   3  293  160  30    9   5   3
112 19 2  70  25    8   35    3  160   7   -4   1  123  173  24    7   4   5
113  4 2 200  65   53   83    0  220   4   -5   2  253  141  40    3   4   3
113  7 2 113  28   28   45   13  100   8   -1   2  320  236  40    7   5   4
114  8 2 175  65   53   58    0  100   6   -4   3  147  107  40   11   4   5
114 21 2 173  65   30   48   30   60   8   -3   3  240  112  40    9   4   4
116 20 2 340  80  153   95   13  280   3   -2   2  413  280  34  -15   5   5
119  8 2 278  78   53   95   53  250   5   -2   2  400  267  40   -7   5   3
122  5 2 463  78  153  158   75  260   5    0   2  307  267  39   -1   5   4
122 10 2 135  28   63   55   -9  110   7   -1   1  127   93  33    1   5   3
123 19 2 200  53   53   58   38   20   4    1   3  177  124  40   15   5   3
```

FIGURE 2.1-1 Problem 1: IEA Science Achievement Study data

123	20	2	175	65	15	70	25	120	-2	-6	2	213	160	40	-7	5	5
123	23	2	138	53	28	70	-12	160	6	-3	2	177	160	34	1	5	2
123	28	2	250	28	90	95	38	-59	7	-1	3	213	181	40	19	5	2
125	6	2	198	40	53	45	60	110	7	-5	2	353	240	40	-3	5	5
125	8	2	145	40	40	75	-9	320	5	-2	3	340	70	35	1	4	2
126	7	2	113	65	-9	45	13	20	3	-1	2	240	140	32	-1	5	5
131	18	2	140	65	43	33	0	100	6	0	1	333	194	40	5	5	5
132	3	2	90	-7	40	33	25	150	7	-6	3	240	170	32	11	4	3
135	25	2	220	43	63	83	33	210	7	-2	2	360	213	26	9	5	3
138	17	2	378	105	65	145	63	220	7	-3	2	387	267	40	7	5	2
138	28	2	338	53	90	145	50	140	4	-4	2	293	150	32	7	5	5
139	20	2	133	18	48	48	20	140	11	-2	1	333	181	33	15	5	3
143	19	2	145	30	35	55	25	0	10	0	2	253	227	32	1	5	3
145	3	2	125	15	53	45	13	200	9	-2	1	187	30	27	-1	3	1
146	10	2	143	78	53	48	-34	210	7	-6	2	253	160	40	9	5	1
148	21	2	220	50	50	110	10	90	7	2	2	297	217	40	7	3	5
151	4	2	108	23	43	33	10	-69	2	-5	4	53	27	35	-9	5	4
151	13	2	145	60	28	58	0	130	7	1	2	337	123	40	1	5	3
153	21	2	488	130	105	170	83	230	0	-11	2	413	310	40	-3	5	5
154	29	2	213	65	40	108	0	240	2	0	3	293	32	40	13	5	5
155	24	2	138	90	15	33	0	80	11	2	2	360	53	30	-3	5	5
155	27	2	63	28	15	45	-24	180	9	1	1	240	147	30	-3	5	5
156	14	2	400	115	103	120	63	240	4	1	2	333	213	36	9	5	2
156	23	2	275	78	103	83	13	80	10	-4	2	200	267	37	15	5	3
160	18	2	213	53	53	120	-12	200	10	0	3	453	187	40	3	5	3
160	23	2	340	90	83	88	80	220	8	-2	2	333	276	40	5	5	5
161	22	2	190	40	68	58	25	100	8	-1	1	240	177	35	17	5	4
162	8	2	250	90	53	70	38	80	4	-6	3	227	280	34	5	5	5
167	25	2	288	65	90	70	63	220	9	-4	2	360	200	34	15	5	4
168	19	2	25	28	-22	20	0	160	14	1	2	80	55	40	5	4	4
169	14	2	210	75	38	98	0	160	5	-4	2	333	267	36	3	4	2
170	26	2	375	78	78	133	88	280	10	-2	4	293	227	30	1	5	5
171	3	2	175	65	15	70	25	60	8	-5	1	413	227	38	-1	4	5
172	21	2	100	43	15	40	3	300	9	-3	1	227	213	35	3	4	3
172	24	2	428	115	68	158	88	280	2	-5	1	413	213	40	-9	5	4
172	25	2	365	90	115	70	90	260	5	-1	2	453	253	40	9	5	1
173	2	2	165	78	40	58	-9	-39	-2	-3	2	177	160	22	1	5	3
173	11	2	200	3	40	95	63	180	2	-3	3	173	200	32	7	5	3
174	22	2	263	53	53	108	50	140	4	-5	3	360	200	40	-5	5	4
176	23	2	240	55	65	83	38	200	8	-2	2	360	225	40	11	5	3
178	28	2	100	28	15	45	13	130	5	-3	3	307	253	40	7	5	3
184	25	2	13	28	15	8	-37	40	9	-2	1	27	53	40	5	5	5
185	27	2	100	28	3	45	25	60	10	-4	3	173	107	28	7	5	5
186	13	2	200	53	40	95	13	120	4	-4	2	293	120	40	1	5	4
189	27	2	375	78	115	108	75	240	7	-2	2	360	187	40	-9	5	5
190	22	2	200	65	15	83	38	100	11	-3	1	360	278	40	13	5	5
193	24	2	338	90	90	83	75	120	8	2	3	347	170	40	1	5	5
193	28	2	215	28	78	45	65	220	9	-6	3	323	227	31	5	5	5
195	3	2	258	73	70	93	23	150	6	-1	1	357	253	26	-7	5	5
199	20	2	313	115	78	70	50	180	5	-4	3	333	227	36	3	4	3
199	24	2	213	40	65	95	13	140	6	-2	2	240	234	40	5	5	1
200	11	2	313	78	90	95	50	300	5	-9	3	347	260	39	-13	5	5

```
            1                   2                   3                   4                   5                   6                   7                   8
   1234567890123456789012345678901234567890123456789012345678901234567890123456789012345678901234567890
```

FIGURE 2.1-2 Problem 1: IEA Science Achievement Study data (cont.)

The factors are any attributes that define the subgroup membership of the subjects. In analysis-of-variance models, these are the design factors—factor *A*, factor *B*, etc. They designate either experimental conditions or sample classes. In regression models the factors define the subclass structure within the data, so that a common within-group variance-covariance matrix may be obtained.

In the present data set, there are nine measured variables including the five Science Achievement scores, plus scores for the four predictor variables. There is a single factor (sex) with two *levels*. The data cards are sorted into sex groups and the cards for each group have a **Header** card giving the group number and the number of subjects. Thus *Data Form* 2 is coded on the Input Description card. If the cards had not been sorted and each had an appropriate sex-group identification number, Data Form 1 could be used instead. The remaining codes on the Input Description card specify the spacing to be used in printing the output, and to what extent optional statistics are to be computed and printed.

The **Factor Identification** card names and defines the factors existing in the design. In this problem there is one factor, sex, with two possible values. Following the Factor Identification card, the program allows the user to enter comments to describe his problem. The comments terminate with a **Finish** card.

In Data Form 2, the **Variable Format** card describes only the measured variables. Since subjects are grouped into sex groups, the group number (1 or 2) is included on the Header cards in the data deck and is not read with the other scores. In other data forms where the subject identification is read from the data cards, an integer field must be included in the format to receive the subgroup identification number.

The **Variable Label** card(s) contain names for all measured variables. Then come the data with a Header card preceding each group. In this instance, the scores of the 50 boys and 69 girls comprise groups 1 and 2, respectively. The end of the data is signaled by a blank Header card.

PHASE II.   The **Estimation Specification** card may be blank for regression runs, and all other Phase II cards may be omitted.

PHASE III.   In Phase III the control cards select the sets of dependent and independent variables and fix their order. These cards may be repeated as many times as desired with different subsets and different orders of variables.

The first **Analysis Selection** card indicates one dependent variable (Science Achievement Total score) and four predictors. Other parameters on this card indicate that these five variables are to be selected from a larger set originally read by the program, and that a **Covariate Grouping** key is to be used. The latter allows the predictors to be entered into the regression equation in sets. With this key, we may test the joint contribution of both Science Interest scores simultaneously. Without the key, each predictor variable is tested for its separate contribution to regression.

The **Variable Select** key indicates both the order of measures and their status as dependent or independent variables. The dependent variables are listed first. In this instance, only the first variable read from the data cards is a dependent variable, while the predictor variables are the *6th*, *9th*, *7th*, and *8th* variables read by Phase I, in that order. These predictors are *Word Knowledge, Hours of Homework,* and the two *Science Interest* measures, respectively. The Covariate Grouping key indicates variable 6 is to be tested first for its contribution to regression. Next, variable 9 is to be tested, eliminating variable 6. The final two variables, 7 and 8, are to be tested for their joint contribution, eliminating both Word Knowledge and Hours of Homework. MULTIVARI-ANCE requires that a **Hypothesis Test** card be included, even for regression runs. Since the parameters of this card apply only to analysis-of-variance problems, the Hypothesis Test card need only carry a period here.

In the example, the Phase III cards appear twice. The second Analysis Selection card indicates four criterion variables and four predictors. The Variable Select key specifies criterion variables 2, 3, 4, and 5 (the science subtest scores) among those read on the input phase. The predictor variables are the same as before, and their grouping for testing contribution to regression is the same.

```
        1         2         3         4         5         6         7         8
1234567890123456789012345678901234567890123456789012345678901234567890

    1. Title cards
PROBLEM 1: UNIVARIATE AND MULTIVARIATE REGRESSION EXAMPLE IE
A-DATA SWEDEN POP 2 GRADE 8  MALES AND FEMALES SEPARATED
    2. Input Description card
    9   1   2                                                         1
        3. Factor Identification card
SEX     2
        4. Comment cards
UNIVARIATE AND MULTIVARIATE REGRESSION
DATA SAMPLE FROM SWEDEN GRADE 8

EXAMPLE 1: 1 DEPENDENT VARIABLE  SC A&B C
EXAMPLE 2: 4 DEPENDENT VARIABLES  SC BIO C, SC CHE C, SC PHY C, SC PRA C

4 INDEPENDENT VARIABLES: WORDK C ,INTR SC ,SC I WLD,HOURS HW


VARIABLE:      FORMAT:    COLUMNS:    DESCRIPTION:


SCHOOL         F3.0        1- 3
STUDENT        F3.0        4- 6
SEX            I2          7- 8
SC A&B C       F4.1        9-12       SCIENCE TOTAL TEST CORRECTED SCORE
SC BIO C       F4.1       13-16       SCIENCE BIOLOGY SUBTEST CORRECTED SCORE
SC CHE C       F4.1       17-20       SCIENCE CHEMISTRY SUBTEST CORRECTED SCORE
SC PHY C       F4.1       21-24       SCIENCE PHYSICS SUBTEST CORRECTED SCORE
SC PRA C       F4.1       25-28       SCIENCE PRACTICAL SUBTEST CORRECTED SCORE
WORD K C       F5.1       29-33       WORD KNOWLEDGE TEST CORRECTED SCORE
INTRO SC       F4.0       34-37       INTEREST IN SCIENCE (LOWER SCORE IS MORE INT)
SC I WLD       F4.0       38-41       SCIENCE IN THE WORLD (LOWER SCORE IS MORE INT)
HOURS HW       F4.0       42-45       HOURS HOMEWORK IN ALL SUBJECTS PER WEEK
RC C&D C       F5.1       46-50       RDG COMPREHENSION TOTAL TEST CORRECTED SCORE
LI W&R C       F4.1       51-54       LITERATURE TOTAL TEST CORRECTED SCORE
READSPE        F4.0       55-58       READING SPEED-ITEM REACHED
LIINTER        F4.0       59-62       LITERARY INTEREST (LOWER SCORE IS MORE INT)
BOOKSHO        F4.0       63-66       NUMBER OF BOOKS IN HOME
REAPLEA        F4.0       67-70       HOURS READING FOR PLEASURE PER WEEK

        5. End-of-comments card
FINISH
        6. Variable Format card
(8X,5F4.1,F5.1,3F4.0)
        9. Variable Label card
SC A&B CSC BIO CSC CHE CSC PHY CSC PRA CWORD K CINTR SC SC I WLDHOURS HW
    10. Data
        (A) Header card
    50   1
        (B) 50 observations, sex group 1
        (A) Header card
    69   2
        (B) 69 observations, sex group 2
        End of data

    12. Estimation Specification card

    18. Analysis Selection card
    1   4   1                       1
    19. Variable Select key
1,6,9,7,8.
    20. Covariate Grouping key
1,1,2.
    21. Hypothesis Test card

    18. Analysis Selection card
    4   4   1                       1
    19. Variable Select key
2,3,4,5,6,9,7,8.
    20. Covariate Grouping key
1,1,2.
    21. Hypothesis Test card

    22. End-of-job card
                                                          STOP
        1         2         3         4         5         6         7         8
1234567890123456789012345678901234567890123456789012345678901234567890
```

FIGURE 2.2 Problem 1: MULTIVARIANCE control cards for regression analysis

2.7 OUTPUT AND INTERPRETATION

PHASE I.   The output from the first phase of the MULTIVARIANCE program is reproduced in Figures 2.3-1 and 2.3-2. As an option, the intercorrelations of all nine variables are printed for each group for the user's inspection. The means and standard deviations are also shown. The decision to separate sex groups is supported by the observation that boys have higher means on all science tests, have better scores on both science interest tests, and appear to do less science homework. There seems to be a systematic difference in science achievement favoring the male population.

PHASE II.   The pooled within-group variance-covariance matrix is produced by the estimation phase of the program and appears in the output listing as indicated in Figure 2.3-2. The estimated parameters shown in the listing apply to analysis-of-variance models and are not applicable here. The "error sum of cross products" is the pooled within-group sum of cross products, given by the numerator of (9). Its elements are the sums of squares and cross products of deviates of the original scores from their subgroup means.

When the elements of this matrix are divided by the degrees of freedom ($N - J = 119 - 2$), we obtain the pooled within-group or "error" variance-covariance matrix. The within-group variances (diagonal elements of the matrix) are listed at the top of Figure 2.3-3. Their square roots are the within-group standard deviations which describe the random variation in the variables, given that there are mean differences between the two sex groups.

Each covariance in the variance-covariance matrix, when divided by the products of the standard deviations of the respective variables, yields an element of the correlation matrix. As this is the pooled within-group correlation matrix, the correlations are generally intermediate between those for the separate male and female samples, and are the best estimates of the common correlations. They describe the linear relationship between the dependent and independent variables and may be interpreted accordingly. Inspecting just the first column, we can see that, as expected, Word Knowledge plays a large role in determining Science Achievement Total. The Science Interest scores have negative correlations with the criteria because they are scored in the reverse direction. Hours of Homework spent by the student does not appear to correlate either with Total Science score or with the subscores. The latter perhaps indicates that total hours of homework is not indicative of the amount of effort spent on science alone.

PHASE III.   The regression analysis results begin in Figure 2.3-3. We will discuss first the results of the univariate analysis with the Science Achievement Total score as the criterion.

2.7.1   Univariate Analysis

The raw regression coefficients, which appear after some intermediate computations, are the least-squares estimates of the weights in univariate regression model (1). The equation for optimally predicting Science Achievement Total is given by (10).

$$\hat{y}_i = \hat{\alpha} + .67x_{i1} + 1.72x_{i2} - .77x_{i3} - .12x_{i4} \tag{10}$$

The raw regression weights apply to the original scores on the x scales. y_i with a caret is the predicted score on the criterion measure for subject i. A caret on α indicates that these are the sample or "estimated" values. If the predicted scores are close to the observed y scores, then the regression is strong; the "best" linear combination of the predictor variables gives us precise information about the outcome variable. If the predicted scores are not close to the observed y scores, then the regression is weak and the information vague and possibly useless. The statistical tests of regression reveal whether there is any useful information to be obtained from the predictors.

The raw regression coefficients reflect the scale of the y and x variables as well as the intercorrelations among the predictors. For this reason, they cannot be easily interpreted as indicating the importance or relative importance of the *x* variables. This "contamination" of units of scale may be removed by obtaining the *standardized* regression weights that apply to standardized *y* and *x* variables, i.e., mean = 0 and variance = 1. Even the standardized weights, however, depend upon the intercorrelations among the predictors and may be difficult to interpret.

With respect to tests of significance, any one regression weight may be tested by comparing the estimated raw weight to its respective standard error. If the outcome variable has a normal distribution, then the regression coefficient divided by its standard error will have a *t* distribution with degrees of freedom equal to the residual degrees of freedom. Thus, for example, to test whether the Word Knowledge coefficient is significantly different from zero, we may divide the coefficient (.67 in Figure 2.3-3) by its standard error (.11 in Figure 2.3-4) to obtain a *t* value of about 6, well over the .05 critical value; the degrees of freedom are equal to 119, minus 2 for the constants, minus 4 for estimating the regression weights—or 113. We may also use these results to construct confidence intervals on particular coefficients. However, the weights are not independently estimated and the number of individual tests or intervals should be kept to a minimum to avoid compounding statistical error rates.

Figure 2.3-4 also shows the variance and standard deviation of the criterion variables, eliminating all of the predictors (or "removing the effects of the predictors"). The variance of the Science Achievement Total score before adjustment is the common within-group variance in Figure 2.3-2—or 150.13. The conditional variance, eliminating the predictors, is 105.47. There is about a one-third reduction in error variance when the effects of the predictors are removed; thus we have an indication that there is a strong relationship between the set of predictors and Science Achievement Total.

The tests of regression are given in Figure 2.3-4. The multiple correlation of .57 is the correlation of Science Achievement Total with the best linear combination of the four predictors. The squared multiple correlation, .32, is the proportion of criterion variation that can be attributed to this combination of predictors. The corresponding *F* statistic, *F* = 13.38, is statistically significant at the .01 level and clearly indicates a significant relationship between the Total score and the four predictors jointly. (The step-down result is not applicable in the univariate case, as it only reproduces the univariate *F* test.)

The stepwise analysis allows us to test the partial relationship of each predictor, or set of predictors, to the criterion. According to the Covariate Grouping key, Word Knowledge is entered into the regression equation first, then Hours of Homework eliminating Word Knowledge, and then the two Interest scores eliminating Word Knowledge and Hours of Homework.

The listing of the stepwise analysis is correctly read beginning from the bottom. That is, we first observe the test of significance for Interest. If Interest scores are not significantly related to the criterion, then we proceed with a test of the Hours-of-homework and Word-knowledge variables. However, if Interest scores *are* significantly related to the criterion, then the Hours-of-homework and Word-knowledge tests are "confounded" with Interest variation. Although the sum of the squares for Interest is obtained holding constant Word Knowledge and Hours of Homework, Interest has not been eliminated from Hours of Homework and Word Knowledge. If Interest proves to be significant, then a factor of importance has not been held constant in Word-knowledge and Hours-of-homework tests of significance.

Conversely, if Interest proves to be nonsignificant and we proceed with the Hours-of-homework test, we may find Hours of Homework to be nonsignificant. In that case we may proceed validly with a test of the Word-knowledge predictor. If we find Hours of Homework to be significant, however, we then have no valid test of the effect of Word Knowledge on the criterion with this order of predictors. If interests are found to be significantly related to criterion variation and we still desire a test of the Hours-of-homework effect, then we must reorder Interest in Science and Science in the World to precede the Hours of Homework score when we select variables. Then we should repeat the stepwise analysis with the predictor variables in the new order. In this order, we can test Hours of Homework and its relationship to Science Achievement Total, holding constant the significant Interest effects. It is essential that the number of alternate orders be kept to a minimum, since tests made in one order are not statistically independent of those in another. The statistical error rates cannot be accurately

PROBLEM

- -

PROBLEM 1: UNIVARIATE AND MULTIVARIATE REGRESSION EXAMPLE IEA-DATA SWEDEN POP 2 GRADE 8 MALES AND FEMALES SEPARATED

- -

PAGE   1

UNIVARIATE AND MULTIVARIATE REGRESSION
DATA SAMPLE FROM SWEDEN GRADE 8

EXAMPLE 1: 1 DEPENDENT VARIABLE SC A&B C
EXAMPLE 2: 4 DEPENDENT VARIABLES SC BIO C, SC CHE C, SC PHY C, SC PRA C

4 INDEPENDENT VARIABLES: WORDK C ,INTR SC ,SC I WLD,HOURS HW

VARIABLE:	FORMAT:	COLUMNS:	DESCRIPTION:
SCHOOL	F3.0	1- 3	
STUDENT	F3.0	4- 6	
SEX	I2	7- 8	
SC A&B C	F4.1	9-12	SCIENCE TOTAL TEST CORRECTED SCORE
SC BIO C	F4.1	13-16	SCIENCE BIOLOGY SUBTEST CORRECTED SCORE
SC CHE C .	F4.1	17-20	SCIENCE CHEMISTRY SUBTEST CORRECTED SCORE
SC PHY C	F4.1	21-24	SCIENCE PHYSICS SUBTEST CORRECTED SCORE
SC PRA C	F4.1	25-28	SCIENCE PRACTICAL SUBTEST CORRECTED SCORE
WORD K C	F5.1	29-33	WORD KNOWLEDGE TEST CORRECTED SCORE
INTRO SC	F4.0	34-37	INTEREST IN SCIENCE (LOWER SCORE IS MORE INT)
SC I WLD	F4.0	38-41	SCIENCE IN THE WORLD (LOWER SCORE IS MORE INT)
HOURS HW	F4.0	42-45	HOURS HOMEWORK IN ALL SUBJECTS PER WEEK
RC C&D C	F5.1	46-50	RDG COMPREHENSION TOTAL TEST CORRECTED SCORE
LI W&R C	F4.1	51-54	LITERATURE TOTAL TEST CORRECTED SCORE
READSPE	F4.0	55-58	READING SPEED-ITEM REACHED
LI INTER	F4.0	59-62	LITERARY INTEREST (LOWER SCORE IS MORE INT)
BOOKSHO	F4.0	63-66	NUMBER OF BOOKS IN HOME
REAPLEA	F4.0	67-70	HOURS READING FOR PLEASURE PER WEEK

INPUT PARAMETERS
================

PAGE   2

NUMBER OF VARIABLES IN INPUT VECTORS=   9

NUMBER OF FACTORS IN DESIGN=   1

  NUMBER OF LEVELS OF FACTOR 1 (SEX   ) =   2

INPUT IS FROM CARDS. DATA OPTION 2

MINIMAL PAGE SPACING WILL BE USED

ADDITIONAL OUTPUT WILL BE PRINTED

*****NUMBER OF VARIABLE FORMAT CARDS NOT SPECIFIED. ASSUMED TO BE 1.

FORMAT OF DATA
   (8X,5F4.1,F5.1,3F4.0)

FIRST OBSERVATION
SUBJECT   1 , CELL   1
                          23.8000   7.8000   6.5000   5.8000   3.8000   16.0000   6.0000   -2.0000
                           1.0000

GROUP   SEX   1
===

SUBCLASS CORRELATION MATRIX
----

	1 SC A&B C	2 SC BIO C	3 SC CHE C	4 SC PHY C	5 SC PRA C	6 WORD K C	7 INTR SC	8 SC I WLD	9 HOURS HW
1 SC A&B C	1.000000								
2 SC BIO C	0.741132	1.000000							
3 SC CHE C	0.836166	0.441797	1.000000						
4 SC PHY C	0.897411	0.541045	0.722921	1.000000					
5 SC PRA C	0.843304	0.562605	0.608170	0.643439	1.000001				
6 WORD K C	0.526262	0.346187	0.317947	0.503956	0.556149	1.000000			
7 INTR SC	-0.292470	-0.124998	-0.244366	-0.306339	-0.270660	-0.316412	1.000000		
8 SC I WLD	-0.357940	-0.310638	-0.336625	-0.258437	-0.309313	-0.445751	0.309826	1.000000	
9 HOURS HW	-0.011465	0.027525	-0.110016	0.042282	-0.014463	-0.146111	-0.103843	0.099590	1.000000

GROUP   SEX   2
===

SUBCLASS CORRELATION MATRIX
----

	1 SC A&B C	2 SC BIO C	3 SC CHE C	4 SC PHY C	5 SC PRA C	6 WORD K C	7 INTR SC	8 SC I WLD	9 HOURS HW
1 SC A&B C	1.000000								
2 SC BIO C	0.770966	1.000000							
3 SC CHE C	0.830330	0.514784	1.000000						
4 SC PHY C	0.858357	0.583910	0.603960	1.000000					
5 SC PRA C	0.787976	0.448946	0.545758	0.580438	1.000000				
6 WORD K C	0.497495	0.354771	0.444633	0.469184	0.337291	1.000000			
7 INTR SC	-0.300704	-0.348831	-0.176927	-0.330975	-0.126637	0.007704	1.000000		
8 SC I WLD	-0.019034	0.000195	0.027728	-0.040881	-0.050015	-0.055440	0.326082	1.000000	
9 HOURS HW	0.203746	0.079930	0.178447	0.132737	0.271047	-0.015796	-0.067184	-0.060855	1.000000

CELL IDENTIFICATION AND FREQUENCIES

PAGE   3

CELL	FACTOR LEVELS SEX	N
1	1	50
2	2	69

TOTAL N=   119.

FIGURE 2.3-1 Problem 1: Phase I output

TOTAL SUM OF CROSS-PRODUCTS
----

	1 SC A&B C	2 SC BIO C	3 SC CHE C	4 SC PHY C	5 SC PRA C	6 WORD K C	7 INTR SC	8 SC I WLD	9 HOURS HW
1 SC A&B C	95075.57								
2 SC BIO C	22485.34	5901.14							
3 SC CHE C	22274.00	5074.37	5757.57						
4 SC PHY C	33051.53	7671.00	7590.62	12014.98					
5 SC PRA C	17488.64	3893.38	3906.03	5854.88	3870.42				
6 WORD K C	53773.46	12884.92	12517.08	18988.59	9526.72	38414.84			
7 INTR SC	12229.10	3188.10	2984.50	4308.10	1796.40	8459.80	4454.00		
8 SC I WLD	-9010.70	-2179.60	-2086.70	-3138.80	-1631.90	-5764.60	-1052.00	2061.00	
9 HOURS HW	6370.50	1573.70	1483.00	2261.10	1072.30	3872.00	1205.00	-646.00	606.00

OBSERVED CELL MEANS --- ROWS ARE CELLS-COLUMNS ARE VARIABLES

	1 SC A&B C	2 SC BIO C	3 SC CHE C	4 SC PHY C	5 SC PRA C	6 WORD K C	7 INTR SC	8 SC I WLD	9 HOURS HW
1	29.54400	6.75600	6.30000	10.64400	5.92000	16.04200	2.62000	-2.92000	1.94000
2	22.15507	5.88986	5.58406	7.80290	2.96232	15.52609	6.39130	-2.42029	2.21739

OBSERVED CELL STD DEVS--ROWS ARE CELLS-COLUMNS VARIABLES
----

	1 SC A&B C	2 SC BIO C	3 SC CHE C	4 SC PHY C	5 SC PRA C	6 WORD K C	7 INTR SC	8 SC I WLD	9 HOURS HW
1	13.86860	3.49011	3.87298	5.11425	4.08427	8.61172	3.76281	3.94782	0.84298
2	10.94112	3.04008	3.61071	3.57182	3.19748	8.81220	2.96657	2.62009	0.80201

ESTIMATION PARAMETERS
=====================

RANK OF THE BASIS = RANK OF MODEL FOR SIGNIFICANCE TESTING =   0

RANK OF THE MODEL TO BE ESTIMATED IS   0

ERROR TERM TO BE USED IS (WITHIN CELLS)

VARIANCE-COVARIANCE FACTORS AND CORRELATIONS AMONG ESTIMATES WILL BE PRINTED

ERROR SUM OF CROSS-PRODUCTS
----

	1 SC A&B C	2 SC BIO C	3 SC CHE C	4 SC PHY C	5 SC PRA C	6 WORD K C	7 INTR SC	8 SC I WLD	9 HOURS HW
1 SC A&B C	17564.71								
2 SC BIO C	3501.56	1225.33							
3 SC CHE C	4431.29	676.87	1621.53						
4 SC PHY C	5399.92	904.36	1231.30	2149.16					
5 SC PRA C	4215.12	689.72	899.85	1109.34	1512.60				
6 WORD K C	6341.49	1156.13	1481.65	2091.79	1604.76	8914.45			
7 INTR SC	-1411.55	-294.36	-303.37	-527.34	-285.50	-488.71	1292.21		
8 SC I WLD	-997.38	-209.62	-234.36	-281.69	-272.87	-829.61	397.87	1230.49	
9 HOURS HW	115.01	17.22	17.54	34.79	44.83	-59.57	-27.01	7.54	78.56

ERROR VARIANCE -COVARIANCE MATRIX
----

	1 SC A&B C	2 SC BIO C	3 SC CHE C	4 SC PHY C	5 SC PRA C	6 WORD K C	7 INTR SC	8 SC I WLD	9 HOURS HW
1 SC A&B C	150.1258								
2 SC BIO C	29.9278	10.4729							
3 SC CHE C	37.8743	5.7852	13.8593						
4 SC PHY C	46.1532	7.7296	10.5240	18.3689					
5 SC PRA C	36.0267	5.8950	7.6910	9.4816	12.9282				
6 WORD K C	54.2008	9.8815	12.6637	17.8786	13.7159	76.1919			
7 INTR SC	-12.0645	-2.5159	-2.5929	-4.5072	-2.4402	-4.1770	11.0446		
8 SC I WLD	-8.5246	-1.7916	-2.0031	-2.4076	-2.3322	-7.0907	3.4006	10.5170	
9 HOURS HW	0.9830	0.1472	0.1499	0.2973	0.3831	-0.5091	-0.2309	0.0645	0.6714

ERROR CORRELATION MATRIX
----

	1 SC A&B C	2 SC BIO C	3 SC CHE C	4 SC PHY C	5 SC PRA C	6 WORD K C	7 INTR SC	8 SC I WLD	9 HOURS HW
1 SC A&B C	1.000000								
2 SC BIO C	0.754770	1.000000							
3 SC CHE C	0.830323	0.480193	1.000000						
4 SC PHY C	0.878886	0.557289	0.659580	1.000001					
5 SC PRA C	0.817762	0.506621	0.574572	0.615275	1.000000				
6 WORD K C	0.506784	0.349811	0.389704	0.477900	0.437018	1.000000			
7 INTR SC	-0.296284	-0.233931	-0.209576	-0.316439	-0.204212	-0.143990	1.000000		
8 SC I WLD	-0.214536	-0.170712	-0.165915	-0.173221	-0.200013	-0.250489	0.315524	1.000000	
9 HOURS HW	0.097904	0.055503	0.049141	0.084665	0.130035	-0.071178	-0.084772	0.024265	1.000000

VARIABLE	VARIANCE (ERROR MEAN SQUARES)	STANDARD DEVIATION
1 SC A&B C	150.125751	12.2526
2 SC BIO C	10.472872	3.2362
3 SC CHE C	13.859251	3.7228
4 SC PHY C	18.368910	4.2859
5 SC PRA C	12.928222	3.5956
6 WORD K C	76.191917	8.7288
7 INTR SC	11.044570	3.3233
8 SC I WLD	10.517022	3.2430
9 HOURS HW	0.671446	0.8194

D.F.=   117.

ERROR TERM FOR ANALYSIS OF VARIANCE (WITHIN CELLS)

FIGURE 2.3-2 Problem 1: Phase I output (continued) and Phase II output

20

ANALYSIS OF VARIANCE
====================

====================

1 DEPENDENT VARIABLE(S)

1 SC A&B C

4 INDEPENDENT VARIABLE(S)
(PREDICTOR VARIABLES, COVARIATES)

6 WORD K C
9 HOURS HW
7 INTR SC
8 SC I WLD

PREDICTORS WILL BE ADDED TO THE STEP-WISE REGRESSION ACCORDING TO USERS KEY

REGRESSION ANALYSIS
=====================

=============

=====

SUM OF PRODUCTS CRITERIA

```
                     1
                  SC A&B C

1 SC A&B C    17564.71
```

SUM OF PRODUCTS - PREDICTORS BY CRITERIA

```
                     1
                  SC A&B C

1 WORD K C     6341.488
2 HOURS HW      115.006
3 INTR SC     -1411.551
4 SC I WLD     -997.379
```

SUM OF PRODUCTS - PREDICTORS

```
                1          2          3          4
             WORD K C   HOURS HW   INTR SC    SC I WLD

1 WORD K C    8914.455
2 HOURS HW     -59.565     78.559
3 INTR SC     -488.706    -27.010   1292.215
4 SC I WLD    -829.611       7.544    397.868   1230.492
```

INVERSE SUM OF PRODUCTS OF PREDICTORS (X'X)INV

```
                1             2             3             4
             WORD K C      HOURS HW      INTR SC       SC I WLD

1 WORD K C   1.209633D-04
2 HOURS HW   9.341777D-05  1.293098D-02
3 INTR SC    2.528305D-05  3.449723D-04  8.729468D-04
4 SC I WLD   7.280705D-05 -1.278422D-04 -2.673281D-04  9.489925D-04
```

CORRELATION MATRIX OF (X-PRIME X) INVERSE

```
                1          2          3          4
             WORD K C   HOURS HW   INTR SC    SC I WLD

1 WORD K C   1.000000
2 HOURS HW   0.074694   1.000000
3 INTR SC    0.077805   0.102677   1.000000
4 SC I WLD   0.214890  -0.036494  -0.293710   1.000000
```

SUM OF PRODUCTS - REGRESSION

```
                     1
                  SC A&B C

1 SC A&B C     5646.101
```

RAW REGRESSION COEFFICIENTS - INDEPENDENT X DEPENDENT VARS

```
                     1
                  SC A&B C

1 WORD K C     0.669527
2 HOURS HW     1.720108
3 INTR SC     -0.765576
4 SC I WLD    -0.122155
```

STANDARDIZED REGRESSION COEFFICIENTS - INDEP X DEPENDENT VAR

```
                     1
                  SC A&B C

1 WORD K C     0.476974
2 HOURS HW     0.115036
3 INTR SC     -0.207651
4 SC I WLD    -0.032332
```

FIGURE 2.3-3 Problem 1: Phase III output

STANDARD ERRORS OF RAW REGRESSION COEFS-IND X DEP VARIABLES

```
            1
          SC A&B C
1 WORD K C   0.112954
2 HOURS HW   1.167856
3 INTR SC    0.303436
4 SC I WLD   0.316377
```

REGRESSION COEFFICIENTS AS T-STATISTICS - INDEP X DEP VARS

```
            1
          SC A&B C
1 WORD K C   5.927442
2 HOURS HW   1.472877
3 INTR SC   -2.523019
4 SC I WLD  -0.386107
```

DEGREES OF FREEDOM =   113.

ERROR SUM OF PRODUCTS ADJUSTED FOR PREDICTORS

```
              1
            SC A&B C
1 SC A&B C   11918.61
```

ERROR VAR-COV MATRIX ADJUSTED FOR PREDICTORS

```
              1
            SC A&B C
1 SC A&B C   105.4744
```

```
     VARIABLE          VARIANCE          STANDARD DEVIATION
                    (ERROR MEAN SQUARES)

     1 SC A&B C        105.474446             10.2701
```

D.F.=   113.

ERROR TERM FOR ANALYSIS OF COVARIANCE (WITHIN CELLS)

4 COVARIATE(S) HAVE BEEN ELIMINATED

LOG-DETERMINANT ERROR SUM OF PRODUCTS BEFORE ADJUSTMENT FOR PREDICTORS = 0.97736464E+01   AFTER = 0.93858557E+01

STATISTICS FOR REGRESSION ANALYSIS WITH   4 PREDICTOR VARIABLE(S)
==

PAGE   8

VARIABLE	SQUARE MULT R	MULT R	F	P LESS THAN	STEP DOWN F	P LESS THAN
1 SC A&B C	0.3214	0.5670	13.3826	0.0001	13.3826	0.0001

```
          DEGREES OF FREEDOM FOR HYPOTHESIS=   4
          DEGREES OF FREEDOM FOR ERROR=   113.
```

STEP-WISE REGRESSION TO ANALYZE THE CONTRIBUTION OF EACH INDEPENDENT VARIABLE
==

(LIKELIHOOD RATIO = 0.74317020E+00   LOG = -0.29683018E+00)

ADDING VARIABLE   1 (WORD K C) THROUGH   1 (WORD K C) TO THE REGRESSION EQUATION
      F=   40.0881 WITH   1. AND   116.0000 D.F.   P LESS THAN 0.0001

PERCENT OF ADDITIONAL VARIANCE ACCOUNTED FOR= 25.6830

(LIKELIHOOD RATIO = 0.97572333E+00   LOG = -0.24576187E-01)

ADDING VARIABLE   2 (HOURS HW) THROUGH   2 (HOURS HW) TO THE REGRESSION EQUATION
      F=   2.8613 WITH   1. AND   115.0000 D.F.   P LESS THAN 0.0935

PERCENT OF ADDITIONAL VARIANCE ACCOUNTED FOR=   1.8041

(LIKELIHOOD RATIO = 0.93577117E+00   LOG = -0.66384315E-01)

ADDING VARIABLE   3 (INTR SC) THROUGH   4 (SC I WLD) TO THE REGRESSION EQUATION
      F=   3.8780 WITH   2. AND   113.0000 D.F.   P LESS THAN 0.0236

PERCENT OF ADDITIONAL VARIANCE ACCOUNTED FOR=   4.6574

FIGURE 2.3-4   Problem 1:   Phase III output (concluded)

computed and may become large. An initial order of variables should be established based on prior knowledge about the importance and complexity of the predictors.

Reading from the bottom, we find that the two Interest scores are significantly related to Science Achievement Total. The two variables are tested jointly because of the final "2" on the Covariate Grouping key. The F ratio is 3.88, which is significant at the .05 level. We conclude that all four predictor variables are necessary to the regression equation and, thus, retain (10) as in the appropriate prediction formula.

Had we been working at the .01 level, we would have concluded that the Interest scores are not significantly related to the criterion and proceeded with the test of the Hours-of-homework variable. We would find that Hours of Homework is not significantly related to Science Achievement at either the .05 or .01 level. Thus, we could proceed with the test of the relationship of Word Knowledge to Science Achievement, although we have so little doubt as to its significance that a test is hardly necessary. We could, therefore, eliminate the three additional variables from the prediction equation and retain only Word Knowledge as the predictor variable.

Before writing such an equation, however, we must re-estimate the regression weights for Word Knowledge only. Because of the intercorrelations of the predictors, the regression weight for Word Knowledge will change when variables are deleted fron the set. We obtain this estimate by setting the rank of model for *estimation* equal to 3, corresponding to the two intercept constants for the sex groups and one regression weight for the predictor variable. The regression weight is obtained by rerunning the program with Word Knowledge as the only predictor.

The summary data from the regression run are displayed by extending Table 2.1 to include columns indicating (1) whether each variable contributes to regression and (2) the percents of variation uniquely attributable to each antecedent. These results are presented under the heading "Test Statistics"—for example, the percent of variation in Science Achievement attributable to Word Knowledge is 25.68. Since Word Knowledge is the first predictor variable, this is the square of the simple correlation between Science and Word Knowledge ($r = .507$) from the error correlation matrix. Hours of Homework accounts for an *additional* 1.8 percent of criterion variation. The two Science Interest scores account for a total of 4.66 percent of criterion variation in addition to Word Knowledge and Hours of Homework. All together, the four variables account for $25.68 + 1.80 + 4.66 = 32.14$ percent of the variation in the criterion variable. This is exactly the square of the multiple correlation of y with the four x measures. Each separate percentage is sometimes referred to as "an increment in the squared multiple correlation."

2.7.2 Multivariate Analysis

The second set of Phase III control cards in Figure 2.2 indicates that a multivariate regression analysis should be performed with the four Science subtest scores as simultaneous criterion variables. The same predictor variables are selected, and in the same order, as in the univariate pass through Phase III of the program. The output for the multivariate analysis is listed in Figures 2.4-1 through 2.4-3.

The regression weights for the multivariate analysis appear in Figure 2.4-1 as a matrix with as many rows as predictor variables and as many columns as criteria. Point estimates in multivariate regression are identical to the univariate estimates for each outcome measure taken separately. That is, each column of the regression matrix at the bottom of Figure 2.4-1 is the univariate set of regression weights for one criterion measure. For example, the Biology subtest score has a regression equation like (10), with weights of .12 for Word Knowledge, .26 for Hours of Homework, and $-.17$ and $-.04$ for the two Interest scores. These are exactly the weights that would have been obtained if Biology were the outcome measure in a univariate analysis. It is in tests of significance and confidence intervals on elements of the matrix that the multivariate results depart from multiple univariate results.

As in the univariate model, the matrix of standardized regression coefficients in Figure 2.4-2 contains the weights that would be applied to the measures if both criteria and predictors were expressed in standardized form. Because standardized variables are all in the same scale, the weights are more easily interpreted as reflecting something of the relative importance of the variables in the regression equations. In this instance, the matrix indicates that both Word Knowledge and Interest in Science play important roles in predicting the four science achievements. However, the predictors are sufficiently interdependent that the addition or deletion of predictors, even those that appear unimportant, may change all of the regression weights. Thus, the simple, multiple, and partial correlations, as well as the stepwise tests of significance, must be inspected to obtain reliable information about the relative importance of predictors.

The standard errors of the regression weights appear next, with the standard error of a particular weight in the same position in the matrix of standard errors as the regression coefficient in its matrix. These may be used for tests of significance and confidence intervals on single regression weights. In the multivariate model, sets of standard errors may be used to construct confidence intervals and test hypotheses about the same set of regression weights. For example, we may wish to construct a confidence interval on the set of four regression weights for predicting the science outcomes from Word Knowledge alone. For this, we would employ the four estimated regression weights and the corresponding set of four standard errors. These procedures are discussed in detail in Finn (1974, Section 4.4) and Bock (1975, Sections 4.1.12 and 4.2.6). These confidence intervals may be useful in interpretation, especially after stepwise tests have indicated which variables are important to the model.

The next-to-last matrix in Figure 2.4-2 is the variance-covariance matrix adjusted for predictors. This is the pooled within-group matrix for the criterion variables, holding constant the four predictors. The diagonal elements, which are the conditional variances, are extracted and listed along with their square roots. The square roots are the standard deviations of the criterion variables, holding constant the effects of the four predictor variables. The conditional variances serve as the residual or "error mean squares" for univariate tests of regression.

Dividing each covariance in the adjusted variance-covariance matrix by the corresponding standard deviations reduces the matrix to the correlational form shown next. The result is the matrix of *partial correlations* among the criterion variables, holding constant the four predictors. These partial correlations estimate what the correlations among the science tests would be if all subjects had the same scores on predictors x_1 through x_4. Even after eliminating all predictable variation, the correlations among the science tests range from .37 to .57. Thus, residual variation is not independent, and multivariate tests of significance are essential. Note that residual variances and covariances are estimated with 113 degrees of freedom (119 total degrees of freedom, minus 2 for constants for males and females, minus 4 for the predictor variables).

The tests of regression appear in Figure 2.4-3. As in the univariate run, these are organized into three sections, the first giving information about the relationship of each criterion variable to all four predictors, the second section giving an overall test of any relationship between all criterion variables and all predictors, and the third presenting the stepwise regression. The lattermost permits us to inspect the relationship between *each* independent variable (or set of independent variables) and all four criteria, jointly and separately.

The multiple correlation coefficients are the univariate coefficients indicating the degree of association of each criterion variable with the best linear combination of the four predictors. For example, the multiple correlation of the Biology test with the four predictors is .40; i.e., about 16 percent of Biology variation can be explained by the four predictors. Likewise, the proportions of variation in Chemistry, Physics, and Practical Science attributable to the four predictors are 18, 30, and 24 percent, respectively. Physics is the most predictable of the four criterion measures.

Corresponding to each multiple correlation is an F ratio for the test that the population correlation is zero. The multiple correlation for each of the four criterion measures is significant at the .01 level, with 4 and 113 degrees of freedom. Note, however, that these statistics are not independent due to the intercorrelations among the criterion variables. They should *not* be interpreted as partial tests of the multivariate hypothesis. But with the protection of an overall multivariate test, these F ratios may be inspected to decide which criterion variables are significantly related to the predictors. Hummel and Sligo (1971) recommend inspecting the univariate statistics once the multivariate hypothesis is rejected. They indicate that this is neither too conservative nor too liberal an approach in finding important criterion variables.

ANALYSIS OF VARIANCE

====================

====================

4 DEPENDENT VARIABLE(S)

2 SC BIO C
3 SC CHE C
4 SC PHY C
5 SC PRA C

4 INDEPENDENT VARIABLE(S)
(PREDICTOR VARIABLES, COVARIATES)

6 WORD K C
9 HOURS HW
7 INTR SC
8 SC I WLD

PREDICTORS WILL BE ADDED TO THE STEP-WISE REGRESSION ACCORDING TO USERS KEY

REGRESSION ANALYSIS

====================

==============

=====

SUM OF PRODUCTS CRITERIA
----

	1 SC BIO C	2 SC CHE C	3 SC PHY C	4 SC PRA C
1 SC BIO C	1225.326			
2 SC CHE C	676.869	1621.532		
3 SC PHY C	904.359	1231.303	2149.163	
4 SC PRA C	689.718	899.849	1109.344	1512.602

SUM OF PRODUCTS - PREDICTORS BY CRITERIA
----

	1 SC BIO C	2 SC CHE C	3 SC PHY C	4 SC PRA C
1 WORD K C	1156.131	1481.649	2091.792	1604.756
2 HOURS HW	17.220	17.539	34.789	44.825
3 INTR SC	-294.362	-303.370	-527.342	-285.503
4 SC I WLD	-209.618	-234.362	-281.692	-272.873

SUM OF PRODUCTS - PREDICTORS
----

	1 WORD K C	2 HOURS HW	3 INTR SC	4 SC I WLD
1 WORD K C	8914.455			
2 HOURS HW	-59.565	78.559		
3 INTR SC	-488.706	-27.010	1292.215	
4 SC I WLD	-829.611	7.544	397.868	1230.492

INVERSE SUM OF PRODUCTS OF PREDICTORS (X'X)INV
----

	1 WORD K C	2 HOURS HW	3 INTR SC	4 SC I WLD
1 WORD K C	1.209633D-04			
2 HOURS HW	9.341777D-05	1.293098D-02		
3 INTR SC	2.528305D-05	3.449723D-04	8.729468D-04	
4 SC I WLD	7.280705D-05	-1.278422D-04	-2.673281D-04	9.489925D-04

CORRELATION MATRIX OF (X-PRIME X) INVERSE
----

	1 WORD K C	2 HOURS HW	3 INTR SC	4 SC I WLD
1 WORD K C	1.000000			
2 HOURS HW	0.074694	1.000000		
3 INTR SC	0.077805	0.102677	1.000000	
4 SC I WLD	0.214890	-0.036494	-0.293710	1.000000

SUM OF PRODUCTS - REGRESSION
----

	1 SC BIO C	2 SC CHE C	3 SC PHY C	4 SC PRA C
1 SC BIO C	198.5145			
2 SC CHE C	239.6925	292.9204		
3 SC PHY C	355.4996	430.4182	645.4381	
4 SC PRA C	259.8072	318.6073	464.8793	358.4625

RAW REGRESSION COEFFICIENTS - INDEPENDENT X DEPENDENT VARS
----

	1 SC BIO C	2 SC CHE C	3 SC PHY C	4 SC PRA C
1 WORD K C	0.118754	0.156130	0.222438	0.171219
2 HOURS HW	0.255928	0.290518	0.499354	0.665941
3 INTR SC	-0.165755	-0.158663	-0.320150	-0.120245
4 SC I WLD	-0.038262	-0.035677	0.021500	-0.071524

FIGURE 2.4-1   Problem 1:   Phase III multivariate output

STANDARDIZED REGRESSION COEFFICIENTS - INDEP X DEPENDENT VAR
----

		1 SC BIO C	2 SC CHE C	3 SC PHY C	4 SC PRA C
1	WORD K C	0.320310	0.366076	0.453025	0.415658
2	HOURS HW	0.064802	0.063945	0.095471	0.151765
3	INTR SC	-0.170219	-0.141638	-0.248248	-0.111141
4	SC I WLD	-0.038342	-0.031079	0.016268	-0.064511

STANDARD ERRORS OF RAW REGRESSION COEFS-IND X DEP VARIABLES
----

		1 SC BIO C	2 SC CHE C	3 SC PHY C	4 SC PRA C
1	WORD K C	0.033154	0.037713	0.040121	0.035149
2	HOURS HW	0.342785	0.389920	0.414821	0.363417
3	INTR SC	0.089064	0.101310	0.107780	0.094424
4	SC I WLD	0.092862	0.105631	0.112377	0.098451

REGRESSION COEFFICIENTS AS T-STATISTICS - INDEP X DEP VARS
----

		1 SC BIO C	2 SC CHE C	3 SC PHY C	4 SC PRA C
1	WORD K C	3.581915	4.140000	5.544179	4.871180
2	HOURS HW	0.746614	0.745070	1.203782	1.832441
3	INTR SC	-1.861082	-1.566106	-2.970395	-1.273459
4	SC I WLD	-0.412030	-0.337748	0.191318	-0.726495

DEGREES OF FREEDOM = 113.

ERROR SUM OF PRODUCTS ADJUSTED FOR PREDICTORS
----

		1 SC BIO C	2 SC CHE C	3 SC PHY C	4 SC PRA C
1	SC BIO C	1026.812			
2	SC CHE C	437.176	1328.612		
3	SC PHY C	548.859	800.885	1503.725	
4	SC PRA C	429.910	581.241	644.464	1154.140

ERROR VAR-COV MATRIX ADJUSTED FOR PREDICTORS
----

		1 SC BIO C	2 SC CHE C	3 SC PHY C	4 SC PRA C
1	SC BIO C	9.08683			
2	SC CHE C	3.86882	11.75763		
3	SC PHY C	4.85716	7.08748	13.30730	
4	SC PRA C	3.80452	5.14373	5.70322	10.21362

MATRIX OF CORRELATIONS WITH PREDICTORS ELIMINATED
----

		1 SC BIO C	2 SC CHE C	3 SC PHY C	4 SC PRA C
1	SC BIO C	1.000000			
2	SC CHE C	0.374293	1.000000		
3	SC PHY C	0.441704	0.566614	1.000000	
4	SC PRA C	0.394915	0.469384	0.489199	1.000000

VARIABLE	VARIANCE (ERROR MEAN SQUARES)	STANDARD DEVIATION
1 SC BIO C	9.086828	3.0144
2 SC CHE C	11.757629	3.4289
3 SC PHY C	13.307297	3.6479
4 SC PRA C	10.213624	3.1959

D.F.= 113.

ERROR TERM FOR ANALYSIS OF COVARIANCE (WITHIN CELLS)

4 COVARIATE(S) HAVE BEEN ELIMINATED

FIGURE 2.4-2   Problem 1:   Phase III multivariate output (continued)

LOG-DETERMINANT ERROR SUM OF PRODUCTS BEFORE ADJUSTMENT FOR PREDICTORS = 0.27914734E+02   AFTER = 0.27474258E+02

STATISTICS FOR REGRESSION ANALYSIS WITH   4 PREDICTOR VARIABLE(S)
===

PAGE 11

VARIABLE	SQUARE MULT R	MULT R	F	P LESS THAN	STEP DOWN F	P LESS THAN
1 SC BIO C	0.1620	0.4025	5.4616	0.0005	5.4616	0.0005
2 SC CHE C	0.1806	0.4250	6.2283	0.0002	2.5771	0.0414
3 SC PHY C	0.3003	0.5480	12.1256	0.0001	3.6985	0.0073
4 SC PRA C	0.2370	0.4868	8.7741	0.0001	1.4263	0.2301

DEGREES OF FREEDOM FOR HYPOTHESIS=   4
DEGREES OF FREEDOM FOR ERROR=   113.

F VALUE FOR TEST OF HYPOTHESIS OF NO ASSOCIATION BETWEEN DEPENDENT AND INDEPENDENT VARIABLES=   3.2636

D.F.= 16. AND   336.6931   P LESS THAN 0.0001

(LIKELIHOOD RATIO = 0.64373028E+00   LOG = -0.44047546E+00)

STEP-WISE REGRESSION TO ANALYZE THE CONTRIBUTION OF EACH INDEPENDENT VARIABLE
==

(LIKELIHOOD RATIO = 0.73360544E+00   LOG = -0.30978394E+00)

ADDING VARIABLE   1 (WORD K C) THROUGH   1 (WORD K C) TO THE REGRESSION EQUATION
F=   10.2584   WITH   4.   AND   113.0000   D.F.   P LESS THAN 0.0001

VARIABLE	UNIVARIATE F	P LESS THAN	STEP DOWN F	P LESS THAN	PERCENT OF ADDITIONAL VARIANCE ACCOUNTED FOR
1 SC BIO C	16.1738	0.0002	16.1738	0.0002	12.2368
			STEP-DOWN MEAN SQUARES =(149.9405/	9.2706)	
2 SC CHE C	20.7714	0.0001	9.0301	0.0033	15.1869
			STEP-DOWN MEAN SQUARES =(90.8346/	10.0591)	
3 SC PHY C	34.3346	0.0001	8.9130	0.0035	22.8388
			STEP-DOWN MEAN SQUARES =(76.3243/	8.5632)	
4 SC PRA C	27.3842	0.0001	3.2525	0.0740	19.0984
			STEP-DOWN MEAN SQUARES =(23.0922/	7.0997)	

D.F.=   1. AND   116.

- -

(LIKELIHOOD RATIO = 0.96430618E+00   LOG = -0.36346436E-01)

ADDING VARIABLE   2 (HOURS HW) THROUGH   2 (HOURS HW) TO THE REGRESSION EQUATION
F=   1.0364   WITH   4.   AND   112.0000   D.F.   P LESS THAN 0.3918

VARIABLE	UNIVARIATE F	P LESS THAN	STEP DOWN F	P LESS THAN	PERCENT OF ADDITIONAL VARIANCE ACCOUNTED FOR
1 SC BIO C	0.8577	0.3564	0.8577	0.3564	0.6497
			STEP-DOWN MEAN SQUARES =(7.9613/	9.2819)	
2 SC CHE C	0.8112	0.3697	0.3342	0.5644	0.5941
			STEP-DOWN MEAN SQUARES =(3.3809/	10.1177)	
3 SC PHY C	2.1494	0.1454	0.9974	0.3202	1.4157
			STEP-DOWN MEAN SQUARES =(8.5412/	8.5634)	
4 SC PRA C	3.8336	0.0527	1.9429	0.1661	2.6099
			STEP-DOWN MEAN SQUARES =(13.6801/	7.0410)	

D.F.=   1. AND   115.

- -

(LIKELIHOOD RATIO = 0.90996867E+00   LOG = -0.94345093E-01)

ADDING VARIABLE   3 (INTR SC) THROUGH   4 (SC I WLD) TO THE REGRESSION EQUATION
F=   1.3283   WITH   8.   AND   220.0000   D.F.   P LESS THAN 0.2305

VARIABLE	UNIVARIATE F	P LESS THAN	STEP DOWN F	P LESS THAN	PERCENT OF ADDITIONAL VARIANCE ACCOUNTED FOR
1 SC BIO C	2.2347	0.1118	2.2347	0.1118	3.3144
			STEP-DOWN MEAN SQUARES =(20.3063/	9.0868)	
2 SC CHE C	1.5746	0.2116	0.5360	0.5866	2.2834
			STEP-DOWN MEAN SQUARES =(5.4679/	10.2007)	
3 SC PHY C	4.6655	0.0114	2.3257	0.1025	5.7776
			STEP-DOWN MEAN SQUARES =(19.4593/	8.3671)	
4 SC PRA C	1.4736	0.2335	0.2751	0.7600	1.9900
			STEP-DOWN MEAN SQUARES =(1.9625/	7.1333)	

D.F.=   2. AND   113.

FIGURE 2.4-3 Problem 1: Phase III multivariate output (concluded)

If the criterion variables have an inherent order, the step-down F ratios provide multivariate tests of the same correlations. Since in this case the four science tests have no particular prior order, the step-down F's are of little value and are not discussed here. An application in which step-down analysis is meaningful is presented in Chapter 4.

The overall multivariate test in this problem is a test that the entire 4×4 matrix of regression coefficients is zero—that is, a test of whether there is significant association between any linear combinations of dependent and independent variables. The F statistic for the multivariate test is, in this instance, 3.26 with 16 and 336.69 degrees of freedom. As this value exceeds the .01 critical value, we conclude that there is a nonzero association of the two sets of variables. The F statistic accurately approximates probability points for the multivariate test and the degrees of freedom may be fractional. If so, the next lowest integer degrees of freedom should be used to enter the F table. The MULTIVARIANCE program contains an accurate algorithm for finding probability levels for all fractional values.

Although the overall test indicates an association between the sets of variables, it does not locate the association in the subtests of predictor or criterion measures. The stepwise regression analysis is more useful for the purpose. In the three parts of this stepwise printout, we first test the contribution of Word Knowledge to four Science Achievement scores; then we test the additional contribution of Homework to four Science scores; finally, we test the additional contribution of the two Interest scores to the four Science Achievements. Because we remove at each step all variation attributable to prior independent variables, this table, like the stepwise table in the univariate analysis, is read from the bottom to the top.

Examining the effects of Interest in Science first, we see that the multivariate test statistic is $F = 1.33$, with 8 and 220 degrees of freedom. Since this value is not significant at α of .05, we conclude that the two scores are *not* related to the four Science Achievements (removing Word Knowledge and Hours of Homework). This is the primary test statistic of the multivariate analysis, and leads us to conclude that H_0 is supported—i.e., science interest scores are not necessary to the model. Any variation in Science Achievement that may be explained by the set of predictors is explained by Word Knowledge and Hours of Homework alone.

We may also inspect the univariate F statistics to see the extent to which Science Interests contribute to variation in the separate achievement subtests. For predicting Biology Achievement alone, the F statistic of 2.23, with 2 and 113 degrees of freedom, is not significant in isolation, and we conclude once more that Interests do not contribute to Science Achievement. The F statistic for Physics alone is 4.67, with 2 and 113 degrees of freedom, and is significant at the .05 level. However, Physics is by definition only a portion of our response data, and not independent of the other measures. The probability of finding one F ratio out of four to be significant by chance alone may be much higher than .05. On the basis of the multivariate test, therefore, we continue to believe that Interest in Science is not an important mediator of cognitive achievement.

From a more descriptive point of view, we see that the two Interest tests account for 3.3, 2.3, 5.8, and 2.0 percent, respectively, of variation in four science subtests. These measures are explained variation above and beyond variation attributable to Word Knowledge and Hours of Homework.

Having found the last set of predictors not to contribute to criterion variation, we proceed with the next-to-last test, or the test of the Hours-of-homework predictor. The multivariate test statistic of 1.04, with 4 and 112 degrees of freedom, is not significant at the .5 level. Once again we accept H_0 and conclude that Hours of Homework is not necessary to our model. Any variation attributable to the predictor variables in this study is attributable to predictors earlier in the order of elimination—namely, Word Knowledge. For the Hours-of-homework predictor variable, none of the univariate F statistics is significant, confirming complete support for our decision. Hours of Homework accounts, respectively, for .6, .6, 1.4, and 2.6 percent of variation in the four science subtests, above and beyond that attributable to Word Knowledge.

Finally, having found the Hours of Homework variable not significant, we proceed with tests of the Word Knowledge predictor variable. The multivariate F statistic of 10.26 indicates that Word Knowledge is significantly related to the set of criterion variables. The verbal ability variable accounts, respectively, for 12.2, 15.2, 22.8, and 19.1 percent of variation in the four science subtests. Given that the multivariate test statistic is significant, we inspect the univariate statistics and find that all four univariate F ratios are significant. That is,

Word Knowledge appears to be significantly related to all of the science subtests (although the univariate F ratios are not independent of one another). The smallest of the univariate ratios is for Biology, which appears to be least dependent upon verbal ability.

The results of the tests of significance may be summarized in a table such as Table 2.2. It is necessary to specify both the order of predictor variables and the predictors eliminated at each stage. The asterisks on the percentages of variation refer to the univariate F statistic corresponding to each measure.

All of the multivariate tests are based upon the likelihood ratio statistic. We note in particular that there is no necessary relationship between the univariate results and the multivariate result for any one hypothesis. It is possible, for example, that Verbal Ability would have a significant multivariate test statistic and no single significant univariate test statistic. It is possible also, as with the Interest variable, that the multivariate test statistic may be nonsignificant while one or more of the univariate results is significant. Only the set of multivariate test statistics for a particular order of predictors has an exactly specified probability level. These are the primary decision making statistics.

The univariate results, including proportions of variation and the multiple correlations, are useful interpretive devices. The percentages of variation for any one criterion sum to the respective squared multiple correlation. For example, $.191 + .026 + .020 = .237$, which is the squared correlation for y_4.

Table 2.2 Summary of Multivariate Multiple Regression Analysis

Source of Variation	d.f.	Multivariate Test	Percent of variation explained; Univariate			
			Biology	Chemistry	Physics	Practical
Constant (2 sexes)	2		—	—	—	—
Word Knowledge, eliminating Constant	1	**	**12.2	**15.2	**22.8	**19.1
Homework, eliminating Constant and Word Knowledge	1		.6	.6	1.4	*2.6
Interest, eliminating Constant, Word Knowledge, and Homework	3		3.3	2.3	*5.8	2.0
Residual	113	Mean squares	9.09	11.76	13.31	10.21

*$p < .05$ **$p < .01$

Having decided that only the first predictor variable is important, we are concerned with interpreting and explaining the findings. The regression model for predicting the four science achievements has been reduced to:

$$\hat{y}_i = \hat{\alpha} + \hat{\beta}_1 x_{i1} \tag{11}$$

That is, science achievement is predicted by summing a vector of constants (or a vector of constants for each sex group) and a weighted function of verbal ability. We should re-estimate the four regression weights for verbal ability alone. The estimates will be different from those for the verbal variable in a set of four predictors because of the interrelationships among the independent variables. The rank of the model for estimation is three, if we allow two degrees of freedom for the constants and one for estimating β_1. We re-estimate β_1 in the MULTI-VARIANCE program by another pass through Phase III. This time we indicate that there are four criterion variables (the science subtests) and one predictor (Word Knowledge).

The descriptive data for the study include the means, standard deviations, and correlations of the variables for both sex groups. In particular, the within-group correlations of Word Knowledge with the four science subtests are .35, .39, .48, and .44, respectively (Figure 2.3-2). If more than a single predictor had been significant, the canonical correlations (correlations of two *sets* of variables) might be useful interpretive measures. They are not necessary in the present example, for, as so often occurs in educational research, general verbal skill alone accounts for student achievement.

3

SOCIAL CLASS, STAGE OF THINKING,
AND READING COMPREHENSION:
TWO-WAY ANALYSIS OF VARIANCE

It is well established that a high proportion of variation in verbal ability is attributable to familial factors and to a child's home environment, both of which are external to the school. It is seldom possible to separate familial and environmental causes however. Children born into middle-class homes, surrounded as they are by sophisticated verbal stimuli and exposed to reading and reading-related material, typically enter school with large verbal advantages over lower-class children.

Within social classes, however, there are also large differences in verbal skills. Piaget explains these differences in terms of three thinking stages that develop sequentially and affect both the child's verbal skills as well as other school achievement. He designates these stages the "preoperational," "concrete operational," and "formal cognitive operations" stages of thinking. According to Piaget's theory, it is a pedagogic error to present material to children that is at too high a thinking level for their developmental stage. For example, children who have developed to the stage of concrete operations will not be able to benefit from, say, science problems that require formal operational processes. Not only will the material not be absorbed, but the experience is likely to be frustrating and result in lowered motivation for the child to attempt further work. It is likely that children develop through the three thinking stages at different rates, as a function of their home and social group backgrounds.

3.1   THE DATA

The present study is an attempt to examine differences in reading skills among children who have developed to different thinking stages within each of three social groups. Psychologist Kurt Bergling drew a random sample of ten-year-old Swedish boys from the data files of the International Association for the Evaluation of Educational Achievement (IEA). He classified each subject into one of three social groups, based on father's occupation. Social group 1 is the highest, corresponding to jobs requiring the greatest amount of education; social group 2 is intermediate; and social group 3 is the lowest of the three.

Bergling also classified each of the boys according to thinking stage. He identified items on the IEA Science Achievement test for which certain of the distractors required thinking at the preoperational stage, others which required concrete operations, and still others which required formal cognitive operations. Each student was classified according to thinking stage from his responses to the distractors. The "right" and "wrong" answers to the items, as well as the total science achievement scores, were ignored. The alternate scoring, based on classifying the response level of the student, was used instead. The purpose of the study was to compare the three social groups, responding at three different cognitive stages, on reading comprehension ability.

The design of the study is represented by the sampling scheme in Table 3.1. This study comprises a 3×3 crossed design, complete but with unequal numbers of subjects in the subclasses. The total $N = 385$.

Table 3.1 Sampling Plan for Reading
Comprehension Study

		Thinking Stage (B)		
		1	2	3
Social Group (A)	1	$N_{11} = 3$	$N_{12} = 7$	$N_{13} = 32$
	2	$N_{21} = 22$	$N_{22} = 23$	$N_{23} = 147$
	3	$N_{31} = 16$	$N_{32} = 27$	$N_{33} = 108$

3.2 THE MODEL

The model employed for comparing means across social groups and across thinking stages is a two-way fixed effects analysis-of-variance model given by (12).

$$y_{ijk} = \mu + \alpha_j + \beta_k + (\alpha\beta)_{jk} + \epsilon_{ijk} \tag{12}$$

The model is univariate since there is only one criterion measure, Reading Comprehension. y_{ijk} represents the Reading Comprehension score for subject i in social group j at thinking stage k. The subscripts j and k have values from 1 to 3. The quantity μ is a population mean, common to all subjects, and α_j is the fixed deviation from μ due to the observation having been drawn from social class j. The quantity β_k is the average deviation from μ of all subjects at thinking stage k; it represents the advantage or disadvantage in reading comprehension due to the child's cognitive stage.

The interaction effect $(\alpha\beta)_{jk}$ is a specific mean deviation of subjects in social group j at thinking stage k from the rest of the model. For example, it is possible that students from the middle social group who operate at the middle thinking level perform better on the reading comprehension scale than we would expect from the additive effect of their group or thinking stage levels. This specific deviation from the additive "main-effect model" is $(\alpha\beta)_{22}$.

Finally ϵ_{ijk} is the specific deviation of one subject's score from the mean of all subjects in group jk. These random residuals or errors are assumed to be normally distributed, with mean zero and common variance σ^2. They are also assumed to be independent, so that the unique response for one subject does not depend in any way on other subjects' responses.

Although model (12) is univariate, it is easily converted to multivariate form. Suppose that instead of a single reading comprehension score, the criterion measures were both a reading comprehension and a reading speed score. Then each of the terms in (12) would be a *vector* having two elements. That is, there would be two outcome measures for each subject, two μ's (one for each dependent variable), two α_j's, and so on. The vector $\underset{\sim}{\alpha}_j$ would consist of an element for each of the variables indicating the extent to which each is affected by the student's social group membership. These social class effects may be different for the two outcome measures, but they may be tested for significance simultaneously. The correlation between the two outcome measures would undoubtedly be positive, so that multivariate confidence intervals and tests of significance would be necessary.

There is no restriction on the number of subjects in the subgroups; an exact least-squares analysis can be obtained even when the numbers are unequal and disproportionate. Furthermore, the assumption that individual errors have equal variance does not require that the *means* have equal variances. Let the mean in subclass jk be represented as y_{jk}. Then y_{jk} has expectation μ_{jk} and variance σ^2/N_{jk} where N_{jk} is the number of subjects in the group. In other words, the variance of the mean is inversely proportional to the number of subjects in the group. The N's themselves may have any values. This assumption may be written as

$$y_{jk} \sim N(\mu_{jk}, \sigma^2/N_{jk}) \tag{13}$$

The independence of individual errors implies that the means are also independent across all nine groups.

There is, however, a restriction that must be considered because the design has only nine subclass means. These nine means are distributed independently of one another, so that we say that there are *nine degrees of freedom among means*. This implies that we may estimate or test the significance of only nine means, or nine linear functions of them. Our model, however, has more than nine parameters. From (12), we would like to estimate one μ, three α's, three β's, and nine $(\alpha\beta)$'s, or a total of sixteen parameters. Thus, we must restrict the parameters so that estimation of only nine independent quantities is required.

For example, if we restrict the sum of the α's to zero, we only need to estimate two α's, and the third is determined. Similarly, if we restrict the sum of the β's to zero, only two β's need be estimated. Finally, if we restrict the sum of the $(\alpha\beta)$'s across rows and across columns, only four $\alpha\beta$'s need be estimated in order to determine all nine values. Thus the number of independent parameters to be estimated and tested equal the between-group degrees of freedom. The assignment of degrees of freedom then takes the form shown in Table 3.2.

The total number of parameters to be estimated (nine) is called the *rank of the model for significance testing*. Its maximum value is J, the total number of groups having at least one subject. It is the first purpose of the analysis to test whether some or all of the terms in the model are zero. For example, we wish to test whether

Table 3.2   Analysis-of-variance Source Table for
3 × 3 Crossed Design

Source of Variation	Degrees of Freedom
Constant	1
Social group (A)	2
Thinking stage (B)	2
Interactions (AB)	4
Degrees of freedom among means	9
Within groups $N - J = 385 - 9 = 376$	
Total $N = 385$	

the restricted α's are zero, or equivalently, whether the means for the three social groups are equal. The hypothesis is represented as

$$H_0(1): \quad \alpha_1 = \alpha_2 = \alpha_3 = 0 \tag{14}$$

We also wish to test whether there are significant mean differences among thinking levels, or equivalently that the restricted β's are zero. This hypothesis is

$$H_0(2): \quad \beta_1 = \beta_2 = \beta_3 = 0 \tag{15}$$

Finally we may wish to test whether the interactions are necessary to the model, above and beyond main effects. To the extent that specific group interactions are found, simple main-effect (social-group-thinking-stage) explanations of the outcomes are inadequate. The interaction hypothesis is

$$H_0(3): \quad (\alpha\beta)_{jk} = 0, \quad \text{for all } j,k \tag{16}$$

Once tests of significance on parameters are obtained, we wish to explain the results in terms of the variables in the model. The most important data for this purpose are estimates of the parameters that are nonzero—that is, those that prove to be significant from the analysis-of-variance tests. The choice of parameters to be estimated is particularly important in unequal-N analysis-of-variance problems. The number of parameters estimated affects both the estimate values and their standard errors; unlike equal-N models, the estimates of μ, α_j and β_k are not simple functions of the observed subclass means $y_{.jk}$.

The number of parameters estimated is important for another reason as well. A most useful device for interpreting analysis-of-variance outcomes, and especially in the unequal-N case, consists of the *predicted* or *estimated* means, analogous to the predicted scores in regression models. The estimated means are obtained by taking the best estimates of the parameters deemed essential to the model, and summing to obtain an estimated mean for each subclass. These means have particular simplicity because they include only the significant effects. Effects that may be attributed to sampling variation are omitted.

For example, let us assume that μ is necessary to the model since the test score is not adjusted to a zero mean. Then, if we find that only social class is significant, and thinking stage and interactions are not significant, we may estimate the means by adding together the best estimate of μ with the best estimates of α_1, α_2, and α_3, respectively. The predicted means in this case are given by (17a).

$$\hat{y}_{jk} = \hat{\mu} + \hat{\alpha}_j \tag{17a}$$

The means predicted by (17a) reflect exactly the differences between the means for the three social groups. We say that they are obtained under a model of rank three, because they include a constant term (having one degree of freedom) and the social class effects (having two degrees of freedom). That is, the *rank of the model for estimation* is $c = 3$.

The circumflex on each term indicates that *estimated* parameters are summed to obtain estimated means. In contrast, the original subclass means, $y_{.jk}$, are obtained from sums of *observed* values.

On the other hand, if we found that thinking levels are significantly different on mean Reading Comprehension, while social groups and interactions are not significant, then we would estimate a mean for each group by summing together the estimate of μ and the estimate of β_1, β_2, or β_3. Again we estimate means for each group based on a model of rank three. In this case they are not the leading three terms in the model, but the first term and the two terms following the social class parameters. The prediction model is represented by (17b).

$$\hat{y}_{jk} = \hat{\mu} + \hat{\beta}_k \qquad (17b)$$

It is also possible that we may find both thinking stages and social groups to be of importance to the model—that is, both significant—while interactions are not. The best estimate of the mean in each subclass is then a sum of the estimate of μ plus estimates of the respective α_j and β_k effect. This model is represented by (17c) with the rank of the model for estimation $c = 5$.

$$\hat{y}_{jk} = \hat{\mu} + \hat{\alpha}_j + \hat{\beta}_k \qquad (17c)$$

The effects that are summed correspond to the first five degrees of freedom in the model.

We may also find that all terms including interactions are significant. In this case, the predicted means are obtained by adding together the best estimates of every parameter in the model. For example, the rank of the model for estimation is nine. This represents the summing of one constant, two independent α effects, two independent β effects, and four independent interactions. The means predicted under a model whose rank is *equal* to the number of groups in the design are identical to the nine observed subclass means. Every possible between-group source variation is included.

The estimated means are sums of estimated population parameters, and may be combined without respect to the subclass N's to obtain row and column marginal means. The predicted row and column (or *combined*) means are not biased by smaller or larger samples—an arbitrary factor that we do not want to affect our findings. This is distinct from the observed row and column means, which are a function of the arbitrary cutting ~~points in~~ the social group and thinking stage classifications. The observed subclass means must be weighted by the respective numbers of subjects to obtain row and column observed means. The mean residuals, also useful for interpreting the outcomes, are the differences between the observed and predicted subclass means.

3.3 ADDITIONAL CONSIDERATIONS REQUIRED BY THE DATA SET

Although the design of this study is complete (i.e., there are no cells devoid of observations), the fact that there are disproportionate numbers of subjects in the cells requires special consideration. When there are disproportionate N's in analysis-of-variance designs, estimates and tests of the various parameters are not independent of one another. This means that if we compute a sum of squares for the constant, a sum of squares between social groups, between thinking stages and for interaction, plus a sum of squares within-groups, their sum would be greater than the sum of the squares of all 385 original scores. If this fact is ignored, tests on various effects would be intercorrelated and likely to inflate the statistical error rates. Moreover, we would be in danger of attributing variation to one effect that is really due to another, because the two are interrelated.

Thus, a general *nonorthogonal* analysis for a disproportionate design, with an independent test of each source of variation in Table 3.2, is required. This analysis depends upon a specified order of the main effects and interactions, such as established in regression models, so that the tests may be made in a stepwise (or blockwise) fashion. With the effects ordered as in Table 3.2, for example, we would test for differences among social groups, eliminating any effect of the constant; for differences among thinking levels, eliminating any variation due to the constant and to differences between social groups; and for any interaction, eliminating the constant and both main class effects. When the numerical results are entered in the analysis-of-variance table, the order of elimination must be indicated. For example, the social group row should be labeled "Social groups, eliminating the constant"; the thinking stage label should read "Thinking stages, eliminating the constant and social groups," and so on. When the sums of squares are partitioned in this manner, the total of the sums of squares for separate effects, plus the within-groups sum of squares will equal the sum of squares of all 385 observations, as it should.

The tests are interpreted, as in the regression model, in the reverse order from the order of elimination. Thus, the F statistic for interaction is examined first. Then the F statistic for thinking stages B is examined. If thinking levels are not significantly different, then we may validly proceed with the test of the differences among means of the social groups A. If thinking-level means are significantly different, however, we have no unconfounded test of the social-group means in this order.

That is, the B sum of squares is obtained eliminating A variation. However, the A sum of squares is not obtained eliminating B. The finding that B variation is significant implies that the test of A is confounded, and the A sum of squares is inflated by some part of the B effect. Thus, if thinking stage is significant, and we still require a test of social groups, we must reorder the B effects to precede A. The sums of squares are recomputed in the new order to obtain a valid F test for social groups, removing the effects of thinking stage.

Failure to consider effect order in a nonorthogonal analysis of variance can adversely affect the conclusions drawn from the data. Yet, the question of order of elimination is often ignored in presentations which teach the regression approach to analysis-of-variance problems through the coding of "dummy variables." Sometimes an *unweighted means* solution for nonorthogonal designs is recommended to get around this problem, but it is only an approximation to the exact analysis and does not make the best use of the data. It is not as sensitive or precise as the exact least-squares analysis. The more disparate are the subclass frequencies, the poorer is the approximation to the exact least-squares solution.

Unequal subclass frequencies arise in empirical studies for a variety of reasons. In the present example, they tend to occur because the sample subclasses represent populations of varying size. In comparative studies of naturally occurring groups, it may happen that certain types of subjects are difficult to find (e.g., female engineers), and efforts to select a balanced sample fail. In experimental studies, unequal cell frequencies may occur because of subject mortality or because of a need to discontinue certain experimental treatments. The common textbook presentation with an equal number of subjects in all treatment groups is not the typical situation. Although it leads to computational simplicity and may be presented through ordinary scalar algebra, it does not generally correspond to the needs of our research. By the same token, discarding observations to make cell frequencies equal or proportional is a wasteful practice that computational simplicity does not justify.

In nonorthogonal designs, tests of analysis-of-variance effects in several orders are not independent of one another. Therefore, the number of alternate orders should be kept to a minimum to avoid compounding statistical error rates. An initial ordering should be established according to the relative importance or complexity of the effects in the model. As in the regression model, the most problematic effects and the most complex effects are ordered last. For example, interactions are always ordered to follow the corresponding main effects, and higher-order interactions should follow lower-order interactions.[1]

Within a given level of complexity, variables known to contribute to criterion variation, or known to have significant mean differences, should be ordered first. These include all control variables, blocking variables, and other factors which do not form the major hypotheses of the study. In educational studies, sex, social class, age, and other common control variables frequently take this position. Design factors of primary importance are placed in later positions—for example, the main experimental variable, the newly developed constructs of the study, and so on.

In the present example, Social Group functions as a control variable because there are known reading comprehension differences across social-class levels. It therefore appears first in the order of elimination, while Thinking Stage appears second because it is the variable of main concern in the study. Thus we shall test for reading achievement differences among students at Piaget's three levels of thinking, after eliminating social-class variation.

It is important to understand that, if thinking-stage effects are significant, we have no unconfounded test of social-group differences in this order. Although the social-group effect is not of particular concern in this study,

---

[1] In fact, to order an interaction ahead of the main effects involves changing the meaning of the terms in the original model. All between-group variation can be attributed to the highest-order interaction, leaving no main-effect variation to test. This serves no useful purpose, however, in terms of explaining the outcomes from the design factors.

for purposes of illustration we will reorder terms in the model and test social group differences, eliminating thinking-stage effects. The MULTIVARIANCE program allows testing of effects in several orders within the same problem run.

3.4 FORMAT OF THE DATA

From a previous analysis of these data, the mean scores and standard deviations for the nine groups are already known. These summary statistics may be used as input to the MULTIVARIANCE program and need not be recalculated. The ability to reconstruct analyses from summary statistics is useful when results have been presented in this form in articles or books and the raw data are not available. The MULTIVARIANCE program also has an option to punch, as summary statistics, the means, variances, and correlations in a form that can be reread by the program as input. Thus, for a very large data set the time required for input and the computation of simple summary statistics need be spent only once.

For the reading comprehension analysis, there are nine means input cards. Each is punched with the following information:

Columns	Variables	
1-2	Social group number,	1 = high group
		2 = middle group
		3 = low group
3-4	Stage of thinking,	1 = preoperational
		2 = concrete operations
		3 = formal operations
5-16	Mean reading comprehension score for the group. (Format F12.5)	

There is also one data card giving the number of subjects in each of the nine groups.

Finally, the pooled within-group variance, or within-group mean square, is required. This is obtained from the standard deviations for the separate groups. Let S_j be the standard deviation in any one group. The number of subjects in the group is N_j.[2] Each standard deviation is squared to obtain the groups variance, S_j^2. Equation (8) of Chapter 2 may then be applied. The second line of (8) is exactly in the correct form for the data as we have them, with $N = 385$ subjects and $J = 9$ groups. The result for this study is $S^2 = 96.54$. The input data cards are listed in Figure 3.1. When there is more than one criterion variable, the MULTIVARIANCE program will accept the correlation matrix among the measures, and the standard deviation of each measure, as input.

The social-group variable is obtained by condensing the nine-point IEA father's-occupation scale into three categories (see Comber and Keeves, 1973; Husén, 1973). The criterion variable is the IEA Reading Comprehension test, versions of which have been administered to ten-year-olds in twenty-two countries (see Thorndike, 1973).

---

[2] We use a single subscript to indicate groups one through nine, even though these arise from the crossing of two design factors.

```
             1         2         3         4         5         6         7         8
    1234567890123456789012345678901234567890123456789012345678901234567890123456789 0

     1  1    17.90000
     1  2    21.04286
     1  3    25.82813
     2  1    16.30455
     2  2    20.98696
     2  3    21.28912
     3  1    10.44375
     3  2    16.01111
     3  3    19.39352
          3       7      32      22      23     147      16      27     108
       96.54049

             1         2         3         4         5         6         7         8
    1234567890123456789012345678901234567890123456789012345678901234567890123456789 0
```

FIGURE 3.1   Problem 2:   Reading Comprehension--means, N's, and variance

3.5   MULTIVARIANCE SETUP

The input data to the MULTIVARIANCE program are listed in Figure 3.2. The control cards are numbered to correspond to the numbers in page 14 of the MULTIVARIANCE *User's Guide*. The **Input Description** card, containing most of the data description, follows the **Title** cards. A distinction is made between measured variables (which include dependent variables, covariables for analysis of covariance, and variables that may be involved in data transformations or that are included for descriptive purposes) and the independent variables that form the analysis-of-variance design. The last are termed *factors*. In the present example there is only one measured variable, namely, the score on the Reading Comprehension test. There are two factors in the analysis-of-variance design: social group *A* and thinking stage *B*. Data Form 4 is the input form for means-and-variance summary data. Additional options on the Input Description card include a single Variable Format card, minimal page spacing for the output, and optional intermediate printout throughout the problem run.

The **Factor Identification** card names the classification factors in the analysis-of-variance design and gives the number of levels of each. In this instance, there are three levels of the social-group variable and three levels of the thinking-stage variable. The order of factors on this card indicates to the program the order of group identification of the data cards. For example, the second mean card shows a mean of 21.04286 for group 12. From the Factor Identification card, the program knows that this refers to social group 1, thinking stage 2.

The **Comments** cards and **End-of-comments** card are followed by the **Variable Format** card for the input data. The group identification numbers (1,1), (1,2), (1,3), and so on are read as integer data, while scores on all measured variables are read as real numbers in F format. The **Variable Label** card provides a name for the measured Reading Comprehension score.

The arrangement of the data for Data Form 4 is listed on page 20 of the MULTIVARIANCE *User's Guide*. The means for all nine groups, each identified by a social-group and a thinking-stage number, are followed by a blank card. The vector of subclass *N*'s is punched in fixed format (13F6.0), with the numbers in the natural order of group indices (i.e., N_{11}, N_{12}, N_{13}, N_{21}, etc.). This card is followed by the Variable Format card for the within-group variance; the final card of the data input contains the variance value punched in this format.

The estimation phase is introduced by the **Estimation Specification** card, containing in column 4 the rank of the model for significance testing. In this case the rank is nine, equal to the number of degrees of freedom among means given in Table 3.2.

The rank of the model for estimation is the *c* pertaining to formulas (17a) to (17c). Strictly speaking, the rank of the model for estimation cannot be known until after the tests of significance have been seen. This is an

```
        1         2         3         4         5         6         7         8
1234567890123456789012345678901234567890123456789012345678901234567890
```

```
     1. Title car s
PROBLEM 2: TWO-WAY VARIANCE ANALYSIS
UNIVARIATE UNEQUAL N FROM MEANS
     2. Input Description card
     1    2    4                                            1
        3. Factor Identification card
GROUP     3STAGE     3
        4. Comment cards
2-WAY ANOVA - SOCIAL GROUP X THINKING STAGE
SWEDEN GRADE 3 BOYS
CRITERION: READING COMPREHENSION CORRECTED
SOCIAL GROUP:   1=SOCIAL GROUP 1,   2=SOCIAL GROUP 2,   3=SOCIAL GROUP 3
THINKING STAGE:   1=PREOPERATIONAL,   2=CONCRETE OPERATIONAL,
     3=FORMAL OPERATIONAL
CLASSIFICATION OF DISTRACTORS BY THINKING STAGE ACCORDING TO PIAGETS THEORY:
A+B = THINKING STAGE 1,   C = THINKING STAGE 2,   D = THINKING STAGE 3


DATA ARE NS, MEAN SCORES AND COMMON WITHIN-GROUP VARIANCE
UNEQUAL N, SO EFFECTS ARE TESTED IN TWO ORDERS.


DATA CARDS:

        COL 1- 2   SOCIAL GROUP
        COL 3- 4   THINKING STAGE
        COL 5-16   MEAN SCORE FOR GROUP
     5. End-of-comments card
FINISH
     6. Variable Format card
(2I2,F12.5)
     9. Variable Label card
RC C&D C
    10. Data
        (A) Cell Means
  1 1    17.90000
  1 2    21.04286
  1 3    25.82813
  2 1    16.30455
  2 2    20.98696
  2 3    21.28912
  3 1    10.44375
  3 2    16.01111
  3 3    19.39352
        End of data

        (B) Cell Frequencies
     3     7    32    22    23    147    16    27    108
        (C) Variable Format card
(F11.5)
        (D) Pooled within-cell variance
  96.54049
    12. Estimation Specification card
     9    9         1                        3
    13. Means key
1,2.
    16. Symbolic Contrast Vectors
D0,D0,                        GRAND MEAN                        CONST.
D1,D0,                        SOCIAL GROUF                      ALPHA1
D2,D0,                        SOCIAL GROUP                      ALPHA2
D0,D1,                        THINKING STAGE                    BETA1
D0,D2,                        THINKING STAGE                    BETA2
D1,D1,                        INTERACTION                       S X T
D1,D2,                        INTERACTION                       S X T
D2,D1,                        INTERACTION                       S X T
D2,D2,                        INTERACTION                       S X T
    17. Contrast Reordering key
1,4,5,2,3.
    18. Analysis Selection card
     1         1
    21. Hypothesis Test card
1,2,2,4.
1,2,2.
    22. End-of-job card
                                                  STOP
```

```
        1         2         3         4         5         6         7         8
1234567890123456789012345678901234567890123456789012345678901234567890
```

FIGURE 3.2   Problem 2:   MULTIVARIANCE control cards for 2-way anova

unfortunate reversal in the logic in MULTIVARIANCE, for it requires setting the parameter prior to seeing the results of the problem run. One of several approaches may be taken in choosing c. The user may make an "educated guess" as to how many terms will prove significant and set the rank of model for estimation to that number. For example, if he expects that main effects in this problem but not interactions will be significant, he would set the rank of the model for estimation at five. Or the user may omit this parameter from the problem run and wait until the results of the significance tests can be inspected. The parameter may be set correctly in a second problem run, and the parameter estimates and other interpretive output obtained. In yet a third approach, the user might set the rank of the model for estimation equal to the rank of the model for significance testing. He would thus obtain estimates of all parameters in the model and inspect them for their initial interpretive value. A second run might then be required to re-estimate the parameters remaining after the nonsignificant terms are eliminated.

On the following control cards, each parameter in the model is named and given a symbolic code. The rank of the model for significance testing determines how many parameters there are in the complete model. The rank of the model for estimation determines how many of the *leading* parameters are to be estimated or combined to obtain the predicted means. For purposes of this example, the rank of the model for estimation is set to include all terms in the model (nine).

We suspect that thinking stages will prove significant but would also like a test of the social-group mean differences. We therefore specify, by punching 1 in column 20 of the Estimation Specification card, that one alternate order of the effects will be coded. In the alternate order, social-group effects will be tested eliminating thinking-stage differences.

The *combined means* in two-way designs are referred to as "row and column means" in many other texts. In other designs there may be more than two dimensions, and the general term "combined" is used. Either the observed means for all nine groups may be combined across rows and columns of the design, or means predicted from one of the forms in (17) may be combined, or both. In this problem both are requested (3 in column 44 of the Estimation Specification card).

The request for combined row and column means must be followed by a **Means Key**, indicating factors of the design for which means are requested. In the example, the Means Key indicates that the means for factor 1 and factor 2 are required, factors being numbered as they appear on the Factor Identification card. The factor-1 request will produce three means, viz., a mean reading comprehension scores for the first, second, and third social groups. The factor-2 request will produce means for each of the three levels of the thinking-stage factor. If the code 1*2 were entered on the Means Key, every combination of social group and thinking stage—that is, nine separate means—would be printed. In this case, these combinations refer to the smallest groups in the design and need not be printed, because predicted and observed means for *all* groups of subjects are always produced by the program.

The following **Symbolic Contract Vectors** (SCV's) serve to code and name the effects in the analysis-of-variance model and to determine the initial order in which sums of squares are computed. Altogether there are as many SCV cards as the rank of the model for significance testing, which is less than or equal to the number of groups in the design. There is one card corresponding to each degree of freedom in the model for significance testing—in this case, one for the constant term, two for the social group-group factor (A), two for the thinking-stage factor (B), and four for the interaction effect (AB). But before examining these codes, let us construct the codes for a simpler one-way model.

Assume that we have a one-way fixed-effects analysis-of-variance design with, say, five levels of the design factor. The model may be stated as:

$$y_{ij} = \mu + \alpha_j + \epsilon_{ij} \qquad (j = 1, 2, ..., 5) \tag{18}$$

The corresponding analysis-of-variance might take the form in Table 3.3. In this instance, the rank of model for significance testing, i.e., the number of degrees of freedom among means, is five. Thus we must code five effects with the SCV's. Of these, the first corresponds to the constant term in the model and is always coded zero by convention. We then code the four A effects that are independently estimable. The effect α_5 can be obtained as minus the sum of the first four α's, since the effects sum to zero. The codes for α_1 through α_4 are the numbers 1, 2, 3, and 4, respectively.

Each of these codes must be preceded by a letter indicating the specific nature of the effect to be estimated. In this example, as in the other analysis-of-variance examples in this text, we estimate only the conventional analysis-of-variance effects such as α_j and β_k, for which the letter code is D. The entire set of five codes for the one-way analysis-of-variance model is therefore given by (19).

$$
\begin{array}{ll}
\text{D0,} & \text{CONSTANT} \\
\text{D1,} & \text{ALPHA 1} \\
\text{D2,} & \text{ALPHA 2} \\
\text{D3,} & \text{ALPHA 3} \\
\text{D4,} & \text{ALPHA 4}
\end{array}
\tag{19}
$$

Note that each letter-number code is followed by a comma to indicate the end of the code for that parameter. The code D0, represents the constant term, and D1, D2, D3, and D4, represent the effects α_1, α_2, α_3, and α_4, respectively. These SCV codes are punched one to a card and should be followed by an up-to-eight character label for the effect, as in (19). These labels will appear on the matrices of effect estimates and standard errors in the printout.

The MULTIVARIANCE *User's Guide* (pages 69-70) gives several "rules of thumb" for simplifying the coding. For example, the letter D may be omitted from all cards except the first. A "repeat code" is also available so that the four α codes, for example, could be coded on one card instead of four. The SCV's are punched in free format—there are no particular card columns for the codes, the commas, or the comments.

This system of coding effects generalizes to multi-way designs. The symbolic contrast codes for a two-way design, as in the example, have two letter-number codes, separated by a comma and terminating in a comma, on each card. These codes may be thought of as arranged in two columns on the card. The first column refers to the social-group factor, and the second to the thinking-stage factor. Corresponding to the first source of variation in Table 3.2, the constant term for all subjects is coded by D0, in the social-group column *and* D0, in the thinking-stage column. Thus, the complete code is D0,D0,.

The α_1 and α_2 social-group effects are indicated by entering cards with D1, and D2, in the social-group column. A zero code D0, acting as a place holder, is entered on both cards in the thinking-stage column. Thus, the two social-group effects, α_1 and α_2, are coded D1,D0, and D2,D0, respectively.

Table 3.3 Analysis-of-variance Source Table
for One-way Fixed Design

Source of Variation	Degrees of Freedom
Constant	1
Between groups	4
Degrees of freedom among means	5
Within groups	$N-5$
Total	N

The two B effects, β_1 and β_2, are coded by inserting D1, and D2, respectively, in the thinking-stage column. A zero code D0, is entered as a place holder in the social-group term of each card. Thus the cards to code β_1 and β_2 in the two-way model read D0,D1, and D0,D2,.

Finally, the four degrees of freedom for interaction are coded as combinations of every A effect and every B effect. That is, for α_1 we have D1, on the left side of each card, while D1, and D2, appear on the right side for the interactions with β_1 and β_2, respectively. For α_2 we have D2, on the left side of the card. This appears with D1, and D2, on the right side of the cards for β_1 and β_2, respectively. Thus the four interactions for the two α's with the two β's are represented as D1,D1,; D1,D2,; D2,D1,; and D2,D2,.

All nine SCV's are included in the input listing, each followed by a label and some comment. The order in which the SCV's appear in the deck establishes the initial order in which tests of significance will be carried out. Note that both the number and order of these cards in the input listing corresponds to the effects as listed in Table 3.2. Note also, however, that on the Estimation Specification card, significance testing in an alternative order is requested. This alternative order is indicated on a **Contrast Reordering Key** which contains the numbers 1,4,5,2,3. These numbers are the indices of the effect codes in the alternate order. That is, effect 1 of the original order (constant) is to appear first in the alternate order; effects 4 and 5 in the original order (β_1 and β_2) will appear next in the alternate order, and effects 2 and 3 (α_1 and α_2) will appear last in the alternate order. The alternate order corresponds to a rearrangement of five of the cards to the order shown in (20).

$$
\begin{array}{lll}
\text{D0,D0,} & \quad & \text{CONSTANT} \\
\text{D0,D1,} & \quad & \text{BETA 1} \\
\text{D0,D2,} & \quad & \text{BETA 2} \\
\text{D1,D0,} & \quad & \text{ALPHA 1} \\
\text{D2,D0,} & \quad & \text{ALPHA 2}
\end{array}
\tag{20}
$$

Since all of the reordering is done internally, the SCV cards do not need to be repunched. Neither need the four interactions appear in the alternate order, for interchanging main effects A and B will not effect the residual sum of squares for any following effect. Since we may not order the AB interaction to precede either factor A or factor B, these may be omitted entirely from the re-analysis.

The Phase III **Analysis Selection** card indicates that there is one dependent variable—the only measured variable in the data set. Tests of significance are to be carried out with one alternative order of effects in addition to the order in which SCV cards were entered in the data deck. That is, in any one pass through Phase III of the program it is not necessary to use all orders of effects if several have been established in the estimation phase.

The **Hypothesis Test** card determines the manner in which the sums of squares will be grouped for tests of significance. For example, in the one-way case with symbolic codes given by (19), we would test the significance of the constant term (if we were interested) and obtain a simultaneous test of all four α's—that is, the test of (21).

$$
H_0: \quad \mu_1 = \mu_2 = \mu_3 = \mu_4 = \mu_5
\tag{21}
$$

This is the standard four-degrees-of-freedom test that all five means are equal. The Hypothesis Test card reads 1,4. The *1* indicates a test of the first SCV alone (that the constant is zero); the *4* indicates a simultaneous test of all four following SCV's [the test of (21)]. The numbers on the Hypothesis Test card also correspond to the degrees of freedom between groups in Table 3.3.

In the two-way model the Hypothesis Test Card reads 1,2,2,4. The *1* indicates that a test of the constant term is to be made—i.e., the first SCV. The first *2* indicates that a test of the two A effects (D1,D0, and D2,D0,) is to be made simultaneously. This is the two-degrees-of-freedom test of hypothesis 1 (14) concerning differences among social groups. The second *2* on this card indicates that the *next* two B effects, D0,D1, and D0,D2, are to be tested for significance jointly. These effects are the differences among the three thinking stages specified in hypothesis 2 (15). Finally the *4* on this card indicates that the next four effects coded, those attributable to interaction, are to be tested simultaneously as specified in hypothesis 3 (16).

These numbers on the Hypothesis Test card correspond to the between-group degrees of freedom in Table 3.2 and indicate to the program how coded effects are to be grouped for the tests of significance. Although in most designs the numbers on this card correspond to the degrees of freedom between groups in the analysis-of-variance table, it is also possible to test specific contrasts, and specific subsets of contrasts, by choosing other groupings of the coded effects. Examples are given in Finn (1974).

A second Hypothesis Test card is entered to indicate the grouping of effects in the alternate order, as listed in (20). For the alternate order, we wish a test of the constant term, of the two *B* effects eliminating the constant, and of the two *A* effects eliminating the constant and *B*. Thus, the Hypothesis Test card for the alternate order reads also 1,2,2. The numbers are the same as the degrees of freedom for the original order, only because both factors in this study have three levels.

3.6   OUTPUT AND INTERPRETATION

PHASE I.   The descriptive output for this problem is shown in Figure 3.3-1 through Figure 3.3-5. After listing the input parameters, the program counts the number of subjects on each group and assigns each subclass a unique internal identification number, from one through nine. These numbers are used throughout the problem run to identify group means, standard deviations, and other output. In this instance, the total number of observations is 385.

The observed means for all groups are listed and are combined across rows and columns to yield the observed combined means, as requested on the Means Key. The combined observed means are weighted by the numbers of subjects in the groups. For example, the mean of 24.46 for the first social group is obtained according to (22).

$$24.46 = \frac{3 \times 17.90 + 7 \times 21.04 + 32 \times 25.83}{3 + 7 + 32} \tag{22}$$

This value is exactly the mean of all 42 subjects in social group 1. Although it is biased upward because of the large number of subjects in the third thinking stage relative to the first two, a strong trend can be seen for higher social groups to have higher mean reading comprehension scores, and for lower social groups to have lower means. The trend can be seen in the array of nine means at all three stages of thinking. Similarly, children at the higher thinking stages have higher reading comprehension scores both for each social group separately and for all social groups combined.

PHASE II.   The results of the estimation phase of the MULTIVARIANCE run are listed in Figures 3.3-2 through 3.3-4. The estimation parameters are reproduced from the input cards, as are the SCV codes for the *A* and *B* effects. The error sum-of-squares and cross-products matrix in the univariate case is simply the within-group sum of squares of the two-way fixed-effects design. The value 36299.22 is divided by the error degrees of freedom to obtain the within-group variance, or error mean square. In this case, the within-group degrees of freedom are 376, obtained from 385 independent observations, minus 9 parameters estimated, and the within-group mean square is 96.54. The square root of the latter is 9.83, the common within-group standard deviation. This is the single estimate of the standard deviation of the scores, unbiased by group mean differences. It is this estimate of the standard deviation that should be used to describe variation in the outcome measure. A standard deviation computed without considering the subclass membership of the observations would be artificially inflated by group-mean differences (see Chapter 2).

PROBLEM

- -

PROBLEM 2: TWO-WAY VARIANCE ANALYSIS   UNIVARIATE UNEQUAL N FROM MEANS

- -

PAGE   1

```
2-WAY ANOVA - SOCIAL GROUP X THINKING STAGE
SWEDEN GRADE 3 BOYS
CRITERION: READING COMPREHENSION CORRECTED
SOCIAL GROUP:  1=SOCIAL GROUP 1,  2=SOCIAL GROUP 2,   3=SOCIAL GROUP 3
THINKING STAGE:  1=PREOPERATIONAL,  2=CONCRETE OPERATIONAL,
     3=FORMAL OPERATIONAL
CLASSIFICATION OF DISTRACTORS BY THINKING STAGE ACCORDING TO PIAGETS THEORY:
A+B = THINKING STAGE 1,  C = THINKING STAGE 2,  D = THINKING STAGE 3

DATA ARE NS, MEAN SCORES AND COMMON WITHIN-GROUP VARIANCE
UNEQUAL N, SO EFFECTS ARE TESTED IN TWO ORDERS.

DATA CARDS:

     COL 1- 2  SOCIAL GROUP
     COL 3- 4  THINKING STAGE
     COL 5-16  MEAN SCORE FOR GROUP
```

INPUT PARAMETERS
================

PAGE   2

NUMBER OF VARIABLES IN INPUT VECTORS=   1

NUMBER OF FACTORS IN DESIGN=   2

   NUMBER OF LEVELS OF FACTOR 1 (GROUP) =   3
   NUMBER OF LEVELS OF FACTOR 2 (STAGE) =   3

INPUT IS FROM CARDS. DATA OPTION 4

MINIMAL PAGE SPACING WILL BE USED

ADDITIONAL OUTPUT WILL BE PRINTED

COMPUTATION OF COVARIANCE MATRIX FOR EACH GROUP
IMPOSSIBLE DUE TO FORM OF DATA INPUT

*****NUMBER OF VARIABLE FORMAT CARDS NOT SPECIFIED. ASSUMED TO BE 1.

FORMAT OF DATA
(2I2,F12.5)

CELL IDENTIFICATION AND FREQUENCIES

PAGE   3

CELL	FACTOR LEVELS		N
	GROUP	STAGE	
1	1	1	3
2	1	2	7
3	1	3	32
4	2	1	22
5	2	2	23
6	2	3	147
7	3	1	16
8	3	2	27
9	3	3	108

TOTAL N=   385.

TOTAL SUM OF CROSS-PRODUCTS

```
           1
         RC C&D C
1 RC C&D C    1.935967D+05
```

FIGURE 3.3-1 Problem 2: Phase I output

OBSERVED CELL MEANS --- ROWS ARE CELLS-COLUMNS ARE VARIABLES

```
          1
   RC C&D C

 1     17.90000
 2     21.04286
 3     25.82813
 4     16.30455
 5     20.98696
 6     21.28912
 7     10.44375
 8     16.01111
 9     19.39352
```

OBSERVED COMBINED MEANS   PAGE   4
==============================

- -

FACTORS   1 (GROUP   )

   LEVEL   1
   N =   42.

      MEANS   RC C&D C= 24.46

   LEVEL   2
   N =   192.

      MEANS   RC C&D C= 20.68

   LEVEL   3
   N =   151.

      MEANS   RC C&D C= 17.84

- -

FACTORS   2 (STAGE   )

   LEVEL   1
   N =   41.

      MEANS   RC C&D C= 14.13

   LEVEL   2
   N =   57.

      MEANS   RC C&D C= 18.64

   LEVEL   3
   N =   287.

      MEANS   RC C&D C= 21.08

ESTIMATION PARAMETERS
=====================
                        PAGE   5

RANK OF THE BASIS = RANK OF MODEL FOR SIGNIFICANCE TESTING =   9
RANK OF THE MODEL TO BE ESTIMATED IS   9
ERROR TERM TO BE USED IS (WITHIN CELLS)
NUMBER OF ORDERS OF THE BASIS VECTORS OTHER THAN THE FIRST IS 1
VARIANCE-COVARIANCE FACTORS AND CORRELATIONS AMONG ESTIMATES WILL BE PRINTED
ESTIMATED COMBINED MEANS WILL BE PRINTED

SYMBOLIC CONTRAST VECTORS
=========================
                        PAGE   6

(1)			
	D0,D0,	GRAND MEAN	CONST
(2)			
	D1,D0,	SOCIAL GROUP	ALPHA1
(3)			
	D2,D0,	SOCIAL GROUP	ALPHA2
(4)			
	D0,D1,	THINKING STAGE	BETA1
(5)			
	D0,D2,	THINKING STAGE	BETA2
(6)			
	D1,D1,	INTERACTION	S X T
(7)			
	D1,D2,	INTERACTION	S X T
(8)			
	D2,D1,	INTERACTION	S X T
(9)			
	D2,D2,	INTERACTION	S X T

FIGURE 3.3-2 Problem 2: Phase I and II output

ERROR SUM OF CROSS-PRODUCTS

```
                 1
              RC C&D C

  1 RC C&D C   36299.22
```

ERROR VARIANCE -COVARIANCE MATRIX

```
                 1
              RC C&D C

  1 RC C&D C   96.54049
```

```
       VARIABLE          VARIANCE            STANDARD DEVIATION
                     (ERROR MEAN SQUARES)

       1 RC C&D C        96.540487                   9.8255
```

D.F.=   376.

ERROR TERM FOR ANALYSIS OF VARIANCE (WITHIN CELLS)

LEAST SQUARE ESTIMATES OF EFFECTS -- EFFECTS X VARIABLES

```
                 1
              RC C&D C

  1   CONST.    18.80000
  2   ALPHA1     2.79033
  3   ALPHA2     0.72688
  4   BETA1     -3.91723
  5   BETA2      0.54698
  6   S X T      0.22690
  7   S X T     -1.09445
  8   S X T      0.69491
  9   S X T      0.91311
```

ESTIMATES OF EFFECTS IN STANDARD DEVIATION UNITS-EFF X VARS

```
                 1
              RC C&D C

  1   CONST.    1.913388
  2   ALPHA1    0.283989
  3   ALPHA2    0.073979
  4   BETA1    -0.398680
  5   BETA2     0.055669
  6   S X T     0.023093
  7   S X T    -0.111388
  8   S X T     0.070725
  9   S X T     0.092932
```

STANDARD ERRORS OF LEAST-SQUARES ESTIMATES--EFFECTS BY VARS

```
                 1
              RC C&D C

  1   CONST.    0.921178
  2   ALPHA1    1.631858
  3   ALPHA2    1.091274
  4   BETA1     1.557699
  5   BETA2     1.283454
  6   S X T     2.795781
  7   S X T     2.234734
  8   S X T     1.804526
  9   S X T     1.567145
```

LEAST-SQUARES ESTIMATES AS T-STATISTICS - EFFECTS X VARS

```
                 1
              RC C&D C

  1   CONST.    20.40864
  2   ALPHA1     1.70991
  3   ALPHA2     0.66608
  4   BETA1     -2.51476
  5   BETA2      0.42618
  6   S X T      0.08116
  7   S X T     -0.48974
  8   S X T      0.38509
  9   S X T      0.58266
```

DEGREES OF FREEDOM =   376.

VARIANCE-COVARIANCE FACTORS OF ESTIMATES
----

		1 CONST.	2 ALPHA1	3 ALPHA2	4 BETA1	5 BETA2	6 S X T	7 S X T
1	CONST.	8.789781D-03						
2	ALPHA1	1.000431D-02	2.758387D-02					
3	ALPHA2	-5.244021D-03	-1.355007D-02	1.233554D-02				
4	BETA1	7.554214D-03	1.068873D-02	-6.049469D-03	2.513378D-02			
5	BETA2	-5.167281D-04	-2.404348D-03	1.801886D-03	-1.582727D-02	1.706283D-02		
6	S X T	1.068873D-02	-2.404348D-03	1.801886D-03	3.069735D-02	-1.828869D-02	8.096491D-02	
7	S X T	-2.404348D-03	-3.437804D-03	1.119190D-03	-1.828869D-02	1.760427D-02	-4.994323D-02	5.172994D-02
8	S X T	-6.049469D-03	-1.219348D-02	9.058959D-03	-1.653751D-02	9.491605D-03	-3.929362D-02	2.462436D-02
9	S X T	1.801886D-03	1.119190D-03	7.684295D-04	9.491605D-03	-8.686157D-03	2.462436D-02	-2.598095D-02

		8 S X T	9 S X T
8	S X T	3.373004D-02	
9	S X T	-2.216293D-02	2.543951D-02

FIGURE 3.3-3 Problem 2: Phase II output (continued)

```
                              INTERCORRELATIONS AMONG THE ESTIMATES
                  --------------------------------------------------------------------

                      1         2         3         4         5        6        7        8        9
                    CONST.    ALPHA1    ALPHA2    BETA1     BETA2    S X T    S X T    S X T    S X T

     1  CONST.     1.000000
     2  ALPHA1     0.642496  1.000000
     3  ALPHA2    -0.503612 -0.734573  1.000000
     4  BETA1      0.508243  0.405947 -0.343565  1.000000
     5  BETA2     -0.042194 -0.110827  0.124200 -0.764278  1.000000
     6  S X T      0.400672  0.545878 -0.385834  0.680493 -0.492049  1.000001
     7  S X T     -0.112755 -0.091009  0.044305 -0.507204  0.592545 -0.771716  1.000000
     8  S X T     -0.351334 -0.399753  0.444110 -0.567980  0.395645 -0.751909  0.589502  1.000000
     9  S X T      0.120499  0.042250  0.043378  0.375367 -0.416915  0.542578 -0.716192 -0.756597  1.000000
```
                                                                                              PAGE   7
```
                  ESTIMATED COMBINED MEANS BASED ON FITTING A MODEL OF RANK        9
                  ================================================================================
```

- -

```
FACTORS      1 (GROUP   )

    LEVEL         1

        MEANS        RC C&D C=   21.59
        -------

    LEVEL         2

        MEANS        RC C&D C=   19.53
        -------

    LEVEL         3

        MEANS        RC C&D C=   15.28
        -------
```

- -

```
FACTORS      2 (STAGE   )

    LEVEL         1

        MEANS        RC C&D C=   14.88
        -------

    LEVEL         2

        MEANS        RC C&D C=   19.35
        -------

    LEVEL         3

        MEANS        RC C&D C=   22.17
```

FIGURE 3.3-4   Problem 2:   Phase II output (concluded)

The array entitled "Least Squares Estimates of Effects" contains the estimates of the parameters in the model for the particular sampling design. Each estimate corresponds to one coded Symbolic Contrast Vector. Because we have set the rank of the model for estimation at nine, all parameters are estimated. In particular, the least-squares estimate of μ in this model is 18.8. The least-squares estimate of α_1 is 2.79. That is, on the average, subjects in social class 1 scored 2.79 points higher than the total group on the reading comprehension test, while subjects in social class 2 averaged about .73 points higher than the total group. From these we can compute α_3 as $-(2.79 + .73) = -3.52$. That is, on the average, subjects in social class 3 scored about 3.5 points below the the total group on the reading comprehension test. Similarly, the best estimate of β_1 is -3.92, indicating that children at the lowest stage of thinking averaged 3.92 points below the total group on the reading comprehension test. Similar interpretations apply to the other estimates.

The interactions may be interpreted in much the same way. From the fact that the entire sample of subjects averaged 18.80 points on the reading test while subjects in social class 1 averaged 2.79 points above that value, and subjects at thinking stage 1 averaged 3.92 points below that, a "main-effects model" would lead us to predict that subjects in group 1,1 (the highest social class, the lowest thinking group) have a mean score of $18.80 + 2.79 - 3.92 = 17.67$ points. The interaction of .23 points indicates that in reality the subjects averaged about two-tenths of a point *higher* than that predicted from the main-effects model. In fact, the observed mean of 17.9 points is exactly $17.67 + .23$.

The estimated effects may be put in the metric of the within-group standard deviation for interpretation. For example, subjects in social class 1 averaged in raw score units about 2.79 points above the total group mean in reading comprehension, or about .28 within-group standard deviation units. The latter figure allows us to compare the effects of social class on reading achievement scores with its effect on other variables expressed in standard deviation units.

The MULTIVARIANCE program also prints the standard errors of the estimated effects, which appear in a separate array, in the same relative position as each effect in the estimate array. Thus, the standard error of the estimate 2.79 for α_1 is about 1.63 points. It may be used in constructing confidence intervals on the effect, or in making univariate tests of significance on individual parameters. It appears that α_1 alone is not significant since the estimate is less than two standard errors above zero. However, a simultaneous test of all α's may prove that there are significantly different means among the three social classes.

The matrix of variance-covariance factors of the estimates is an intermediate stage in computing the intercorrelations among the estimates. This matrix is read like a correlation matrix and indicates the extent to which the α estimates, the β estimates, and the interaction estimates are all interdependent because of unequal N's in the analysis-of-variance design. In this instance the nonorthogonality of the design introduces correlations between the estimates of the A effects and the B effects ranging from $-.34$ to $+.41$. If B effects were omitted from the model, we might expect a fairly large change in the least-squares estimates of the A terms.

In this example the estimated means are predicted from a model having all terms (the rank of the model for estimation is equal to nine); and estimated means for all subclasses are, therefore, identical to the observed means. The estimated marginal means, however, are combined across rows and columns of the design without respect to the subclass frequencies and are not equal to the observed marginal means. Thus, the estimated mean for the first social class of $21.59 = (17.90 + 21.04 + 25.83)/3$ is exactly the unweighted average of the means for the three social-group-1 subclasses. This is true only of the full rank model, and the estimated mean will change if the significance tests indicate that some of the effects must be omitted. The remaining effects and predicted means will then have to be re-estimated from the reduced-rank model.

PHASE III. The results of the significance tests are presented in the top half of Figure 3.3-5 for the original order of effects. In that order, after the one degree of freedom for the constant term, we have the two-degree-of-freedom test of social groups, the two-degree-of-freedom test of stages of thinking, and the four-degree-of-freedom interaction test. As in the regression model, these results are interpreted from the bottom of the table upward.

This means that the interactions are tested for significance first, eliminating all main effects. Since the mean square for interaction is 60.27 with 4 degrees of freedom, and the within-group mean square (given in Figure 3.3-3 as part of the estimation output) is 96.54 with 376 degrees of freedom, the F ratio for interaction is $60.27/96.54 = .62$ with 4 and 376 degrees of freedom. This value is less than expectation, and interaction is deemed nonsignificant; beyond the main effects there is no group-specific interaction that contributes to criterion variation.

Having found interaction nonsignificant, we may validly proceed with the test of significant differences among means for the three stages of thinking. The relevant mean square, eliminating the constant and social-group effect, is 866.88 with 2 degrees of freedom. Dividing by the within-group mean square, we obtain an F ratio of 8.98, with 2 and 376 degrees of freedom, which is significant at $p < .01$. Thus there is a significant effect of cognitive thinking stages on reading achievement, and Hypothesis 2 is rejected.

Because stages of thinking is significant, we now have no valid test of social-group mean differences *in this order of eliminating effects*. Stages of thinking have been tested eliminating social-group differences, but social groups have not been tested eliminating stages of thinking. Since thinking stages have different means, these differences confound all preceding tests. We must, if we are interested in the social group test, reorder the α's and β's and test social groups, eliminating stages of thinking. Before doing so, however, let us summarize the analysis-of-variance results from the first order of effects as in Table 3.4.

In preparing tables such as 3.4, it is important to include labels in the table indicating which effects have been eliminated when each test is conducted. The SCV codes name the effects in each hypothesis on the printout, while the numbers on the Hypothesis Test card indicate the grouping of effects in the tests. Thus the Hypothesis Test card contains the numbers in the "Degrees of Freedom" column of Table 3.4.

```
                         ANALYSIS OF VARIANCE
                         ===================
                                                                    PAGE    8
                         ===================

                         1 DEPENDENT VARIABLE(S)
                           1 RC C&D C
                NUMBER OF ALTERNATE BASIS ORDERS=   1
              LOG-DETERMINANT ERROR SUM OF CROSS-PRODUCTS =  0.10499552D+02
                     HYPOTHESIS   1      1 DEGREE(S) OF FREEDOM
                     ========================================
                                                                    PAGE    9
          D0,D0,                    GRAND MEAN                    CONST.
          - - - - - - - - - - - - - - - - - - - - - - - - - - - - - - - - - -

              UNIVARIATE ANALYSIS OF VARIANCE FOR (RC C&D C)

     HYPOTHESIS MEAN SQUARE=   153692.187    F=    1591.9971   WITH   1. AND     376. DEGREES OF FREEDOM   P LESS THAN 0.0001
. . . . . . . . . . . . . . . . . . . . . . . . . . . . . . . . . . . . . . . . . . . . . . . . . . . . . . . . . . . .

                     HYPOTHESIS   2      2 DEGREE(S) OF FREEDOM
                     ========================================
          D1,D0,                    SOCIAL GROUP                 ALPHA1
          D2,D0,                    SOCIAL GROUP                 ALPHA2
          - - - - - - - - - - - - - - - - - - - - - - - - - - - - - - - - - -

              UNIVARIATE ANALYSIS OF VARIANCE FOR (RC C&D C)

     HYPOTHESIS MEAN SQUARE=    815.1958    F=       8.4441   WITH   2. AND     376. DEGREES OF FREEDOM   P LESS THAN 0.0003
. . . . . . . . . . . . . . . . . . . . . . . . . . . . . . . . . . . . . . . . . . . . . . . . . . . . . . . . . . . .

                     HYPOTHESIS   3      2 DEGREE(S) OF FREEDOM
                     ========================================
          D0,D1,                    THINKING STAGE               BETA1
          D0,D2,                    THINKING STAGE               BETA2
          - - - - - - - - - - - - - - - - - - - - - - - - - - - - - - - - - -

              UNIVARIATE ANALYSIS OF VARIANCE FOR (RC C&D C)

     HYPOTHESIS MEAN SQUARE=    866.8833    F=       8.9795   WITH   2. AND     376. DEGREES OF FREEDOM   P LESS THAN 0.0002
. . . . . . . . . . . . . . . . . . . . . . . . . . . . . . . . . . . . . . . . . . . . . . . . . . . . . . . . . . . .

                     HYPOTHESIS   4      4 DEGREE(S) OF FREEDOM
                     ========================================
          D1,D1,                    INTERACTION                  S X T
          D1,D2,                    INTERACTION                  S X T
          D2,D1,                    INTERACTION                  S X T
          D2,D2,                    INTERACTION                  S X T
          - - - - - - - - - - - - - - - - - - - - - - - - - - - - - - - - - -

              UNIVARIATE ANALYSIS OF VARIANCE FOR (RC C&D C)

     HYPOTHESIS MEAN SQUARE=     60.2722    F=       0.6243   WITH   4. AND     376. DEGREES OF FREEDOM   P LESS THAN 0.6456
. . . . . . . . . . . . . . . . . . . . . . . . . . . . . . . . . . . . . . . . . . . . . . . . . . . . . . . . . . . .

                         ORDER OF EFFECTS (CONTRASTS)
       -----------------------------------------------------------------------       PAGE   10

          1   4   5   2   3

                     HYPOTHESIS   1      1 DEGREE(S) OF FREEDOM
                     ========================================
                                                                    PAGE   11
          D0,D0,                    GRAND MEAN                    CONST.
          - - - - - - - - - - - - - - - - - - - - - - - - - - - - - - - - - -

              UNIVARIATE ANALYSIS OF VARIANCE FOR (RC C&D C)

     HYPOTHESIS MEAN SQUARE=   153692.187    F=    1591.9971   WITH   1. AND     376. DEGREES OF FREEDOM   P LESS THAN 0.0001
. . . . . . . . . . . . . . . . . . . . . . . . . . . . . . . . . . . . . . . . . . . . . . . . . . . . . . . . . . . .

                     HYPOTHESIS   2      2 DEGREE(S) OF FREEDOM
                     ========================================
          D0,D1,                    THINKING STAGE               BETA1
          D0,D2,                    THINKING STAGE               BETA2
          - - - - - - - - - - - - - - - - - - - - - - - - - - - - - - - - - -

              UNIVARIATE ANALYSIS OF VARIANCE FOR (RC C&D C)

     HYPOTHESIS MEAN SQUARE=    926.2129    F=       9.5940   WITH   2. AND     376. DEGREES OF FREEDOM   P LESS THAN 0.0001
. . . . . . . . . . . . . . . . . . . . . . . . . . . . . . . . . . . . . . . . . . . . . . . . . . . . . . . . . . . .

                     HYPOTHESIS   3      2 DEGREE(S) OF FREEDOM
                     ========================================
          D1,D0,                    SOCIAL GROUP                 ALPHA1
          D2,D0,                    SOCIAL GROUP                 ALPHA2
          - - - - - - - - - - - - - - - - - - - - - - - - - - - - - - - - - -

              UNIVARIATE ANALYSIS OF VARIANCE FOR (RC C&D C)

     HYPOTHESIS MEAN SQUARE=    755.8662    F=       7.8295   WITH   2. AND     376. DEGREES OF FREEDOM   P LESS THAN 0.0005
. . . . . . . . . . . . . . . . . . . . . . . . . . . . . . . . . . . . . . . . . . . . . . . . . . . . . . . . . . . .
CORE USED FOR DATA=  158 LOCATIONS OUT OF 3072 AVAILABLE
```

FIGURE 3.3-5 Problem 2: Phase II output

Table 3.4 Summary of Analysis-of-variance Results for 3 × 3 Crossed Design

Source of Variation	Degrees of Freedom	Mean Square	F
Constant	1	—	—
Social group, eliminating constant	2	815.20	**8.44
(Social group, eliminating constant and thinking stage)	(2)	(755.87)	(**7.83)
Thinking stage, eliminating constant and social group	2	866.88	**8.98
Interaction, eliminating all above	4	60.27	.62
Within groups	376	96.54	
Total	385		

**significant at $p < .01$

The tests of significance in the alternative order appear in the bottom half of Figure 3.3-5. In this output the constant is tested as previously. The sum of squares is obtained for stages of thinking, eliminating the constant, and the sum of squares is obtained for social groups, eliminating both the constant and stages of thinking. The latter is the only test in this order that we are interested in.

In this order, the mean square among social groups is 755.87 and the F statistic is 7.83. Hypothesis 2 is therefore rejected at $p < .01$, and we claim significant differences among reading comprehension means for the three social groups. While the F has not changed dramatically with reordering in this study, in other research it may mean the difference between significance or the lack of it. To report this result, a line or a footnote may be added to Table 3.4 indicating the F for the alternate order.

To summarize, we conclude that there are significant differences in reading comprehension among ten-year-old children from three different social groups, and at different operational levels of thinking as defined by Piaget. In testing the hypothesis of group-mean differences, we have concluded that both social group and thinking stage main effects are significant, while interaction is not. The terms μ, α_j, and β_k are therefore all that are necessary to the analysis-of-variance model.

In the general unequal-N case, the estimates of these effects depend on the number of terms included. Thus, to obtain best estimates of the three terms in the model and the corresponding predicted means, we should assume the main-effects model of rank 5 (17c). To obtain these estimates and means, the MULTIVARIANCE program can be rerun with the rank of the model for estimation set to 5. The predicted means that result will have smaller standard errors than the observed means, since fewer terms are summed in the equation. In those cases where the interaction is significant, the residuals, or the differences between the observed and predicted means, may indicate subgroups in the design for which the main-class model does not hold.

In addition to the information in Table 3.4, the write-up of a study such as this should include the sample sizes and observed means in each of the nine groups, the five estimated effects and their standard errors in the final model, and the estimated combined row and column means. The estimated means, in particular, indicate the direction of mean differences and the strength of the effects—that is, the number of points on the reading comprehension test which separate the various groups. Although the standard deviations for separate groups may also be included, the common within-group standard deviation is usually adequate.

4

ATTITUDES AND ACHIEVEMENT: THREE-WAY MULTIVARIATE ANALYSIS OF VARIANCE

Several confounding factors must be dealt with in studies of school attitudes and achievement. First, according to Jackson (1968), strong attitudes toward school and school subjects are not formed until children have had five to eight years' experience with school. These attitudes universally decline fron the time they are formed, at least through grade nine or ten in most western countries. Second, in measuring attitudes, global reactions such as "attitude toward school" are apt to be highly transitory and should be avoided. Better results will be obtained with attitudes toward specific aspects of school, e.g., specific subjects or specific types of activity, than with "like-school" scales. On the whole, the IEA studies (Comber and Keeves, 1973) have shown that, when more specific attitudes are measured, correlations with achievement are both higher and more consistent.

The present study applies these principles in an investigation of the relationship between science attitudes and achievement. Students are classified on the basis of their interest in science as characterized by one of the three categories—like science "more than," "about as much as," or "less than" other school subjects. Children were selected for the study at an age level where these attitudes are likely to be well established, viz., grades seven through nine. Since attitudes toward school work systematically decline in this age range, however, grade level is included in the study as a control variable. In addition, systematic differences between boys and girls are expected both in science attitudes and science achievement, and sex is also included as a control factor.

The dependent variables for the study are four subtests of the IEA science achievement battery. The cognitive items are divided into groups according to the complexity of the process necessary to answer them. The first group, entitled "Functional Information," tests the student's knowledge of simple facts and relationships in a variety of science fields. A second subtest, entitled "Comprehension," measures the extent to which the student is able to understand scientific principles and explain them in his own words. The third subtest, "Application," requires the student to apply the principles and knowledge in new situations as, for example, in designing his own experiment. A fourth subtest, entitled "Higher Mental Processes," requires more complex thought processes such as the ability to evaluate scientific experiments and presentations that have been prepared by others.

The design of the study may be diagrammed as shown in Figure 4.1. Each student is classified according to three sampling factors, namely, sex, grade level, and attitude toward science. Attitude level 1 is comprised of those who like science best, while attitude level 3 is those who like science least. In total there are $2 \times 3 \times 3 = 18$ subgroups of students. Each student is represented by the following four measures:

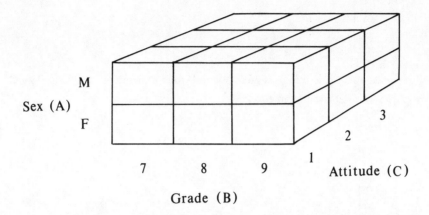

FIGURE 4.1   Sampling Diagram for Three-way Crossed Design

$y_1 =$ Functional information

$y_2 =$ Comprehension

$y_3 =$ Application

$y_4 =$ Higher mental processes

Because these subtest scores are four aspects of the same construct, i.e., science achievement, they are treated as simultaneous dependent variables and a multivariate model is adopted. That the correlations among the four measures are undoubtedly all positive and perhaps high, and the variances possibly unequal, are additional arguments for applying multivariate techniques.

The purpose of the analysis is to investigate mean differences among sex groups, grade levels, and attitude groups on the four science achievement tests. For this purpose, we will attempt to fit the data to the three-way fixed-effects analysis-of-variance model given by (23).

$$\mathbf{y}_{ijkl} = \underset{\sim}{\mu} + \underset{\sim}{\alpha}_j + \underset{\sim}{\beta}_k + \underset{\sim}{\gamma}_l + (\underset{\sim}{\alpha}\underset{\sim}{\beta})_{jk} + (\underset{\sim}{\alpha}\gamma)_{jl} + (\underset{\sim}{\beta}\gamma)_{kl} + (\underset{\sim}{\alpha}\underset{\sim}{\beta}\gamma)_{jkl} + \underset{\sim}{\epsilon}_{ijkl} \tag{23}$$

In (23) $\underset{\sim}{\mu}$ is a population constant, common to all observations. $\underset{\sim}{\alpha}_j$, $\underset{\sim}{\beta}_k$, and γ_l are the systematic deviations from $\underset{\sim}{\mu}$ due to the subject being a member of sex group j, grade k, and attitude group l, respectively. $(\underset{\sim}{\alpha}\underset{\sim}{\beta})_{jk}$ is the unique interaction effect of sex group j and grade k, while $(\underset{\sim}{\alpha}\gamma)$ and $(\underset{\sim}{\beta}\gamma)$ are interactions of other factors. Finally, $(\underset{\sim}{\alpha}\underset{\sim}{\beta}\gamma)_{jkl}$ is a unique interaction for each cell, or a so-called high-order interaction. To the extent that the $(\underset{\sim}{\alpha}\underset{\sim}{\beta}\gamma)$'s are large, main effects and simple interactions do not suffice to explain the outcomes. Finally, $\underset{\sim}{\epsilon}_{ijkl}$ is the unique deviation of the achievement score for subject i in group jkl from his subgroup mean.

All of the terms in (23) are vectors, having an element for each of the four criterion measures. For example, the observed vector for subject i in group jkl is $\mathbf{y}_{ijkl}$, and contains that subject's scores on all four dependent variables, as shown in (24):

$$\mathbf{y}_{ijkl} = \begin{bmatrix} y_{ijkl}^{(1)} \\ y_{ijkl}^{(2)} \\ y_{ijkl}^{(3)} \\ y_{ijkl}^{(4)} \end{bmatrix} \qquad (24)$$

Also, each analysis-of-variance effect is a vector of effects for all four dependent variables. The effect of being a male is α_1; the vector α_1 may be depicted as in (25):

$$\alpha_1 = \begin{bmatrix} \alpha_1^{(1)} \\ \alpha_1^{(2)} \\ \alpha_1^{(3)} \\ \alpha_1^{(4)} \end{bmatrix} \qquad (25)$$

α_1 contains the deviation from μ for the average of all males on the four dependent variables. The effect of sex on each of the dependent, variables may be different so that the four α_1's have different numerical values. We shall wish to estimate four α_1's and to test that the vector of α_1's is equal to the vector of α_2's. This is the test of significance that the two are equal on the multiple outcome measures.

We shall similarly test the grade effects in terms of the three β vectors, test attitude effects in terms of the equality of the three γ vectors, and, finally, test the two and three factor interactions in terms of the $(\alpha\beta)$, $(\alpha\gamma)$, $(\beta\gamma)$, and $(\alpha\beta\gamma)$ vectors. Each of these tests involves vectors with four components corresponding to the respective criterion scores.

The hypotheses to be tested may be succinctly represented as the null hypotheses (26) through (32):

$$H_0(1): \quad \alpha_1 = \alpha_2 \qquad (26)$$

$$H_0(2): \quad \beta_1 = \beta_2 = \beta_3 \qquad (27)$$

$$H_0(3): \quad \gamma_1 = \gamma_2 = \gamma_3 \qquad (28)$$

$$H_0(4): \quad (\alpha\beta)_{jk} = 0, \quad \text{for all } j,k \qquad (29)$$

$$H_0(5): \quad (\alpha\gamma)_{jl} = 0, \quad \text{for all } j,l \qquad (30)$$

$$H_0(6): \quad (\beta\gamma)_{kl} = 0, \quad \text{for all } k,l \qquad (31)$$

$$H_0(7): \quad (\alpha\beta\gamma)_{jkl} = 0, \quad \text{for all } j,k,l \qquad (32)$$

Once tests of significance indicate which effects are zero and which are not, we may drop the nonsignificant effects from the model and obtain best estimates of those that remain. These estimates may be used to predict the subclass means or for interpretive purposes. There are many possible prediction models implied by (23). In the event that all main effects prove significant and all interactions nonsignificant, we will predict the mean in each subclass by summing the population constant and the sex, grade, and attitude deviations from the constant term. This prediction equation is given by (33).

$$\hat{y}_{jkl} = \hat{\underline{\mu}} + \hat{\underline{\alpha}}_j + \hat{\underline{\beta}}_k + \hat{\gamma}_l \qquad (33)$$

The circumflex over each term indicates that it is estimated from the sample data. Alternatively, some of the main effects may not be significant and would be dropped from the model, or some of the interactions may be significant and need to be included. Note, however, that if all terms in (23) are significant, then there is little reason for a prediction model; the results tell us that each mean can only be explained as a function unique to the particular group. That is, the best and only prediction of the mean for group jkl is the observed mean itself. There is no useful information in the classification of subjects with respect to the various dimensions of the design.

For purpose of significance tests, we assume that the subjects are responding independently of one another and that the error vectors have a four-variate normal distribution with mean zero and general variance-covariance matrix. Specifically, the four dependent variables may have different variances and any pattern of covariances. Correlations among the science scores are not restricted to being zero or equal. Although individual errors must have the same variance-covariance matrix for all observations, the subclass frequencies need not be equal. This implies that the means of the 18 groups may have unequal variances, inversely proportional to the number of subjects in the group, as shown in (13).

There are two restrictions to consider before proceeding further with the analysis. First, the dependent variables must not be linear functions of one another. They may not, for example, consist of subtest scores and a total score for each subject, nor may they have the same total for every subject. Since in the sample data there is no such relationship among the four science subtests, this restriction is not a problem.

The second restriction concerns the number of parameters that may be uniquely estimated and tested, i.e., the degrees of freedom in the model. Although the model has 48 parameters if we count μ, two α's, three β's, three γ's, six $(\alpha\beta)$'s, and so on, there are at most 18 independent means, so that there are at most 18 effects that we may estimate. Thus, it is necessary either to restrict the effects (assume that the sum of the α's equals the sum of the β's equals the sum of the γ's equals zero, and so on) or to choose 18 linear functions of the 48 effects as the parameters to be estimated. The number of effects that are estimable corresponds to the between-group degrees of freedom specified by the rank of the model for significance testing. In Table 4.1, these degrees of freedom are partitioned for each main effect and interaction.

4.1 SPECIAL CONSIDERATIONS REQUIRED BY THE DATA SET

Prior to the problem run, three aspects of the data set must be given special attention—the inequality of subclass N's, the order of criterion measures, and the presence of cells in the design containing no deviations.

4.1.1 Unequal N

Because the sample was drawn from naturally occurring groups, it is unlikely that there will be equal or proportionate numbers of subjects in the sex-grade combinations. Thus, a general nonorthogonal analysis of variance will be required and can be obtained without difficulty if we establish a prior ordering of the effects listed in Table 4.1.

The unequal subclass frequencies induce correlations among the estimates of the α's, β's, γ's, and interactions. Therefore, to obtain an exact additive partition of total sum of squares and cross-products, we shall test: the constant term; sex eliminating the constant; grade eliminating the constant and sex; attitude eliminating sex, grade, and constant; interactions eliminating mean effects; and three-way interaction eliminating the two-way

Table 4.1   Analysis of Variance for Three-way
Crossed Design

Source of Variation	Degrees of Freedom	
	Full Model	Revised
Constant	1	1
Sex (A)	1	1
Grade (B)	2	2
Attitude (C)	2	2
AB	2	2
AC	2	2
BC	4	4
ABC	4	3
Among means	18	17
Within groups	$N - 18$	$N - 17$
Total	N	N

interactions. According to the principles described in Chapter 3, this order is chosen because the main focus of the present study is on differences in achievement among the three attitude groups. Attitude is therefore the last main effect, and is tested unconfounded with sex and grade-level variation. Sex and grade are known, or strongly suspected, of having large achievement differences and are placed early in the order of elimination, as control variables.

The interactions follow the main effects because they are more complex explanations of the behavior being studied. By the same logic, the three-way interaction follows all the two-way interactions and is tested eliminating all main effects and all simple interactions of two design factors.

In reading the output, the last effects in the order of elimination are interpreted first. If they prove nonsignificant, they may be quickly omitted from the model; if not, they are an early warning that main-effect interpretations may be ambiguous. Significant interactions indicate that generalizations about one main effect do not apply across levels of the other design factors.

If interactions are nonsignificant and we find significant differences among attitude-group means, we shall have no valid test of the sex or grade main effects in this order of elimination. This is not a problem, because sex and grade are included in the design as control variables. For the sake of continuing the example, we shall test the significance of effects in an alternative order in which grade differences follow the attitude levels. This order would be necessary if grade differences were of interest and attitude were found significant. We should then test the grade effect free of the confounding with attitude-group differences.

If sex were also of primary importance to the study, a third order of effects would be required in order to test sex-group differences without confounding by grade and attitude effects. The tests in these three orders of elimination would not be statistically independent however.

4.1.2   Order of Criterion Variables

Because this study has multiple criterion measures, we must resort to tests of multivariate hypothesis for decisions about the significance of effects. Most such tests are invariant under permutations of the *order* of the criterion measures. In particular, the univariate results, and the F approximation to the distribution of the likelihood ratio (see Chapter 2), are not affected by the order of the dependent variables. This invariance also applies to other multivariate techniques, such as discriminate analysis and canonical correlation.

In the present study, however, the dependent variables have an inherent order according to their complexity. On both theoretical and empirical grounds, the attainment of functional information may be considered the simplest process of those observed. Information is necessary in order for a student to perform well on the other tests. *Comprehension* of this information is necessary in order for the student to apply his knowledge, or to operate upon it at some higher mental level. Likewise, *application* of the principles of science requires that the information be known and comprehended, and is itself a requisite for more complex mental processing.

If we choose to test mean differences using a test criterion that is appropriate to ordered variables, we have in the output of the MULTIVARIANCE program the step-down F statistics. The tests based on these statistics reveal the presence of a significant difference among group means on the first criterion variable, on the second criterion variable holding constant the first, on the third criterion variable holding constant the first two, and so on to the last criterion variable holding constant all those preceding. The step-down tests reveal whether significant differences among groups are concentrated in the earliest and simplest measures.

Obviously, the results of the step-down analysis will change if the order of dependent variables is altered. It is therefore important to establish an order of variables according to some logical rule. In this example, the variables are ordered because the corresponding level of attainment depends upon preceding levels having been mastered. If there is no basis for ordering the set of dependent variables, the step-down results are not of much interest.

Performing a step-down analysis of p dependent variables is like computing $p - 1$ consecutive analyses of covariance: the step-down statistic for y_1 is the conventional univariate F ratio for the first variable; the step-down statistic for y_2 is the univariate F ratio for the second criterion variable, holding constant the first (just as if it were a covariate); and so on to the last step-down statistic, which is an F ratio for variable y_p holding constant all preceding criterion measures.

4.1.3 Null Subclasses

When classifying data on a number of dimensions, it is possible that some groups turn up with no observations. This is the case in the present example: there are no girls in grade 9 who chose option "like science best." Thus, group 2,3,1 has no observations, the interaction $(\alpha\beta\gamma)$ cannot be estimated, and the interaction degrees of freedom for ABC are reduced from four to three. As a result, the total number of degrees of freedom among means is reduced from 18 to 17. In other words, it is the number of groups with *at least one observation* that determines the maximum number of degrees of freedom among means.

If it happens in a design that several groups have no observations and the missing observations conform to no regular pattern, it may be difficult to draw up an analysis-of-variance table like Table 4.1 or to determine which interactions may or may not be estimated. In a complex design with many empty cells, both low-order and high-order interactions, and possibly some main effects, may be inestimable. In this case, the identification of inestimable parameters can be done empirically. The computer run is first set up as if the design were complete. The MULTIVARIANCE program counts the number of subjects in the cells of the design and tallies the number of cells with and without observations. The effect codes are also written as if the design were complete. For example, in the attitude study, codes are written for all 18 degrees of freedom. The MULTIVARIANCE program will accept all of the codes, and will print a list of effects which may not be estimated due to the missing cells. The user may then eliminate the codes for inestimable effects from the card deck, adjust the degrees of freedom on the Hypothesis Test card accordingly, and rerun the problem with only the remaining effects to be tested. In the present example, these runs are obtained for demonstration purposes, even though we know in advance the one effect that must be eliminated.

4.2 FORMAT OF THE DATA

Columns	Variables	
1-6	Identification	
7	Sex,	1 = male
		2 = female
8	Grade,	1 = grade 7
		2 = grade 8
		3 = grade 9
9	Science attitude,	1 = science favorite subject
		2 = science same as other subjects
		3 = science least favorite subject
11-13	Science functional information achievement score	
14-16	Science comprehension achievement score	
17-19	Science application achievement score	
20-22	Science higher mental process score	

The data are drawn from the sample of fourteen- and fifteen-year-olds of the IEA data bank (Husén, 1973).[1] The students are in grades 7, 8, and 9 of the Swedish schools. The number of items in the tests range from 9 in the higher process scale to 22 items in the comprehension scale. Each subtest score is corrected for guessing. As can be seen in the data list, this procedure sometimes results in negative scores.

4.3 MULTIVARIANCE SETUP

The input to the MULTIVARIANCE program, exclusive of the data cards, is listed in Figures 4.3-1 and 4.3-2. The Input Description card follows the Title cards. A distinction is made on the Input Description card between measured variables and those used to group the observations. Measured variables include all criterion scores, covariates, variables used in data transformations, and variables which are not part of the analysis but for which summary statistics are required. The nominal variables that describe the sampling design (factors in factorial designs) comprise the last. In the present data there are four measured variables (the science achievement subtest scores) and three factors in the analysis-of-variance design (sex of the student, grade of the student, and attitude toward science).

The program's **Data Form 1** is used. This is the simplest data form when each data card has a sex code 1 or 2, a grade code 1, 2, or 3, and an attitude code 1, 2, or 3. If other coding systems are used, a different input data form may be necessary.

The Factor Identification card names the three factors in the sampling design and gives the number of levels of each. This card also establishes the order of factors as they are named on the data cards. That is, the program will expect the sex code, grade code, and attitude code in that order. Thus, a data card with the numbers 2,2,3 would represent a girl in eighth grade for whom science was the least favorite subject.

[1]Swedish Populations II and III. See (Husén, 1973, Chapter 3).

```
         1         2
12345678901234567890123456

101  3112 108 85 70 53      101 23222  45 50 58 40      201 14232 120 58 95 40
101  6112 120108 58 28      101 25222  70 33-29 -7      202  9131  45 95 48 40
101  8212  33 20 33 28      101 26223  70108 58 28      202 17233  83 70 45 15
101 10112  58 83 58 15      101 31122  58 58 58 65      203  1132 133 95 60 40
102  1112  35 20 58 -9      102 23221  20120 70  3      203  2131 158158108 53
102  4212  73 40 20 20      105  3122  95 45 45 15      205  5132 145108 70 78
102  7112  50 80 38  5      105  6222  58 45 70  3      208  2131 108108 83 40
102 10113  58-17 58  3      106 17222  95 58 58 40      208 13132 120 95 83 90
102 12112  58 58 70 15      107  8122  58 95 70 15      208 19232  95 58 33 40
103  1112  33-42 20 15      109 15122  88133 88 40      208 20232  33 20 48 43
103  4213  33  8 -4  3      109 20122 108 70 58 28      208 21233 108108 45 65
103  7113  20 20 33  3      109 23123 108 83 70 40      210 15132  45 70 45 40
105 14112  20-29 -4  3      110 15222  95108 33 40      211  1133  70158 58 18
105 18112  45 33 58 15      110 17221  58 58 70 40      211  2131 108133 60 28
105 24212  83 70 45 40      111 12222  58 33 58 65      211 11232  33 45 33 15
106  4212  95 58 33  3      111 16223  33 70 33 28      211 15232  45 33 20 15
106  8212  58 83 45  3      111 20122  60 20  8 15      213 11132  83 95 70 28
106  9113  45 33  8  3      111 24221  58 83 70 15      214 14232 133108 33  3
107  6213  23 38 20 28      112 13122  45 20 20  3      214 21232  45 45 -4 40
107  7212  83 20 58 53      112 15221  83 83 83 40      215  2132  83 95 95 40
109  1212  63 73 30 20      112 16223  83 33 58 15      215  6232  70 45 70 15
109  2112  58 45 70 18      113  1122  95120 58 28      215 11232  45 45  8 40
109  4111  45 35 45 -9      113  3223  70 83 20 28      215 14232  95108 83 28
109  6112  20 83 45 15      114  1123  83 83 20  3      215 22132 108195 70 53
110  1112  45 -4  8 28      114  4122  58 95 45 28      220 13132  45 -4  8 28
110  3113  58 20 33 28      114  5122  70 70 20 40      220 20132  48 33 25 -2
110  8113  58  8 33 15      114  8222  58 45 58 15      221  3133  70 45 45 15
110  9112   8 10  8-17      114  9222  45 -4 70  3      221  4132 108108108 15
110 10112  95120 58 15      114 10222  70133 45 28      221  5131  58 83 45 40
110 11212  30 78 50 48      114 13223  58133 33 53      224 15232  58 83 58 53
110 12212  70 45  8 28      114 14222  10  8-17 -9      224 17132 123108 83 15
110 14212  83  8 20 28      115  6122 158170 95 65      224 25131 108158 95 90
111  4212  45 20 33 -9      115  9222  83145 58 40      225 10132 120145 95 15
112  5112  45 95 95 15      116 24223  10 23 20 18      226 16233  58 33 20  3
112  6213  -4 33 20 -9      117 20222  95 83 83 -7      226 18233  33 33 33  3
113 10112  58 95 33  3      117 29122  60 45  8  3      228 16233  70 45 45 33
113 11112  70  8  8 28      118  6223  45 43 43  8      228 24232  78 18 65  8
113 15213  70 70 58  3      118  7122  20  8-17  3      230  1131 135170 83 65
113 18112  95 20 20 28      118 16222  45 20 20 15      230 13232  83120 20 15
113 23112  85 45 73 28      119  7122  83 70 20 -7      230 21232 108145 58 28
113 25213   8 20 -4-22      121 17223 108 20 20 18      231 19232 108133108 40
114 22212  58 70 -4 28      121 22122  58 83 20 28      233  2133  70 45 45  3
114 24112  70 95 33  3      122  1122 108183 70 65      233  4132  95 70 58 28
114 25112   8  8 23 53      122  4222  60100 95 28      233 20132  95 48 33  3
115 16111  98 70 70 18      122 10222  95 -9 23 38      233 21131 108 58 73  3
115 17112  45-17 58 15      122 13123 -17-27  8 15      234  1132  83 95108 -7
115 25111  75123 53 28      123 15121  70 33 20  3      234 16232 135145 65 53
115 28112  70120 70 28      123 18222 108 70 33 28      235  9132  58 58 58 15
115 29112  73 13 23 28      123 29222  58 95 33 28      235 15132 108 70 83 65
115 30211  83 58 45 43      124 18223  33 70 20 -9      235 21232  45 58 45  3
```

FIGURE 4.2 Problem 3: Science Achievement data

Comments describe the problem and are followed by an End-of-Comments card. The Variable Format specifies bypassing the subject number, reading the factor identification numbers in I (integer) format, and the measured variables in F (decimal) format. Labels are then inserted for the four measured criterion variables.

One blank observation concludes the data for Data Form 1. That is, there are as many final blank cards as cards containing any one subject's scores (one blank card in this case).

The Estimation Specification card introduces the program's estimation phase. The rank of the model for significance testing is 18, including all main-effect and interaction degrees of freedom. In this case we know in advance that one of the 18 effects is not estimable, but we shall proceed with the run in order to inspect the error message that is produced. On a second run, we delete the inestimable effect in order to complete the analysis-of-variance tests.

Until the results of the significance tests are seen, the rank of the model for estimation cannot be exactly determined. However, by making an "educated guess" that all main effects and none of the interactions will be significant, we may set the rank of the model for estimation to 6. This instructs the program to estimate the 6 effects described by the 6 leading effect codes entered in the data deck. According to the order of the effects in Table 4.1, estimates will be obtained of the constant, the first sex effect, the first two grade effects, and the first two attitude effects. [Later these six effects will be summed in order to obtain predicted means for every subclass according to the model given by (33).] As an alternative, we might leave this parameter undefined for the first run, or set it equal to 18 to estimate all possible between-group effects.

Column 12 is left blank to indicate that the pooled within-group variance-covariance matrix is the error term, or denominator, for the test statistics. Other alternatives for this parameter are discussed in Chapter 5. One alternate order of effects is to be established, so that we may also test grade differences in achievement eliminating attitude effects (1 in column 20). If attitude groups have different means, then the alternate order is necessary for a valid test of the grade factor.

The numeral 1 is entered in column 32 to request that the estimated (or predicted) means be computed for the entire set of 18 cells. This is particularly useful in the present example because, applying (33), we are able to estimate the mean in the missing group 2,3,1. Even though there is no observed mean in that group, we may obtain estimates of μ and α_2 if there is at least one girl, of β_3 if there is at least one ninth grade student, and of γ_1 if there is at least one student who likes science best. If (33) proves to be correct, we may then sum the respective effects to get a best estimate of the mean for the missing group. For this estimate to be valid, it is necessary to assume that group 2,3,1 would yield no unique interaction if we had observations in this cell. We may be willing to make this assumption if the remaining 17 groups all yield no significant interactions.

The 3 in column 44 indicates that combined observed and combined predicted means are to be computed. A code in column 44 requires that the following control card be a Means Key, noting which "row and column means" are wanted.

The zero in the Means Key of this example indicates that the mean of all subjects, regardless of subclass membership, is to be computed for each outcome measure. The "1" refers to factor 1, or the sex factor, on the Factor Identification card. It causes the observed and predicted means on the four criterion measures be computed and printed for all males and all females, regardless of grade or attitude group. The "2" has the same effect for the means of all seventh, eighth, and ninth grade students, regardless of sex or attitude group. Similarly, the "3" causes computation and printing of means for each attitude group, regardless of sex or grade level. To obtain the means for the cross-classification by sex and attitude group, "1*3" is punched next. This means that the four criterion means will be computed for males in attitude group 1, males in attitude group 2, and so on, across all grade levels.

The Symbolic Contrast Vector codes indicate the effects to be estimated. In a three-way design, each code has three terms separated by commas. The order in which the cards are entered in the deck establishes the initial order of effects, corresponding in this case to the order in Table 4.1. The first symbolic contrast code designates the grand mean for all subjects (i.e., across all factors). The mean for a factor is represented by code zero, and in this instance the zero is preceded by the letter D. Thus the grand mean on all factors is D0,D0,D0,. The code should be followed by a label of up to eight characters.

```
            1         2         3         4         5         6         7         8
   1234567890123456789012345678901234567890123456789012345678901234567890

       1. Title cards
   PROBLEM 3: 3-WAY ANALYSIS OF VARIANCE - UNEQUAL N
   IEA SCIENCE AND ATTITUDE STUDY
       2. Input Description card
      4    3    1
       3. Factor Identification card
   SEX       2GRADE      3ATTUDE    3
       4. Comment cards
   3 FACTORS          1.   SEX      1 = MALE
                                    2 = FEMALE
                      2.   GRADE    1 = GRADE 7
                                    2 = GRADE 8
                                    3 = GRADE 9
                      3.   ATTITUDE    1 = LIKE SCIENCE BEST
                                       2 = LIKE SCIENCE SAME
                                       3 = LIKE SCIENCE WORST


   DEPENDENT VARIABLES ARE SCIENCE ACHIEVEMENT TEST SCORES
          A = KNOWLEDGE TEST
          B = COMPREHENSION TEST
          C = APPLICATION TEST
          D = HIGHER MENTAL PROCESSES

   ONE ALTERNATE ORDER OF EFFECTS TO TEST GRADE AS LAST MAIN EFFECT.

   ONE NULL SUBCLASS.

   VARIABLE     FORMAT     COLUMNS

   SCHOOL       I3          1-3
   STUDENT      I3          4-6
   SEX          I1          7
   GRADE        I1          8
   LIKE SC.     I1          9
   SCIENCE A    F3.1       11-13
   SCIENCE B    F3.1       14-16
   SCIENCE C    F3.1       17-19
   SCIENCE D    F3.1       20-22
       5. End-of-comments card
   FINISH
       6. Variable Format card
   (6X,3I1,1X,4F3.1)
       9. Variable Label card
   SCI A   SCI B   SCI C   SCI D
      10. Data
     DATA DECK   (DATA FORM 1)
          End of data
                                                            BLANK CARD

      12. Estimation Specification card
      18   6         1         1            3
      13. Means key
   0,1,2,3,1*3.   MEANS KEY

            1         2         3         4         5         6         7         8
   1234567890123456789012345678901234567890123456789012345678901234567890
```

FIGURE 4.3-1 Problem 3: MULTIVARIANCE control cards for 3-way anova

```
              1         2         3         4         5         6         7         8
     12345678901234567890123456789012345678901234567890123456789012345678901234567890
16. Symbolic Contrast Vectors
     D0,D0,D0,  CONST
     1,0,0,     SEX
     0,1,0,     GRADE
     0,2,0,
     0,0,1,     ATTUDE
     0,0,2,
     1,1,0,     S X G
     1,2,0,
     1,0,1,     S X A
     1,0,2,
     0,1,1,     G X A
     0,1,2,
     0,2,1,
     0,2,2,
     1,1,1,     SXGXA
     1,1,2,
     1,2,1,
     1,2,2,
17. Contrast Reordering key
1,2,5,6,3,4.        CONTRAST REORDERING KEY
18. Analysis Selection card
     4         1
21. Hypothesis Test card
-1,1,2,2,2,2,4,4.
-4,2.        HYPOTHESIS TEST CARD - ALTERNATE ORDER
22. End-of-job card
                                                      STOP
              1         2         3         4         5         6         7         8
     12345678901234567890123456789012345678901234567890123456789012345678901234567890
```

FIGURE 4.3-2   Problem 3:   MULTIVARIANCE control cards for 3-way anova (cont.)

To estimate α_1, a "1" is punched as the first term (sex) of the next card. Zeros are entered as space holders in the other two positions, indicating that this effect does not involve grade or attitude differences. Although the letter D may precede every code, the MULTIVARIANCE program requires only that the letter be punched on the first (grand-mean) card. Thus the 1,0,0, code represents D1,D0,D0,. The label SEX is appropriate for this card.

To instruct the program to estimate β_1 and β_2, we enter the numbers "1" and "2" in the second position of successive symbolic contrast cards and enter zeros in the first and third positions. Two cards are necessary because there are two degrees of freedom for grade levels. With the D's omitted, the grade codes are 0,1,0, and 0,2,0,. Similarly γ_1 and γ_2, the two attitude effects, are coded by putting the numbers 1 and 2 on two successive cards in the third position. Zeros now appear in the first and second positions resulting in the codes 0,0,1, and 0,0,2,.

The interaction effects of sex and grade are coded by inserting two successive cards with combinations of the "1" in the sex position and "1" and "2" in the grade position, respectively. These effects indicate interactions $(\alpha\beta)_{11}$ and $(\alpha\beta)_{12}$. Because these two degrees of freedom are not interactions with attitude, a zero is put in the third position.

In like manner, the interactions of the first and third factors are combinations of the "1" for the sex effect and the "1" and "2" for the attitude effects, with zeros in the middle (grade) position. These cards are punched 1,0,1, and 1,0,2, respectively.

For the interaction effects of grade and attitude, corresponding to the four degrees of freedom indicated in Table 4.1, the codes require four cards containing every combination of the β_1 and β_2 codes for grade with the

γ_1 and γ_2 codes for attitude groups. Zero appears in the first position on each of the four cards. The grade-by-attitude symbolic codes are therefore:

```
0 , 1 , 1 ,
0 , 1 , 2 ,
0 , 2 , 1 ,
0 , 2 , 2 ,
```

Finally, to estimate the four three-factor interaction effects, we punch on successive cards every combination of the "1" and "2" for grades and the "1" and "2" for attitudes:

```
1 , 1 , 1 ,
1 , 1 , 2 ,
1 , 2 , 1 ,
1 , 2 , 2 ,
```

The number of effect codes corresponds exactly to the degrees of freedom in Table 4.1.

The Contrast Reordering Key following the Symbolic Contrast cards determines an alternative order of effects, assuming that the symbolic vectors are numbers from 1 through 18 in the original order. The sequence 1,2,5,6,3,4 on this card specifies that vectors 1 and 2 (grand mean and sex) are first, 5 and 6 (attitude) next, and 3 and 4 (grade) last in the alternative order. In this order, the grade sum of squares and cross-products will be obtained holding constant attitude effects. Interactions are not included on the key, as they are not affected by interchanging factors earlier in the order of elimination.

The analysis-phase cards are entered next. There are four dependent variables; no further information is required because they are the original four measures in the same order as on the data cards. The one alternate order of effects that is established in Phase II is to be used with this set of four variables in Phase III (1 in column 16).

The Hypothesis Test card determines the groups in which the coded effects are to be tested for significance. Specifically, the first effect (grand mean) and the second effect (sex) are to be tested for significance separately. The next two effects (grade) are then to be tested jointly, as are the following two effects (attitude). The AB interactions (sex $\times$ grade) are then tested jointly, as are the AC (sex $\times$ attitude) interaction and the four effects for the BC interaction. Finally, the four ABC interaction effects are tested jointly. (We know in advance that this test will not work due to the missing subclass and deficient degrees of freedom.)

The minus sign preceding the first "1" on the hypothesis test card instructs the program to bypass a test of significance of that one effect. Because the origin of the scale of measurement is arbitrary in most psychological tests, we have no particular interest in testing that the constant term is equal to zero. The option to suppress testing saves computer time and pages.

In the alternative order of effects (grand mean, sex, attitude, grade), we require a test only of the two degrees of freedom for grade differences. Although a second Hypothesis Test card is necessary for this order, we may utilize the minus sign to instruct the computer to bypass testing the first four effects (grand mean, sex, and attitude). The card therefore reads "$-4,2$."

4.4 OUTPUT AND INTERPRETATION

PHASE I. The data for this example are summarized in the Phase I output in Figures 4.4-1 through 4.4-3. At the top of Figure 4.4-2 are listed the number of observations in each subclass and a unique cell number for each group of subjects. Group 2,3,1 is seen to have no subjects. For the other groups, with observations numbered 1 through 17, means and standard deviations are printed. The standard deviations are zero for the two groups

PROBLEM

- -

PROBLEM 3: 3-WAY ANALYSIS OF VARIANCE - UNEQUAL N   IEA SCIENCE AND ATTITUDE STUDY

- -

```
          3 FACTORS        1.  SEX      1 = MALE
                                        2 = FEMALE
                           2.  GRADE    1 = GRADE 7
                                        2 = GRADE 8
                                        3 = GRADE 9
                           3.  ATTITUDE    1 = LIKE SCIENCE BEST
                                           2 = LIKE SCIENCE SAME
                                           3 = LIKE SCIENCE WORST

          DEPENDENT VARIABLES ARE SCIENCE ACHIEVEMENT TEST SCORES
                A  =  KNOWLEDGE TEST
                B  =  COMPREHENSION TEST
                C  =  APPLICATION TEST
                D  =  HIGHER MENTAL PROCESSES

          ONE ALTERNATE ORDER OF EFFECTS TO TEST GRADE AS LAST MAIN EFFECT.

          ONE NULL SUBCLASS.

          VARIABLE      FORMAT      COLUMNS

          SCHOOL         I3          1-3
          STUDENT        I3          4-6
          SEX            I1           7
          GRADE          I1           8
          LIKE SC.       I1           9
          SCIENCE A     F3.1        11-13
          SCIENCE B     F3.1        14-16
          SCIENCE C     F3.1        17-19
          SCIENCE D     F3.1        20-22
```

INPUT PARAMETERS
================

```
          NUMBER OF VARIABLES IN INPUT VECTORS=               4

          NUMBER OF FACTORS IN DESIGN=                        3

             NUMBER OF LEVELS OF FACTOR 1 (SEX     )  =       2
             NUMBER OF LEVELS OF FACTOR 2 (GRADE   )  =       3
             NUMBER OF LEVELS OF FACTOR 3 (ATTUDE  )  =       3

          INPUT IS FROM CARDS. DATA OPTION 1

          MINIMAL PAGE SPACING WILL BE USED

     *****NUMBER OF VARIABLE FORMAT CARDS NOT SPECIFIED. ASSUMED TO BE 1.

          FORMAT OF DATA
             (6X,3I1,1X,4F3.1)
```

FIRST OBSERVATION
SUBJECT   1 , CELL   1 1 2
                                  10.8000   8.5000   7.0000   5.3000

FIGURE 4.4-1   Problem 3: Phase I output

CELL IDENTIFICATION AND FREQUENCIES

CELL	FACTOR LEVELS			N
	SEX	GRADE	ATTUDE	
1	1	1	1	3
2	1	1	2	24
3	1	1	3	5
4	1	2	1	1
5	1	2	2	16
6	1	2	3	3
7	1	3	1	8
8	1	3	2	17
9	1	3	3	3
10	2	1	1	1
11	2	1	2	12
12	2	1	3	5
13	2	2	1	4
14	2	2	2	17
15	2	2	3	9
EMPTY	2	3	1	0
16	2	3	2	17
17	2	3	3	5

TOTAL N=   150.

1 NULL SUBCLASS(ES).

OBSERVED CELL MEANS --- ROWS ARE CELLS-COLUMNS ARE VARIABLES
----

	1 SCI A	2 SCI B	3 SCI C	4 SCI D
1	7.26667	7.60000	5.60000	1.23333
2	5.71667	4.71667	4.37917	1.78333
3	4.78000	1.28000	3.30000	1.04000
4	7.00000	3.30000	2.00000	0.30000
5	7.63750	8.03125	4.16250	2.71250
6	5.80000	4.63333	3.26667	1.93333
7	10.35000	12.03750	7.43750	4.48750
8	9.41176	8.72941	6.77647	3.20000
9	7.00000	8.26667	4.93333	1.20000
10	8.30000	5.80000	4.50000	4.30000
11	6.45000	4.87500	3.09167	2.41667
12	2.60000	3.38000	1.80000	0.06000
13	5.47500	8.60000	7.32500	2.45000
14	6.75294	5.95882	4.40588	2.28235
15	5.66667	6.47778	3.38889	2.07778
16	7.81765	7.45294	4.92941	2.81765
17	7.04000	5.78000	3.76000	2.38000

OBSERVED CELL STD DEVS--ROWS ARE CELLS-COLUMNS VARIABLES
----

	1 SCI A	2 SCI B	3 SCI C	4 SCI D
1	2.657693	4.430576	1.276715	1.913984
2	2.965991	4.852580	2.623138	1.617746
3	1.652876	1.886001	1.767767	1.112654
4	0.0	0.0	0.0	0.0
5	3.227564	5.111649	3.162884	2.307921
6	6.614378	6.350853	3.288363	1.887679
7	3.690915	4.059887	2.227066	2.568178
8	3.110643	4.408481	2.829649	2.729927
9	0.0	6.524058	0.750555	0.793725
10	0.0	0.0	0.0	0.0
11	2.069036	2.669057	1.781449	1.843827
12	2.836371	2.337092	2.537716	1.847431
13	2.599199	2.554734	0.650000	1.855622
14	2.519950	4.574530	3.248552	2.091123
15	2.983287	3.896081	1.588588	1.693205
16	3.474053	4.325234	3.043798	1.680861
17	2.795174	3.187005	1.112654	2.609981

OBSERVED COMBINED MEANS
================================

- -

OVERALL
  N =   150.

    MEANS   SCI A = 6.985   SCI B = 6.589   SCI C = 4.628   SCI D = 2.372

- -

FACTORS   1 (SEX   )

  LEVEL   1
  N =   80.

    MEANS   SCI A = 7.416   SCI B = 6.970   SCI C = 5.079   SCI D = 2.439

  LEVEL   2
  N =   70.

    MEANS   SCI A = 6.493   SCI B = 6.154   SCI C = 4.113   SCI D = 2.296

- -

FACTORS   2 (GRADE)

  LEVEL   1
  N =   50.

    MEANS   SCI A = 5.632   SCI B = 4.472   SCI C = 3.780   SCI D = 1.706

  LEVEL   2
  N =   50.

    MEANS   SCI A = 6.686   SCI B = 6.794   SCI C = 4.262   SCI D = 2.336

  LEVEL   3
  N =   50.

    MEANS   SCI A = 8.638   SCI B = 8.502   SCI C = 5.842   SCI D = 3.074

FIGURE 4.4-2 Problem 3: Phase I output (continued)

```
- - - - - - - - - - - - - - - - - - - - - - - - - - - - - - - - - - - - - - - - - - - - - - - - - - - - - - - - -
FACTORS      3 (ATTUDE  )
    LEVEL       1
    N =    17.

       MEANS         SCI A  =   8.341       SCI B  =   9.565       SCI C  =   6.594       SCI D  =   3.176
    -------

    LEVEL       2
    N =   103.

       MEANS         SCI A  =   7.228       SCI B  =   6.569       SCI C  =   4.686       SCI D  =   2.488
    -------

    LEVEL       3
    N =    30.

       MEANS         SCI A  =   5.383       SCI B  =   4.973       SCI C  =   3.313       SCI D  =   1.517
    -------
- - - - - - - - - - - - - - - - - - - - - - - - - - - - - - - - - - - - - - - - - - - - - - - - - - - - - - - - -
FACTORS      1 (SEX    )    3 (ATTUDE  )
    LEVEL       1            1
    N =    12.

       MEANS         SCI A  =   9.300       SCI B  =  10.20        SCI C  =   6.525       SCI D  =   3.325
    -------

    LEVEL       1            2
    N =    57.

       MEANS         SCI A  =   7.358       SCI B  =   6.844       SCI C  =   5.033       SCI D  =   2.467
    -------

    LEVEL       1            3
    N =    11.

       MEANS         SCI A  =   5.664       SCI B  =   4.100       SCI C  =   3.736       SCI D  =   1.327
    -------

    LEVEL       2            1
    N =     5.

       MEANS         SCI A  =   6.040       SCI B  =   8.040       SCI C  =   6.760       SCI D  =   2.820
    -------

    LEVEL       2            2
    N =    46.

       MEANS         SCI A  =   7.067       SCI B  =   6.228       SCI C  =   4.257       SCI D  =   2.515
    -------

    LEVEL       2            3
    N =    19.

       MEANS         SCI A  =   5.221       SCI B  =   5.479       SCI C  =   3.068       SCI D  =   1.626
```

FIGURE 4.4-3 Problem 3: Phase I output (concluded)

having only one observation. The means for combinations of subclasses are also printed. From these it can be seen that the 80 boys scored higher than the 70 girls on all four of the science tests. There may be some confounding in these mean values however. For example, the 80 boy students may have a higher proportion of students with more positive attitudes toward science. Or, there may be more girls in the lower grades. The combined *estimated* means, produced in Phase II, give a more accurate picture of the outcomes, unbiased by different subgroup sizes.

Even in the observed means, however, there can be seen not only the expected increase over grade levels for all four subtests, but also a decrease in these scores with lower attitudes toward science. The latter trend can be seen for both girls and boys in the means for different combinations of factor 1 (sex) and factor 3 (attitude). For example, on the comprehension subtest the boys' means decrease from 10.20 to 6.84 to 4.10, and the girls' mean scores decrease from 8.04 to 6.23 to 5.48 for the three attitude groups. Again, there may be some bias in these values if the lower attitude groups contain a preponderance of students at one grade level.

PHASE II.   The estimation results for this run are presented in Figure 4.4-4. First, the parameters set by the user are listed, followed by the symbolic effect codes (Symbolic Contrast Vectors). At the same time the program is internally constructing columns of the matrices necessary for the estimation of effects. If there are effects that cannot be estimated due to missing subclasses, these are identified when the codes are encountered in the input deck. In this example, this occurs when the 18*th* effect is read. If more than one effect had been inestimable, several such messages would occur in the list of symbolic vectors. (Note that the same type of error might occur if vectors are incorrectly coded, or degrees of freedom incorrectly computed.)

ESTIMATION PARAMETERS
=====================

RANK OF THE BASIS = RANK OF MODEL FOR SIGNIFICANCE TESTING = 18
RANK OF THE MODEL TO BE ESTIMATED IS   6
ERROR TERM TO BE USED IS (WITHIN CELLS)
NUMBER OF ORDERS OF THE BASIS VECTORS OTHER THAN THE FIRST IS   1
ESTIMATED CELL MEANS, RESIDUALS AND RESIDUALS IN FORM OF T-STATISTICS WILL BE PRINTED
ESTIMATED COMBINED MEANS WILL BE PRINTED

SYMBOLIC CONTRAST VECTORS
=========================

(1)
| | D0,D0,D0, | CONST |

(2)
| | 1,0,0, | SEX |

(3)
| | 0,1,0, | GRADE |

(4)
| | 0,2,0, | |

(5)
| | 0,0,1, | ATTUDE |

(6)
| | 0,0,2, | |

(7)
| | 1,1,0, | S X G |

(8)
| | 1,2,0, | |

(9)
| | 1,0,1, | S X A |

(10)
| | 1,0,2, | |

(11)
| | 0,1,1, | G X A |

(12)
| | 0,1,2, | |

(13)
| | 0,2,1, | |

(14)
| | 0,2,2, | |

(15)
| | 1,1,1, | SXGXA |

(16)
| | 1,1,2, | |

(17)
| | 1,2,1, | |

(18)
| | 1,2,2, | |

**********ABOVE VECTOR IS LINEAR COMBINATION OF PRECEDING VECTORS**********
SEE DEPENDENCY TABLE BELOW

THERE IS AT LEAST ONE DEPENDENCY AMONG BASIS/CONTRAST VECTORS
CREATED BY DESIGN HAVING MORE EFFECTS THAN SUBCLASSES WITH OBSERVATIONS

DEPENDENCIES IN BASIS

BASIS VECTOR 18 IS A LINEAR COMBINATION OF

VECTORS	WEIGHTS
1	1.000000
2	-1.000000
3	-1.000000
4	-1.000000
5	2.000000
6	-1.000000
7	1.000000
8	1.000000
9	-2.000000
10	1.000000
11	-2.000000
12	1.000000
13	-2.000000
14	1.000000
15	2.000000
16	-1.000000
17	2.000000

ERROR   40 HAS OCCURRED. CONSULT PROGRAM WRITE-UP.
SKIPPING TO NEXT PROBLEM.

FIGURE 4.4-4 Problem 3: Phase II output (first run)

For each of the effects that cannot be estimated, a list of weights entitled "Dependencies in Basis" is produced indicating which preceding vectors in the set the inestimable effect is dependent upon. Inestimability of an effect occurs because all of the information required to estimate it has already been incorporated in earlier effects in the order of elimination. In the present example all of the earlier effects (1 through 17) contain the information that would be attributed to interaction effect 1,2,2,.

Since we cannot estimate the additional interaction, the sum of squares for this interaction is distributed among the other 17 effects and can affect to some extent their sum of squares. If the missing interaction is null, there is of course no confounding to be concerned with. But if we suspect that the interaction is large or important, then the confounding with other effects may be cause for concern. Failure to estimate the interaction would then bias the sum of squares for other effects to the point where they might appear significant. If we have reason to believe in this case that the empty cell contributes an important source of variation to the model, then we have no choice but to return to the sample and to locate females in grade nine who feel that science is their most preferred subject.

4.5 MULTIVARIANCE SETUP REVISED

Figure 4.5 lists the input to Phase II and Phase III of the MULTIVARIANCE program, as revised to eliminate the inestimable interaction. The terms and ranks now correspond to the right hand column of Table 4.1. The rank of the model for significance testing is 17 rather than 18, while the rank of the model for estimation remains at 6. The former 18th Symbolic Contrast Vector has been eliminated. The Contrast Reordering Key need not be altered, as only the leading 6 effects are reordered, and the Analysis Selection card remains the same. However, the Hypothesis Test card is altered because there are now only three degrees of freedom for the three high-order interaction effects.

The results of Phase I for the revised model are the same as given in Figures 4.4-1 through 4.4-3 and are not reproduced here. The Phase II output produced by the program listed in Figures 4.6-1 through 4.6-3 includes the 17 effects in the revised model that can now be tested for significance; the error message encountered in the earlier run is not seen.

The pooled within-group variances, standard deviations, and correlations are presented in Figure 4.6-1. These are best estimates for the four science subtest variables, given the analysis-of-variance model we assume. In this case, we can see that the correlations among the subtests are all positive, ranging from .29 to .53. The correlations between the three lower process subtests and the Higher Process test are the lowest, while the correlation between Functional Information and Comprehension is highest. This table of correlations should be included among the descriptive data in the written report of the study.

The common within-group variance is obtained as a weighted average of the variances for each variable in the 17 separate groups. The corresponding standard deviation is a convenient measure of dispersion of the scores about their subclass means, and also should be included in reports of the study. The within-group variance (or mean square) is the error (denominator) mean square for all univariate analysis-of-variance tests. The F ratios for testing the mean differences one subtest at a time have these values as their denominators. These mean squares are estimated with 133 degrees of freedom, or the total number of subjects, 150, minus the number of degrees of freedom among means, 17.

In order to estimate the constant, sex effect, two grade effects, and two attitude effects, we have set the rank of the model for estimation to 6. These resulting estimates appear in the matrix of "Least-squares Estimates of Effects" for all four criterion measures. For example, the least-squares estimate of the overall mean on the Functional Information test is 6.88. The least squares estimate of α_1 for the same subtest is .39, indicating that, on the average, boys are about four-tenths of a score point higher than the mean of all subjects on the first science achievement test. Similarly on this measure, grade-seven students are about 1.4 points below the mean of all subjects on the first test, and grade-eight students ($\hat{\beta}_2$) are about one-tenth of a point below the mean of all students. By subtraction, grade-nine students have $\hat{\beta}_3 = 1.54$.

The estimates of the effects in the model are useful interpretive devices. Each may be divided by the standard deviation of the respective criterion variable to obtain "estimates of effects in standard deviation units," which give the number of standard deviations separating the particular group from the mean for all subjects. For example, grade-seven students are about 2.1 score points below the mean of all students on the Comprehension subtest. The standard deviation of the Comprehension test, from above, is 4.33 score points. Therefore, grade-seven students are almost one-half standard deviation below the mean of all subjects on the Comprehension test.

The standard errors of the estimated effects, given next, are also useful. If the observations are distributed normally, then the estimated effects (as linear combinations of the cell means) also have normal distributions. Using the estimated standard errors, we may draw confidence intervals for any of the effects (α, β, γ) using the appropriate critical value from the t distribution. The degrees of freedom for this distribution are the within-group degrees of freedom, 133.

We may also test the significance of an individual effect. For example, males are about four-tenths of a score point above the mean of all subjects on the first outcome measure, and the corresponding standard error is .257. Since the effect does not exceed 1.96 standard errors, we should conclude that there is no significant difference between sex groups on this variable alone. Only a small number of such tests should be made, however, because the effects are interdependent—across rows due to the unequal cell frequencies, and across columns due to the intercorrelated outcome measures. More useful, perhaps, are confidence intervals drawn on

```
         1         2         3         4         5         6         7         8
1234567890123456789012345678901234567890123456789012345678901234567890123456789012
     1. Title cards to 10.  See Figure 4.3
    12. Estimation Specification card
   17   6         1         1         3
    13. Means key
0,1,2,3,1*3.   MEANS KEY
    16. Symbolic Contrast Vectors
D0,D0,D0, CONST
1,0,0,    SEX
0,1,0,    GRADE
0,2,0,
0,0,1,    ATTUDE
0,0,2,
1,1,0,    S X G
1,2,0,
1,0,1,    S X A
1,0,2,
0,1,1,    G X A
0,1,2,
0,2,1,
0,2,2,
1,1,1,    SXGXA
1,1,2,
1,2,1,
    17. Contrast Reordering key
1,2,5,6,3,4.       CONTRAST REORDERING KEY
    18. Analysis Selection card
    4         1
    21. Hypothesis Test card
-1,1,2,2,2,2,4,4.
-4,2.     HYPOTHESIS TEST CARD - ALTERNATE ORDER
    22. End-of-job card
                                                  STOP

         1         2         3         4         5         6         7         8
1234567890123456789012345678901234567890123456789012345678901234567890123456789012
```

FIGURE 4.5 Problem 3: MULTIVARIANCE control cards for run 2 of Problem 3

ESTIMATION PARAMETERS
======================

RANK OF THE BASIS = RANK OF MODEL FOR SIGNIFICANCE TESTING =   17

RANK OF THE MODEL TO BE ESTIMATED IS   6

ERROR TERM TO BE USED IS (WITHIN CELLS)

NUMBER OF ORDERS OF THE BASIS VECTORS OTHER THAN THE FIRST IS   1

ESTIMATED CELL MEANS, RESIDUALS AND RESIDUALS IN FORM OF T-STATISTICS WILL BE PRINTED

ESTIMATED COMBINED MEANS WILL BE PRINTED

SYMBOLIC CONTRAST VECTORS
=========================

(1)		
(2)	D0,D0,D0,	CONST
(3)	1,0,0,	SEX
(4)	0,1,0,	GRADE
(5)	0,2,0,	
(6)	0,0,1,	ATTUDE
(7)	0,0,2,	
(8)	1,1,0,	S X G
(9)	1,2,0,	
(10)	1,0,1,	S X A
(11)	1,0,2,	
(12)	0,1,1,	G X A
(13)	0,1,2,	
(14)	0,2,1,	
(15)	0,2,2,	
(16)	1,1,1,	SXGXA
(17)	1,1,2,	
	1,2,1,	

ERROR CORRELATION MATRIX
----

	1 SCI A	2 SCI B	3 SCI C	4 SCI D
1 SCI A	1.000000			
2 SCI B	0.525188	1.000001		
3 SCI C	0.473045	0.509848	1.000000	
4 SCI D	0.358960	0.331857	0.291808	1.000000

VARIABLE	VARIANCE (ERROR MEAN SQUARES)	STANDARD DEVIATION
1 SCI A	9.158040	3.0262
2 SCI B	18.760450	4.3313
3 SCI C	6.870840	2.6212
4 SCI D	4.157115	2.0389

D.F.=   133.

ERROR TERM FOR ANALYSIS OF VARIANCE (WITHIN CELLS)

LEAST SQUARE ESTIMATES OF EFFECTS -- EFFECTS X VARIABLES
----

	1 SCI A	2 SCI B	3 SCI C	4 SCI D
1 CONST	6.878667	6.905872	4.786478	2.359424
2 SEX	0.392396	0.374218	0.369956	0.025383
3 GRADE	-1.416639	-2.116900	-0.875642	-0.654207
4	-0.121976	0.393047	-0.200236	0.014989
5 ATTUDE	0.946083	2.076011	1.413936	0.655309
6	0.333906	-0.331984	-0.124521	0.139064

FIGURE 4.6-1 Problem 3: Phase II output (second run)

ESTIMATES OF EFFECTS IN STANDARD DEVIATION UNITS-EFF X VARS
----

	1 SCI A	2 SCI B	3 SCI C	4 SCI D
1 CONST	2.273019	1.594399	1.826043	1.157204
2 SEX	0.129665	0.086398	0.141138	0.012449
3 GRADE	-0.468121	-0.488741	-0.334058	-0.320863
4	-0.040306	0.090745	-0.076390	0.007352
5 ATTUDE	0.312628	0.479301	0.539417	0.321403
6	0.110337	-0.076647	-0.047505	0.068205

STANDARD ERRORS OF LEAST-SQUARES ESTIMATES--EFFECTS BY VARS
----

	1 SCI A	2 SCI B	3 SCI C	4 SCI D
1 CONST	0.323164	0.462534	0.279915	0.217730
2 SEX	0.257423	0.368441	0.222972	0.173437
3 GRADE	0.355158	0.508325	0.307627	0.239285
4	0.356162	0.509762	0.308497	0.239962
5 ATTUDE	0.542377	0.776286	0.469791	0.365423
6	0.365823	0.523589	0.316865	0.246471

LEAST-SQUARES ESTIMATES AS T-STATISTICS - EFFECTS X VARS
----

	1 SCI A	2 SCI B	3 SCI C	4 SCI D
1 CONST	21.28536	14.93052	17.09973	10.83647
2 SEX	1.52432	1.01568	1.65920	0.14635
3 GRADE	-3.98876	-4.16446	-2.84644	-2.73400
4	-0.34247	0.77104	-0.64907	0.06247
5 ATTUDE	1.74433	2.67429	3.00971	1.79329
6	0.91275	-0.63405	-0.39298	0.56422

DEGREES OF FREEDOM =   133.

ESTIMATED CELL MEANS, ALL GROUPS - CELLS X VARIABLES
----

	1 SCI A	2 SCI B	3 SCI C	4 SCI D
1	6.80051	7.23920	5.69473	2.38591
2	6.18833	4.83121	4.15627	1.86966
3	4.57444	3.41916	2.99138	0.93623
4	8.09517	9.74915	6.37013	3.05511
5	7.48299	7.34115	4.83168	2.53886
6	5.86910	5.92911	3.66678	1.60542
7	9.75576	11.07995	7.64625	3.67933
8	9.14358	8.67196	6.10779	3.16309
9	7.52969	7.25992	4.94290	2.22965
10	6.01572	6.49076	4.95482	2.33514
11	5.40354	4.08277	3.41636	1.81890
12	3.78964	2.67073	2.25146	0.88546
13	7.31038	9.00071	5.63022	3.00434
14	6.69820	6.59272	4.09176	2.48809
15	5.08431	5.18067	2.92687	1.55466
16	8.97097	10.33152	6.90634	3.62857
17	8.35879	7.92352	5.36788	3.11232
18	6.74490	6.51148	4.20299	2.17889

MEANS ESTIMATED BY FITTING MODEL OF RANK   6

ESTIMATED COMBINED MEANS BASED ON FITTING A MODEL OF RANK   6   PAGE   7
===

- -

OVERALL

    MEANS   SCI A = 6.879   SCI B = 6.906   SCI C = 4.786   SCI D = 2.359

- -

FACTORS   1 (SEX   )

  LEVEL   1

    MEANS   SCI A = 7.271   SCI B = 7.280   SCI C = 5.156   SCI D = 2.385

  LEVEL   2

    MEANS   SCI A = 6.486   SCI B = 6.532   SCI C = 4.417   SCI D = 2.334

- -

FACTORS   2 (GRADE)

  LEVEL   1

    MEANS   SCI A = 5.462   SCI B = 4.789   SCI C = 3.911   SCI D = 1.705

  LEVEL   2

    MEANS   SCI A = 6.757   SCI B = 7.299   SCI C = 4.586   SCI D = 2.374

  LEVEL   3

    MEANS   SCI A = 8.417   SCI B = 8.630   SCI C = 5.862   SCI D = 2.999

FIGURE 4.6-2 Problem 3: Phase II output (second run continued)

```
FACTORS      3 (ATTUDE  )

   LEVEL        1

     MEANS       SCI A  =  7.825      SCI B  =  8.982      SCI C  =  6.200      SCI D  =  3.015
     -------

   LEVEL        2

     MEANS       SCI A  =  7.213      SCI B  =  6.574      SCI C  =  4.662      SCI D  =  2.498
     -------

   LEVEL        3

     MEANS       SCI A  =  5.599      SCI B  =  5.162      SCI C  =  3.497      SCI D  =  1.565
     -------
```

- -

```
FACTORS      1 (SEX    )    3 (ATTUDE  )

   LEVEL        1          1

     MEANS       SCI A  =  8.217      SCI B  =  9.356      SCI C  =  6.570      SCI D  =  3.040
     -------

   LEVEL        1          2

     MEANS       SCI A  =  7.605      SCI B  =  6.948      SCI C  =  5.032      SCI D  =  2.524
     -------

   LEVEL        1          3

     MEANS       SCI A  =  5.991      SCI B  =  5.536      SCI C  =  3.867      SCI D  =  1.590
     -------

   LEVEL        2          1

     MEANS       SCI A  =  7.432      SCI B  =  8.608      SCI C  =  5.830      SCI D  =  2.989
     -------

   LEVEL        2          2

     MEANS       SCI A  =  6.820      SCI B  =  6.200      SCI C  =  4.292      SCI D  =  2.473
     -------

   LEVEL        2          3

     MEANS       SCI A  =  5.206      SCI B  =  4.788      SCI C  =  3.127      SCI D  =  1.540
```

```
                      RAW RESIDUALS - ROWS ARE FULL CELLS - COLUMNS ARE VARIABLES
                 ----------------------------------------------------------------

                    1          2          3          4
                 SCI A      SCI B      SCI C      SCI D

         1        0.466160   0.360799  -0.094728  -1.152576
         2       -0.471663  -0.114539   0.222896  -0.086330
         3        0.205564  -2.139164   0.308623   0.103774
         4       -1.095169  -6.449148  -4.370133  -2.755105
         5        0.154508   0.690097  -0.669176   0.173641
         6       -0.069098  -1.295777  -0.400116   0.327911
         7        0.594240   0.957545  -0.208748   0.808167
         8        0.268182   0.057452   0.668679   0.036913
         9       -0.529689   1.006749  -0.009564  -1.029651
        10        2.284285  -0.690764  -0.454815   1.964856
        11        1.046462   0.792231  -0.324692   0.597769
        12       -1.189644   0.709273  -0.451464  -0.825461
        13       -1.835378  -0.400711   1.694779  -0.554340
        14        0.054741  -0.633892   0.314118  -0.205741
        15        0.582360   1.297104   0.462019   0.523120
        16       -0.541144  -0.470582  -0.438467  -0.294675
        17        0.295103  -0.731481  -0.442985   0.201115
```

```
                      RESIDUALS IN STD. DEV. UNITS - FULL CELLS X VARIABLES
                 -----------------------------------------------------------

                    1          2          3          4
                 SCI A      SCI B      SCI C      SCI D

         1        0.154040   0.083300  -0.036139  -0.565293
         2       -0.155858  -0.026444   0.085035  -0.042341
         3        0.067928  -0.493881   0.117740   0.050897
         4       -0.361893  -1.488952  -1.667208  -1.351270
         5        0.051056   0.159327  -0.255291   0.085164
         6       -0.022833  -0.299164  -0.152644   0.160827
         7        0.196363   0.221074  -0.079638   0.396374
         8        0.088619   0.013264   0.255101   0.018104
         9       -0.175033   0.232434  -0.003649  -0.505003
        10        0.754830  -0.159481  -0.173512   0.963684
        11        0.345798   0.182907  -0.123870   0.293182
        12       -0.393111   0.163754  -0.172234  -0.404856
        13       -0.606491  -0.092514   0.646559  -0.271882
        14        0.018089  -0.146350   0.119836  -0.100908
        15        0.192438   0.299470   0.176260   0.256570
        16       -0.178818  -0.108646  -0.167275  -0.144526
        17        0.097515  -0.168881  -0.168999   0.098639
```

```
                      RESIDUALS AS T-STATISTICS - FULL CELLS X VARIABLES
                 --------------------------------------------------------

                    1          2          3          4
                 SCI A      SCI B      SCI C      SCI D

         1        0.304678   0.164760  -0.071479  -1.118101
         2       -1.236713  -0.209832   0.674739  -0.335972
         3        0.178081  -1.294775   0.308671   0.133433
         4       -0.377176  -1.551831  -1.737615  -1.408335
         5        0.298193   0.930541  -1.491017   0.497396
         6       -0.043709  -0.572684  -0.292205   0.307869
         7        0.834350   0.939346  -0.338381   1.684197
         8        0.512412   0.076696   1.475040   0.104682
         9       -0.335144   0.445052  -0.006986  -0.966952
        10        0.794064  -0.167770  -0.182531   1.013774
        11        1.575555   0.833377  -0.564388   1.335822
        12       -1.028097   0.428263  -0.450440  -1.058812
        13       -1.490282  -0.227329   1.588738  -0.668074
        14        0.104549  -0.845866   0.692622  -0.583221
        15        0.754512   1.174165   0.691084   1.005961
        16       -1.102481  -0.669843  -1.031315  -0.891059
        17        0.255288  -0.442120  -0.442428   0.258230
```

FIGURE 4.6-3 Problem 3: Phase II output (second run concluded)

```
                        ANALYSIS OF VARIANCE
                        ====================                              PAGE    8
                        ====================


                        4 DEPENDENT VARIABLE(S)

                            1 SCI A
                            2 SCI B
                            3 SCI C
                            4 SCI D

        NUMBER OF ALTERNATE BASIS ORDERS=  1

                    HYPOTHESIS   1      1 DEGREE(S) OF FREEDOM
                    ==========================================
                                                                         PAGE    9

        DO,DO,DO,                                              CONST

- - - - - - - - - - - - - - - - - - - - - - - - - - - - - - - - - - - - -

                        TESTS OF HYPOTHESIS BEING SKIPPED

                    HYPOTHESIS   2      1 DEGREE(S) OF FREEDOM
                    ==========================================
                                                                         PAGE   10

        1,0,0,                                                 SEX

- - - - - - - - - - - - - - - - - - - - - - - - - - - - - - - - - - - - -



        F-RATIO FOR MULTIVARIATE TEST OF EQUALITY OF MEAN VECTORS=    1.5213

              D.F.=    4.  AND    130.0000    P LESS THAN 0.1998
```

VARIABLE	HYPOTHESIS MEAN SQ	UNIVARIATE F	P LESS THAN	STEP DOWN F	P LESS THAN
1 SCI A	31.8324	3.4759	0.0645	3.4759	0.0645
2 SCI B	24.8412	1.3241	0.2520	0.0393	0.8432
3 SCI C	34.8301	5.0693	0.0260	2.4064	0.1233
4 SCI D	0.7638	0.1837	0.6689	0.1875	0.6658

```
                    DEGREES OF FREEDOM FOR HYPOTHESIS=   1
                    DEGREES OF FREEDOM FOR ERROR=     133.

                    HYPOTHESIS   3      2 DEGREE(S) OF FREEDOM
                    ==========================================
                                                                         PAGE   11

        0,1,0,                                                 GRADE
        0,2,0,

- - - - - - - - - - - - - - - - - - - - - - - - - - - - - - - - - - - - -



        F-RATIO FOR MULTIVARIATE TEST OF EQUALITY OF MEAN VECTORS=    4.3133

              D.F.=    8.  AND    260.0000    P LESS THAN 0.0001
```

VARIABLE	HYPOTHESIS MEAN SQ	UNIVARIATE F	P LESS THAN	STEP DOWN F	P LESS THAN
1 SCI A	120.0043	13.1037	0.0001	13.1037	0.0001
2 SCI B	215.1123	11.4663	0.0001	3.0664	0.0500
3 SCI C	59.3669	8.6404	0.0003	1.0530	0.3519
4 SCI D	23.8901	5.7468	0.0041	0.5228	0.5942

```
                    DEGREES OF FREEDOM FOR HYPOTHESIS=   2
                    DEGREES OF FREEDOM FOR ERROR=     133.

                    HYPOTHESIS   4      2 DEGREE(S) OF FREEDOM
                    ==========================================
                                                                         PAGE   12

        0,0,1,                                                 ATTUDE
        0,0,2,

- - - - - - - - - - - - - - - - - - - - - - - - - - - - - - - - - - - - -



        F-RATIO FOR MULTIVARIATE TEST OF EQUALITY OF MEAN VECTORS=    2.1418

              D.F.=    8.  AND    260.0000    P LESS THAN 0.0325
```

VARIABLE	HYPOTHESIS MEAN SQ	UNIVARIATE F	P LESS THAN	STEP DOWN F	P LESS THAN
1 SCI A	35.8565	3.9153	0.0223	3.9153	0.0223
2 SCI B	75.4856	4.0237	0.0202	2.1130	0.1250
3 SCI C	38.2898	5.5728	0.0048	1.7834	0.1722
4 SCI D	13.4670	3.2395	0.0423	0.7887	0.4567

```
                    DEGREES OF FREEDOM FOR HYPOTHESIS=   2
                    DEGREES OF FREEDOM FOR ERROR=     133.
```

FIGURE 4.6-4 Problem 3: Phase III output

HYPOTHESIS   5   2 DEGREE(S) OF FREEDOM
==

<pre>
1,1,0,   S X G
1,2,0,
</pre>

- -

F-RATIO FOR MULTIVARIATE TEST OF EQUALITY OF MEAN VECTORS=   1.2377

D.F.=   8. AND   260.0000   P LESS THAN 0.2772

VARIABLE	HYPOTHESIS MEAN SQ	UNIVARIATE F	P LESS THAN	STEP DOWN F	P LESS THAN
1 SCI A	6.0276	0.6582	0.5195	0.6582	0.5195
2 SCI B	12.4610	0.6642	0.5164	0.2077	0.8127
3 SCI C	17.4660	2.5421	0.0826	3.9733	0.0212
4 SCI D	1.8106	0.4355	0.6479	0.1872	0.8296

DEGREES OF FREEDOM FOR HYPOTHESIS=   2
DEGREES OF FREEDOM FOR ERROR=   133.

HYPOTHESIS   6   2 DEGREE(S) OF FREEDOM
==

<pre>
1,0,1,   S X A
1,0,2,
</pre>

- -

F-RATIO FOR MULTIVARIATE TEST OF EQUALITY OF MEAN VECTORS=   0.8233

D.F.=   8. AND   260.0000   P LESS THAN 0.5827

VARIABLE	HYPOTHESIS MEAN SQ	UNIVARIATE F	P LESS THAN	STEP DOWN F	P LESS THAN
1 SCI A	3.9598	0.4324	0.6499	0.4324	0.6499
2 SCI B	10.9675	0.5846	0.5588	0.8592	0.4258
3 SCI C	5.8260	0.8479	0.4306	2.0210	0.1367
4 SCI D	0.1781	0.0429	0.9581	0.0144	0.9858

DEGREES OF FREEDOM FOR HYPOTHESIS=   2
DEGREES OF FREEDOM FOR ERROR=   133.

HYPOTHESIS   7   4 DEGREE(S) OF FREEDOM
==

<pre>
0,1,1,   G X A
0,1,2,
0,2,1,
0,2,2,
</pre>

- -

F-RATIO FOR MULTIVARIATE TEST OF EQUALITY OF MEAN VECTORS=   0.4978

D.F.= 16. AND   397.7942   P LESS THAN 0.9482

VARIABLE	HYPOTHESIS MEAN SQ	UNIVARIATE F	P LESS THAN	STEP DOWN F	P LESS THAN
1 SCI A	4.5709	0.4991	0.7364	0.4991	0.7364
2 SCI B	7.6355	0.4070	0.8034	0.1779	0.9495
3 SCI C	0.5789	0.0843	0.9872	0.1241	0.9736
4 SCI D	6.3487	1.5272	0.1979	1.2084	0.3105

DEGREES OF FREEDOM FOR HYPOTHESIS=   4
DEGREES OF FREEDOM FOR ERROR=   133.

HYPOTHESIS   8   3 DEGREE(S) OF FREEDOM
==

<pre>
1,1,1,   SXGXA
1,1,2,
1,2,1,
</pre>

- -

F-RATIO FOR MULTIVARIATE TEST OF EQUALITY OF MEAN VECTORS=   0.9356

D.F.= 12. AND   344.2390   P LESS THAN 0.5113

VARIABLE	HYPOTHESIS MEAN SQ	UNIVARIATE F	P LESS THAN	STEP DOWN F	P LESS THAN
1 SCI A	7.2852	0.7955	0.4985	0.7955	0.4985
2 SCI B	16.8154	0.8963	0.4450	1.9339	0.1272
3 SCI C	3.1058	0.4520	0.7163	0.4664	0.7062
4 SCI D	3.1052	0.7470	0.5260	0.5885	0.6236

DEGREES OF FREEDOM FOR HYPOTHESIS=   3
DEGREES OF FREEDOM FOR ERROR=   133.

FIGURE 4.6-5   Problem 3:   Phase III output (continued)

```
                                    ORDER OF EFFECTS (CONTRASTS)
-------------------------------------------------------------------------------------------        PAGE   17

   1    2    5    6    3    4

                                    HYPOTHESIS   1       4 DEGREE(S) OF FREEDOM
                                    ==================================================        PAGE   18

              DO,DO,DO,                                                        CONST
              1,0,0,                                                           SEX
              0,0,1,                                                           ATTUDE
              0,0,2,
-------------------------------------------------------------------------------------------
                                 TESTS OF HYPOTHESIS BEING SKIPPED
                                 HYPOTHESIS   2       2 DEGREE(S) OF FREEDOM
                                 ==================================================        PAGE   19

              0,1,0,                                                           GRADE
              0,2,0,
-------------------------------------------------------------------------------------------


        F-RATIO FOR MULTIVARIATE TEST OF EQUALITY OF MEAN VECTORS=        3.8056
             D.F.=   8.  AND    260.0000      P LESS THAN 0.0004


      VARIABLE      HYPOTHESIS MEAN SQ     UNIVARIATE F     P LESS THAN       STEP DOWN F     P LESS THAN
      --------      -----------------     ------------     -----------       -----------     -----------
      1  SCI A           107.8972           11.7817          0.0001            11.7817          0.0001
      2  SCI B           185.9705            9.9129          0.0001             2.6221          0.0765
      3  SCI C            48.3681            7.0396          0.0013             0.8236          0.4411
      4  SCI D            20.5340            4.9395          0.0086             0.4499          0.6387

                          DEGREES OF FREEDOM FOR HYPOTHESIS=    2
                          DEGREES OF FREEDOM FOR ERROR=       133.
 CORE USED FOR DATA=  332 LOCATIONS OUT OF 3072 AVAILABLE
```

FIGURE 4.6-6 Problem 3: Phase III output (concluded)

an entire row of the matrix of effects and based on the corresponding entire row of the matrix of standard errors. Procedures for this purpose are discussed in Finn (1974, Chapter 8).

The estimated cell means for all 18 groups, including the group without any observed data, follow in the printout. For example, the mean for the missing group (group 16 in this table) on the Comprehension test is 10.332. These means are estimated from the general prediction model given by (33). The missing group in sex group 2, grade level 3, attitude level 1; the model for any one variable for this group is given by (34):

$$\hat{y}_{.231} = \hat{\mu} + \hat{\alpha}_2 + \hat{\beta}_3 + \hat{\gamma}_1 \tag{34}$$

The circumflex indicates that a mean predicted from the sample is obtained from effects estimated in the example.

To focus on one variable, the estimate of μ for the second subtest is 6.906. Since the deviation estimate of α_1 is .374 (for males), the value for α_2 is $-.374$ for females. Similarly, the estimates of β_1 and β_2 are -2.117 and .393, respectively. Summing these and subtracting from zero, we have the estimate of β_3 for the ninth-grade group equal to 1.724. The estimate of γ_1 for the high attitude group is 2.076. Summing these estimated effects, we obtain the predicted mean for the group of $6.906 - .374 + 1.724 + 2.076 = 10.332$.

Like the observed means, the estimated means are more useful when combined across subclasses. But unlike the observed means, the estimated means are combined without weighting by sample sizes, and so are not biased by unequal numbers of subjects in levels of the other factors. Although the estimated means in this study show the same pattern of sex differences, grade differences, and attitude differences as the observed means, in other instances not only the magnitude but also the direction of the differences might be altered.

The means for each combination of sex and attitude group show the same differences among attitude levels for males as for females. Thus, for the first science subtest, the difference between 8.217 and 7.605 is identical to the difference between 7.432 and 6.820. This is true because all interactions of sex and attitude have been eliminated from these estimates. When the interaction reflects only random variation (i.e., it is not significant), these means give a clearer picture of the effects than do the observed means.

The mean residuals are the differences between the observed and estimated means; they can be obtained only for subclasses having observations. For purposes of interpretation, they may be put in the metric of the common within-group standard deviation or converted to *t*-statistic form by dividing each by its respective standard error.

The residuals in this study are the sums of the estimates of all interactions (i.e., of effects omitted from the model). Examining the table of *t* statistics, we see that none exceeds the 1.96 critical *t* value (assuming 133 degrees of freedom), a fact consistent with the absence of any interaction in the data. When the residuals are shown to be significant in the overall test, they may be useful in identifying one or more subclasses that do not follow the model. Such subclasses may be subjected to further study.

PHASE III.   The results of the significance tests are listed in Figures 4.6-4 and 4.6-5 for the original order of effects. In Figure 4.6-4 is the test of the grand mean, which has not been conducted due to the minus sign preceding the first "1" on the Hypothesis Test card. This is followed by the test of the sex effect, eliminating the grand mean, then the grade effect eliminating the grand mean and sex, and so on. As in the stepwise regression model, these results are read in the reverse order starting fron the last test at the bottom of Figure 4.6-5. In this case, the last effect in the order of elimination is the three-way interaction comprising three degrees of freedom tested jointly because of the final three on the (revised) Hypothesis Test card. For this hypothesis, as for the others, three sets of test statistics are produced.

4.5.1   Multivariate *F* Test

Immediately following the label for the hypothesis is the "*F* ratio for the multivariate test of equality of mean vectors." This test statistic is based on the likelihood ratio criterion, and is distributed approximately as an *F* statistic with, in this case, 12 and 344.24 degrees of freedom. The value of the statistic may be referred to the table of the *F* distribution with 12 and 344 degrees of freedom, or may be evaluated by numerical approximation as in the MULTIVARIANCE program.

The result indicates that the three-way interaction is not significant at $\alpha = .05$. This test gives us one statistic for testing the significance of all three-way interaction terms for all four dependent variables simultaneously, as stated in hypothesis (32). The test statistic is computed from the within-group matrix of variances and covariance of the measures, and a similar matrix of mean squares and products for interaction eliminating all preceding effects. These matrices are compared to determine if interaction effects are large relative to within-group sampling variation. The computations are described in detail in most texts on multivariate analysis.

4.5.2   Univariate *F* Statistics

The second test criterion provides a set of univariate results. These are the conventional *F* ratios (mean square between)/(mean square within) for each criterion variable separately. They are the results that would have been obtained if each science subtest score had been considered in isolation in a simple one-variable analysis. For example, the univariate *F* statistic for interaction for the Higher Mental Process score is .747, which is a ratio of the mean square, 3.105, to the respective mean square within, 4.157 (given in Figure 4.6-1). The other three statistics follow the same pattern. The degrees of freedom for the two mean squares, and thus for each univariate *F* test of interaction, are 3 and 133.

To the extent that the variables have nonzero intercorrelations, the univariate *F* statistics are not independent of one another, and should not be used as partial tests of the multivariate hypotheses (26) through (32). Nevertheless, they have interpretive value: relative to their respective error variables, the largest univariate *F* statistic indicates the variable most affected by the independent variables (in this case the three-factor interaction), while the smallest univariate *F* statistic indicates the variable least affected. Should the multivariate test statistic prove significant, the univariate statistics will usually give some guide to locating the measures responsible for the significant effect. (See Hummel and Sligo, 1971.) In this example we have not found the multivariate test statistic to be significant and the univariate test statistics are of little interest. In fact, none is significant.

It is important to note that there is no strong relationship between the multivariate test criterion and the separate univariate results. A multivariate statistic may be significant when none of the univariate statistics is significant; conversely, one or more of the univariate statistics may be significant when the multivariate statistic is not.

We rely upon the multivariate test statistic for the initial decision about H_0. Without the protection of the multivariate test, separate univariate decisions are likely to inflate statistical error rates dramatically; the probability of finding one test statistic significant by chance alone, out of a list of many, may be very high. Furthermore, if we make a type I or type II error for one of the simple univariate results, we are likely to make additional errors of the same type for other correlated outcomes.

The multivariate test statistic reflects variation in the data as a whole and is influenced by relationships between variables. If we obtain a significant multivariate result and no significant univariate results, we must resort to other techniques for discovering the combinations of variables that produce the significant effect. The discriminant functions or canonical analysis of effects may be useful in this connection.

4.5.3 Step-down Analysis

The step-down results are the third set of test criteria provided. The first step-down F ratio is a univariate test of significance for the first outcome measure. Note that the F ratio of .7955 for Functional Information is identical to the univariate F ratio for the same variable. The second step-down test statistic is a univariate test for the second outcome measure (Comprehension), holding constant the first (Functional Information). It reflects variation among groups in the second outcome measure, eliminating that which is seen in the first variate. Similarly, the third step-down result is a test of variable y_3 eliminating variation due to y_1 and y_2, and the fourth is a test of variation for y_4 holding constant y_1, y_2, and y_3.

The step-down analysis is a multivariate procedure that depends on a prior ordering of the criterion variables. When no prior ordering is inherent in the measures, the step-down statistics should be ignored. The multivariate hypothesis is rejected if, and only if, one of the step-down F statistics exceeds its respective critical value. Note that one degree of freedom for the denominator of the step-down F is "lost" for each prior variable eliminated.

The step-down tests are statistically independent under the null hypothesis. This means that a fixed type I error rate may be maintained for the set of four F statistics, given a single ordering of criterion variables. The appropriate test procedure is to begin with the last step-down statistic and proceed in a backward order. For example, we should inspect the value $F_4 = .5885$ first. We refer F_4 to the table of F with 3 and 130 degrees of freedom. Finding it to be nonsignificant, we inspect the preceding statistic $F_3 = .4664$, and so on.

Testing stops when a significant test statistic is found. No variable earlier in the order of elimination may be validly tested. Generally it does not make sense to conduct step-down tests in more than a single order of variables. The initial use of the procedure is dependent on an underlying logic which determines the original order. If other orders are equally sensible, the step-down analysis is not an advisable testing procedure. In the present example, there is a strong basis for ordering the criterion variables according to the complexity of the measures. All four step-down tests for the three-way interaction are nonsignificant, and $H_0(7)$ is accepted.

4.5.4 Other Hypotheses

Having found the three-way interaction to be nonsignificant, we may proceed to the test of the next-to-the-last, or grade-by-attitude, interaction. The multivariate F statistic for this hypothesis is also nonsignificant. None of the step-down statistics exceeds its critical value, and we accept $H_0(6)$ that there is no interaction of grade and attitude levels affecting the four science achievement scores. We may therefore proceed to the next earlier hypothesis in the order of elimination, the sex-by-attitude interaction. The two interaction parameters are tested jointly because of the "2" in the corresponding position on the Hypothesis Test card. The multivariate F statistic of .8233 with 8 and 260 degrees of freedom does not exceed the .05 critical value. Neither are any of the step-down F statistics for this hypothesis significant. We accept $H_0(5)$ that there is no interaction of sex and attitude in the four science outcomes. If there is any significant difference among means on the four tests it must be due to effects earlier in the order of elimination.

Having found no significance to this point, we proceed with a test of the sex-by-grade interaction. Again, there are two degrees of freedom tested jointly for significance because of the "2" in the corresponding position on the Hypothesis Test card. The multivariate test statistic of 1.2377, with 8 and 260 degrees of freedom, does not exceed the .05 critical value.

However, were we to rely on the step-down results, we would obtain different information. The step-down F statistic for the higher mental process variable is not significant at the .01 level (with 2 and 130 degrees of freedom). Therefore, we proceed backward to the step-down test for Application of Science Principles. The step-down statistic is 3.9733, which is referred to the F distribution with 2 and 131 degrees of freedom. This statistic exceeds the .05 critical value, but not the .01 value. $H_0(4)$ is rejected if we assume $\alpha = .05$. There is a significant sex-by-grade interaction on the Application subtest.

We may inspect other results for an interpretation of this finding. For example, none of the univariate F statistics, including the one for Application, is significant. The significant effect occurs after elimination of correlation with the earlier Functional Information and Comprehension subtests. That is, there appears to be a significant sex-by-grade interaction on just those aspects of the Application subtest which are unique and not dependent upon simpler skills. The analysis necessary to identify the nature of this interaction would be to create the conditional variable for inspection. This can be done in the MULTIVARIANCE program by coding the Application variable as a dependent variable, and Functional Information and Comprehension as covariates. Estimated means should be obtained for every combination of sex and grade, using a model including the sex-by-grade interaction term. The means will indicate the direction of the effect, and the estimates and the standard errors can be used to place confidence intervals on the interaction terms.

To continue the example, let us use the .01 level of significance and consider that there is no sex-by-grade interaction. There is some justification for a small α level for interactions, and even more so for step-down tests. However, it must be recognized that this small aspect of the data requires further exploration. In any event, we proceed with the test of the two-degrees-of-freedom attitude main-class effect. The null hypothesis $H_0(3)$ is that the means are equal across all three attitude groups on the four criterion measures simultaneously. The multivariate F statistic of 2.1418, with 8 and 260 degrees of freedom, is significant at an α value of .05. We reject $H_0(3)$ and conclude that attitude mean vectors are significantly different.

The univariate F statistics, each with 2 and 133 degrees of freedom, indicate that there is a significant difference among attitude groups on each of the four science subtests. The effect is largest for the Application subtest, for which there is also some indication of a sex-by-grade interaction. The differences are smallest for the Higher Mental Process subtest. These relative measures cover all differences among the three groups, however, and not any specific contrast of attitude groups with one another.

If we use the step-down F's to test this hypothesis, we find first that there is no significant difference among attitude groups on Higher Mental Processes when the other three tests are eliminated. Further, we find no significant differences among the attitude groups on Application when Functional Information and Comprehension differences are eliminated, nor any significant differences among the three attitude groups on Comprehension when variation attributable to Functional Information is eliminated. There is a clearly significant difference among the three group means on the Functional Information test however.

In this case the step-down results and the general multivariate test criterion agree with each other. In particular, the step-down result indicates that all significant differences among attitude groups are attributable to simple differences in the student's knowledge of functional information. When the amount of functional information is controlled for, the cognitive operations of comprehension, application, and other higher processess do not reflect important between-group variation.

Referring to the observed or estimated means, we find that the students who like science better attain larger reserves of functional scientific information. Those who dislike science, relative to other school subjects,

Table 4.2   Summary of Analysis of Variance for Three-way Science Achievement Study

Source of Variation	d.f.	Multivariate F	Step Down y_1	$y_2 \mid y_1$	$y_3 \mid y_1, y_2$	$y_4 \mid y_1, y_2, y_3$
Constant (M)	1					
Sex (A), eliminating M	1	1.52	3.48	.04	2.41	.19
Grade (B), eliminating M and A	2	**4.31	**13.10	*3.07	1.05	.52
(Grade (B), eliminating M, A, and C)	(2)	(**3.81)	(**11.78)	(2.62)	(.82)	(.45)
Attitude (C), eliminating M, A, and B	2	2.14	3.92	2.11	1.78	.79
AB, eliminating M, A, B, and C	2	1.24	.66	.21	*3.97	.19
AC, eliminating M, A, B, C, and AB	2	.82	.43	.86	2.02	.01
BC, eliminating M, A, B, C, AB, and AC	4	.50	.50	.18	.12	1.21
ABC, eliminating all else	3	.94	.80	1.93	.47	.59
Among means	17	Univariate Mean				
Within groups	133	Squares:	9.16	18.76	6.87	4.16
Total	150					

*$p < .05$ **$p < .01$

have less functional information to rely upon. Of course, we must recognize that the attitudes may also follow achievement in such a way that students who perform better in science may subsequently hold more positive attitudes. Unfortunately, performance seems to mean only attaining knowledge of simple scientific facts and principles. But in any case, the main research hypothesis is supported.

Having found the attitude effect significant, we have no valid test of preceding effects (i.e., sex or grade) in this order. Since both sex and grade are included primarily as control variables, we might stop and not test either. An analysis-of-variance table, summarizing the results of the significance tests, may be prepared in a form such as Table 4.2. It is essential to list the effects that have been eliminated at each stage in the significance testing. The vertical bars in the heading to the step-down tests indicate which variables have been held constant. For example, $y_3 \mid y_1, y_2$ indicates the test of the third criterion variable, eliminating the differences due to the first two.

To complete the example, let us assume that we have some particular interest in the grade effect. Having found attitude significant, we must reorder attitude and grade effects, and test the grade-effect holding constant the attitude differences. The results of the reordering appear in Figure 4.6-6. The first four effects coded in the alternate order are not tested because of the "−4" on the second Hypothesis Test card. Although we eliminate from grade, variation due to the grand mean, sex, and attitude differences, we do not require additional test statistics here. The two-degrees-of-freedom test of grade differences results from the "2" on the same card.

There are significant differences among grade levels, as we might expect. The multivariate F statistic of 3.8056 exceeds its .05 critical value. Examining the step-down results, we see again that significant differences are concentrated only in the Functional Information subtest. It is unfortunate that older children do not improve in functioning at the higher mental levels.

Although the test of the grade effect has not been greatly altered by the reordering, in other instances the effect of reordering may be dramatic. The matrix of "variance-covariance factors among the estimates" gives some indication of the degrees of interdependency of the various effect estimates. This matrix appears in the Phase II output. As a general rule, the number of reorderings should be kept to a minimum to avoid compounding statistical error rates. A number of lines may be added to the analysis-of-variance table to present the results from the alternate order (in parentheses in Table 4.2).

Utilizing the general multivariate test criterion, the rank-six model (33) is not rejected for these data. Sex is necessary to the model as a control variable and grade and attitude differences have been shown to be significant. Interactions, by and large, are nonexistent, although we may suspect some sex-by-grade interaction for the Application variable. The major finding of the study may be simply summarized in the estimated means for the three attitude groups (Table 4.3). More complex presentations are seldom necessary.

Table 4.3   Estimated Means for Three Attitude Groups on Four Science Cognitive Tests

Group	N	Subtest			
		Functional Information	Comprehension	Application	Higher Processes
Like Science best	17	7.83	8.98	6.20	3.02
Like Science same	103	7.21	6.57	4.66	2.50
Like Science least	30	5.60	5.16	3.50	1.56
Pooled within-group standard deviation		3.03	4.33	2.62	2.04

5

GROWTH IN VOCABULARY: UNIVARIATE ANALYSIS OF REPEATED MEASURES DATA

Whenever each subject in a study is measured with the same instrument at more than one point in time, or under more than one experimental condition, the study is said to be carried out in a *repeated measures* design. This type of design finds many and varied applications in educational and psychological research. In education we see it applied when students are administered the same test both before and after instruction in a course or unit. In these applications, the purpose is to test change from the first measurement to the second, and to compare this change across different instructional groups. In more extended studies, the test may be administered at three or more times during a single school year, or annually for several years. The study described in this and the following chapter is an example of the latter taken from Bock (1975). Data for the study consisted of a scaled vocabulary score obtained on the same students once a year for the four consecutive years corresponding to grade levels 8, 9, 10, and 11. The object of the statistical analysis of these data is to characterize average growth across the four years of development and to compare growth trends for male and female subjects.

Another class of studies that gives rise to repeated-measures data results when each subject is assigned percentage scores on each of a number of behavioral categories. For example, we might categorize the percentage of time per day that a child in elementary school spends in play, in waiting for the teacher or other students, in active participation with the class materials, or out of the room, etc. Each outcome measure is a score on a percentage scale or some transformation of a percentage scale (see Bock, 1975, Section 8.2). We would then be interested in testing differences among the scores to determine whether there is, say, significantly more play or waiting than work time; or we may be interested in comparing the scores (or differences between scores) for two or more classrooms. Similar scores and research questions arise in other studies, such as in the content analysis of verbal material, where the occurrence of objects or events is classified in mutually exclusive and exhaustive categories.

In psychological research, a common type of repeated-measures design arises when each subject is measured with the same instrument under several experimental conditions. For example, a subject may be measured in some manner after having been administered various drugs or treatments at various times. Or, the same experimental subjects may be administered two drugs, each in two different doses. For example, on the first day a subject may receive 5 cc of drug A, and on the second day 10 cc of drug A. On the third day he may receive 5 cc of drug B, and on the fourth day 10 cc of drug B. If each subject is measured each day, the outcomes are repeated measures data, and the conditions under which the drugs have been administered form a simple crossed design—that is, two drugs by two dosages. We may then be interested in differences between drugs, differences between dosages, and interactions of drugs and dosage. In more complex cases, there may also be possible interactions with other design factors (e.g., sex, age, or other external variables).

Data of this kind are frequently analyzed as a "within and between subject design," although the assumptions of such analyses are often difficult to justify. In statistical terms, the model that is fit to these data is an analysis-of-variance *mixed model*, which has "subjects" as an explicit classification factor. It is often said in such analyses that "each subject serves as his own control."

All of the research described here has one property in common—namely, that differences among the *measures* are of experimental interest. In other words, the researcher is interested in differences and systematic trends across the multiple response variables. Comparisons are to be made between several outcomes for the same subjects as well as, perhaps, among distinct groups of observations. Unlike outcomes for independent groups, multiple outcomes for the same subject are generally intercorrelated.

Two types of analysis-of-variance models—one univariate and one multivariate—may be applied to such data. If the assumptions of the univariate model can be met, then the univariate analyis should be employed; some of the resulting test statistics are more powerful than those given by the multivariate analysis. Also, if the number of subjects is small relative to the number of measures, only a univariate analysis will be possible. Some comparison of these possibilities is provided in Davidson (1972), McCall and Applebaum (1973), and Poor (1973).

In many real-data situations, however, the strong assumptions of the univariate analysis cannot be met. In these cases, only the multivariate model can provide valid test statistics. For ease of computation with MULTI-VARIANCE, it is usually preferable to set up the univariate *or* multivariate analysis so that it is performed by the computer as a multivariate run. This reduces the size of the problem, usually by a large factor. The univariate results are simple by-products of the multivariate computations and may be extracted from the multivariate output. For illustrative purposes, the present study is analyzed through both the univariate and multivariate models in this and the following chapter, respectively.

The data for this example have been drawn from Chapter 7 of *Multivariate Statistical Methods in Behavioral Research* (Bock, 1975). A sample of 36 boys and 28 girls was selected from the population of students attending the University of Chicago Laboratory School. A scaled vocabulary score based on various forms of the Cooperative Reading Test was obtained for each student when he or she attended the eighth, ninth, tenth, and eleventh grades. The purpose of the study was to examine changes in vocabulary scores with age, differences of male and female vocabulary scores, and possible interactions of sex and growth in vocabulary (i.e., whether the growth curves for males and females were parallel).

Although these data were collected in a nonexperimental setting, the purposes of the study are essentially the same as in an experimental study of change. For example, if we administer two drugs to subjects having mild and severe cases of a disease, we may be interested in differences among drug effectiveness, differences in outcomes due to severity, and the interaction of severity and drug effectiveness. Even when the dimensions are more complex, the form of the questions to be asked of the data remains the same; for example, there may be three or more drugs administered at different dosages, and there may be two or more sampling factors (e.g., three degrees of disease severity and two age groups). We still need to test the fixed main effects and interactions in the model.

The univariate analysis of the present data (the within-and-between-subjects analysis) is obtained by considering the design to have three dimensions as diagrammed in Figure 5.1. Sex and Grade are fixed dimensions and Subjects are random. Since the same subject does not occur in both sex groups, we say that subjects are *nested* within sex groups. Subjects are crossed with grade level, however, because a score for each subject is obtained at every grade. Sex is also crossed with grade. The observation on any one cell is a single vocabulary score for a particular individual at one point in time.

The linear model for the data is given by (34).

$$y_{ijk} = \mu + \alpha_i + b_{j(i)} + \gamma_k + (\alpha\gamma)_{ik} + \epsilon_{ijk} \tag{34}$$

y_{ijk} is the scaled vocabulary score for the student j within sex group i at grade level k. μ is the overall population mean of all students in all grades. α_i is the systematic deviation from that mean due to the subject being a member of sex group i; $b_{j(i)}$ is the random deviation from the sex-group mean for student j within sex group i. γ_k is the average deviation from μ of all students at one grade level ($k = 1,2,3,4$) and $(\alpha\gamma)_{ik}$ is the interaction of sex and grade. ϵ_{ijk} is the random deviation of the student at a particular grade level from the mean of all students

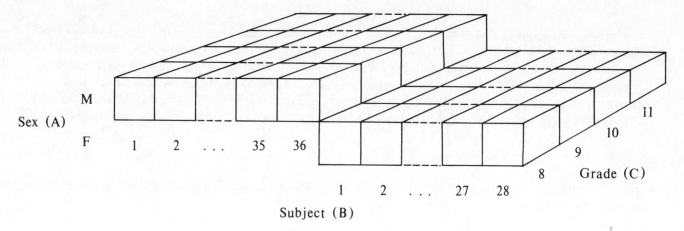

FIGURE 5.1 Sampling Diagram for Vocabulary Growth Study

of that sex group and grade level; this is the only remaining source of variation in the model and is designated the *residual*.

The model includes all of the effects in a three-way crossed design except those that involve the interaction of sex and students. These interactions are not estimable because the same subject is not observed as a member of both sex groups. Thus, neither a sex-by-student nor a sex-by-student-by-grade-level interaction appears in the model.

The sources of variation in the model and the respective degrees of freedom are listed in Table 5.1. This table is often presented with each fixed effect followed by the random interaction of that effect with subjects. It is more convenient for programming purposes to list all the fixed effects in the model first (the effects of major experimental interest), then all of the random effects. Since "subjects" is assumed to be a random factor, the subjects effect and the residual interaction with subjects are both random effects.

In addition to the fixed effects, there are two random sources of variation in the model. Because it contains both fixed and random effects, it is referred to as a *mixed-model*. Of the degrees of freedom for fixed effects, one is employed for estimating the constant term, one is for between sexes, three among the four grade levels, and three for the sex-by-grade interaction. Since the subject classification is not crossed with sex, the estimates of variation among the subjects are obtained separately for each sex group and pooled. There are 35 degrees of freedom for the male group, 27 degrees of freedom for the female group, for a total of 62 degrees of freedom

Table 5.1   Analysis of Variance for Univariate Mixed
Model Analysis

Source of Variation	Degrees of Freedom
Fixed effects:	
Constant	1
Sex	1
Grade	3
Sex × grade interaction	3
Random effects:	
Subjects in sex group 1	35
Subjects in sex group 2	27
Residual (subjects × grade)	186
Total	256

among subjects. Similarly, the random subjects-by-grade interaction has $62 \times 3 = 186$ degrees of freedom. Thus, the total degrees of freedom, 256, equals the total number of observations (that is, 64×4 in Figure 5.1).

Because effects in the model are both fixed and random, and crossed and nested, we must pay attention to which effects appear in the denominators of the F ratios in the test of each hypothesis. As this particular design appears in many texts, the rules for choosing denominators are fairly well known. To test that the means for the two sex groups are equal, we divide the mean square for sex by the mean square for subjects, as given in (35a).

$$F_{\text{sex}} = \text{MS}_{\text{sex}} / \text{MS}_{\text{subjects}} \tag{35a}$$

To test the main effect of grade and the sex-by-grade interaction, we divide the respective mean squares by the mean square for the subjects-by-grade interaction, as in (35b) and (35c).

$$F_{\text{grade}} = \text{MS}_{\text{grade}} / \text{MS}_{\text{residual}} \tag{35b}$$

$$F_{\text{interaction}} = \text{MS}_{\text{interaction}} / \text{MS}_{\text{residual}} \tag{35c}$$

Although other test statistics are possible, the three tests of fixed effects reflect the major questions of interest, and the F statistics of (35a) to (35c) are sufficient for most purposes. In addition to these tests, it may also be of interest to estimate the magnitude of sex and grade effects, and to predict mean scores for each group at all four grade levels.

5.1 ASSUMPTIONS OF THE UNIVARIATE ANALYSIS

Some of the assumptions for a valid univariate analysis of these data are required in all analyses of variance, while others are not. It is assumed that the observations on different subjects are independent and distributed normally with equal error variance. These assumptions are usually met in educational data and, even when they are not, the analysis of variance is sufficiently robust that the resulting test statistics may still be relied upon for most purposes.

However, observations across the four grade levels are not independent, as they are multiple measures of the same subjects. But a substitute assumption, given by (36a), may be made so that the analysis is still valid.

$$\rho_{12} = \rho_{13} = \rho_{14} = \rho_{23} = \rho_{24} = \rho_{34} = \rho \tag{36a}$$

The assumption asserts that the correlation of vocabulary scores between all pairs of grade levels is equal to the same value ρ. The results of the mixed model analysis are valid only if this strong assumption is true. Moreover, violation of this assumption is not compensated for by the robustness of analysis-of-variance tests.

The assumption of equal variances may also be questioned when viewed across time points. It implies that the variance of the scores at grade eight is the same as the variance of the scores at grades nine, ten, and eleven. Each grade level must have the same value σ^2, as represented by (36b).

$$\sigma_1^2 = \sigma_2^2 = \sigma_3^2 = \sigma_4^2 = \sigma^2 \tag{36b}$$

The joint requirement for constant variances and covariances (or correlations) is termed "compound symmetry." It is a critical assumption in the univariate analysis of repeated measures data, and it is one that is not required by the corresponding multivariate analysis.

To determine if the data may be analyzed through the univariate technique, we should first estimate the variances and covariances of the observations. The matrix may be tested to see if it fits the compound symmetry pattern (see Bock, 1975, p. 459). If it does, then we should proceed with the univariate analysis as outlined here. If it does not, we must turn instead to the less restrictive multivariate analysis described in Chapter 6.

In practice, behavioral data rarely meet the assumption of compound symmetry. There is no particular reason why observations made under various experimental conditions should have equal correlations. In longitudinal data especially, we expect a simplex pattern rather than compound symmetry. Time points that are close together will have high intercorrelations, while those more distant have lower intercorrelations. In the development of behavioral traits, the variances across subjects universally increase with age. Thus, longitudinal data may rarely be analyzed through the univariate mixed model, while experimental data must be inspected closely before deciding. In the present example, we refrain from inspecting the correlations and variances, and proceed to demonstrate the computer analysis assuming a univariate model. The reader is cautioned that we proceed in this way only for purposes of illustration.

5.2 ADDITIONAL CONSIDERATIONS REQUIRED BY THE DATA SET

Although it may be of some interest to test mean differences among the four grade levels, there is little doubt that significant differences exist, and it is in a more refined analysis of differences on this dimension that the real interest resides. We will particularly want to investigate the linearity of growth across the four grade levels (that is, are the data consistent with straight line growth). Alternatively, there might be a monotonic increase over the four grade levels, but with decreasing acceleration, or it may even be possible that there is no regular trend in the growth of vocabulary scores.

To test these trends as specific hypotheses, we estimate and test particular linear combinations of the four grade-level means. We obtain these combinations by applying weights—the so-called orthogonal polynomial coefficients—to the four means, $\mu_{..1}$ through $\mu_{..4}$. Tables of orthogonal polynomials are given in many texts (e.g., Bock 1975, Appendix B). The weights for a design factor having four levels (i.e., grade) are given in (37).

$$
\begin{bmatrix}
-3 & -1 & 1 & 3 \\
1 & -1 & -1 & 1 \\
-1 & 3 & -3 & 1
\end{bmatrix}
\quad
\begin{matrix}
\text{P1} & \text{Linear} \\
\text{P2} & \text{Quadratic} \\
\text{P3} & \text{Cubic}
\end{matrix}
\tag{37}
$$

The three rows of the matrix are the weights for linear, quadratic, and cubic trends across grade levels, as indicated. For example, to test whether there is a straight-line or linear trend among the vocabulary means, we should estimate and test the linear combination of the means given by (38).

$$
\text{P1} = -3\mu_{..1} - \mu_{..2} + \mu_{..3} + 3\mu_{..4}
\tag{38}
$$

The weights in (38) are from the first row of (37). To test similarly for decreasing acceleration of vocabulary growth in addition to the linear trend, we employ the weights in the second row of (37). Finally, to test for irregularities in growth in addition to a linear and quadratic trend, we use the cubic or third linear combination of the means. These linear combinations are termed *contrasts*, because the weights in each row sum to zero.

In effect, then, we are testing three contrasts, P1, P2, and P3. The three-degree-of-freedom joint test of significance of all three contrasts is the usual test for $\mu_{..1} = \mu_{..2} = \mu_{..3} = \mu_{..4}$. In addition, to determine the shape of the growth curve, we may obtain separate tests of significance for each contrast. In the computer setup, they are obtained in a second pass through the analysis phase of the program with a second grouping of the degrees of freedom for statistical tests.

The MULTIVARIANCE program is able to generate the orthogonal polynomial coefficients and does not require the transformation matrix to be entered. The design factors for which orthogonal weights will be used are named early in the run so that the program may generate the matrix. The symbolic codes P1, P2, and P3, are entered in place of the codes D1, D2, and D3, to indicate the polynomial grade effects.[1]

5.3 FORMAT OF THE DATA

The scaled vocabulary scores for all subjects are listed in Figure 5.2. For the univariate analysis, subjects are classified on three dimensions and each score is entered on a separate card. There are 256 cards in all, one for each subject in each sex group at each grade level. The format of the cards is as follows:

Columns	Variables	
1	Sex	1 = male
		2 = female
2-3	Subject number	1-36 for males
		1-28 for females
4	Grade level	1 = grade 8
		2 = grade 9
		3 = grade 10
		4 = grade 11
6-10	Scaled vocabulary score (Format F5.2)	

Each subject in the study has four data cards, each containing a score at one grade level. Subjects numbers run 1 through 36 for males and begin again at 1 for females. This allows the complete design to have only 36 levels for the subject factor, rather than 64. However, the variance among subjects must be estimated separately for each sex group. This is indicated in the control cards for Phase II.

5.4 MULTIVARIANCE SETUP

The control cards for the MULTIVARIANCE program, exclusive of the data, are listed in Figure 5.3. The data are described on the Input Description card following the two Title cards for the problem run. There is a single measured variable—the score on the scaled vocabulary measure. There are three factors of classification in the analysis-of-variance design, viz., sex, subject, and grade level. The number of factors is punched in column 8 of the Input Description card, and the names and levels of the factors are punched on the following Factor Identification card.

The data cards are punched so that the score on the measured variable is preceded by an identification number for each factor in the design. In these data, the identification numbers begin with 1 and proceed sequentially, thus permitting Data Form 1 of the program to be used. The data need not be sorted, counted, nor preceded by Header cards. This is the easiest data form to use, and it is generally advisable that the researcher prepare his cards in this manner.

A single Variable Format card may be used to describe the data. A "1" is entered in column 48 of the Input Description card so that the standard deviations for each cell in the design will not be printed. Since there

---

[1] Other codes discussed may also be used to designate other types of contrasts.

```
          1
123456789012345
```

ID	Value	ID	Value	ID	Value	ID	Value
1 11	1.75	1171	2.08	1332	0.93	2132	2.65
1 12	2.60	1172	1.74	1333	1.30	2133	1.72
1 13	3.76	1173	4.12	1334	0.76	2134	2.96
1 14	3.68	1174	3.62	1341	2.18	2141	0.15
1 21	0.90	1181	0.14	1342	6.42	2142	2.69
1 22	2.47	1182	0.01	1343	4.64	2143	2.69
1 23	2.44	1183	1.48	1344	4.82	2144	3.50
1 24	3.43	1184	2.78	1351	4.21	2151	-1.27
1 31	0.80	1191	0.13	1352	7.08	2152	1.26
1 32	0.93	1192	3.19	1353	6.00	2153	0.71
1 33	0.40	1193	0.60	1354	5.65	2154	2.68
1 34	2.27	1194	3.14	1361	8.26	2161	2.81
1 41	2.42	1201	2.19	1362	9.55	2162	5.19
1 42	4.15	1202	2.65	1363	10.24	2163	6.33
1 43	4.56	1203	3.27	1364	10.58	2164	5.93
1 44	4.21	1204	2.73	2 11	1.24	2171	2.62
1 51	-1.31	1211	-0.64	2 12	4.90	2172	3.54
1 52	-1.31	1212	-1.31	2 13	2.42	2173	4.86
1 53	-0.66	1213	-0.37	2 14	2.54	2174	5.80
1 54	-2.22	1214	4.09	2 21	5.94	2181	0.11
1 61	-1.56	1221	2.02	2 22	6.56	2182	2.25
1 62	1.67	1222	3.45	2 23	9.36	2183	1.56
1 63	0.18	1223	5.32	2 24	7.72	2184	3.92
1 64	2.33	1224	6.01	2 31	0.87	2191	0.61
1 71	1.09	1231	2.05	2 32	3.36	2192	1.14
1 72	1.50	1232	1.80	2 33	2.58	2193	1.35
1 73	0.52	1233	3.91	2 34	1.73	2194	0.53
1 74	2.33	1234	2.49	2 41	-0.09	2201	-2.19
1 81	-1.92	1241	1.48	2 42	2.29	2202	-0.42
1 82	1.03	1242	0.47	2 43	3.08	2203	1.54
1 83	0.50	1243	3.63	2 44	3.35	2204	1.16
1 84	3.04	1244	3.88	2 51	3.24	2211	1.55
1 91	-1.61	1251	1.97	2 52	4.78	2212	2.42
1 92	0.29	1252	2.54	2 53	3.52	2213	1.11
1 93	0.73	1253	3.26	2 54	4.84	2214	2.18
1 94	3.24	1254	5.62	2 61	1.03	2221	-0.04
1101	2.47	1261	1.35	2 62	2.10	2222	0.50
1102	3.64	1262	4.63	2 63	3.88	2223	2.60
1103	2.87	1263	3.54	2 64	2.81	2224	2.61
1104	5.38	1264	5.24	2 71	3.58	2231	3.10
1111	-0.95	1271	-0.56	2 72	4.67	2232	2.00
1112	0.41	1272	-0.36	2 73	3.83	2233	3.92
1113	0.21	1273	1.14	2 74	5.19	2234	3.91
1114	1.82	1274	1.34	2 81	1.41	2241	-0.29
1121	1.66	1281	0.26	2 82	1.75	2242	2.62
1122	2.74	1282	0.08	2 83	3.70	2243	1.60
1123	2.40	1283	1.17	2 84	3.77	2244	1.86
1124	2.17	1284	2.15	2 91	-0.65	2251	2.28
1131	2.07	1291	1.22	2 92	-0.11	2252	3.39
1132	4.92	1292	1.41	2 93	2.40	2253	4.91
1133	4.46	1293	4.66	2 94	3.53	2254	3.89
1134	4.71	1294	2.62	2101	1.52	2261	2.57
1141	3.30	1301	-1.43	2102	3.04	2262	5.78
1142	6.10	1302	0.80	2103	2.74	2263	5.12
1143	7.19	1303	-0.03	2104	2.63	2264	4.98
1144	7.46	1304	1.04	2111	0.57	2271	-2.19
1151	2.75	1311	-1.17	2112	2.71	2272	0.71
1152	2.53	1312	1.66	2113	1.90	2273	1.56
1153	4.28	1313	2.11	2114	2.41	2274	2.31
1154	5.93	1314	1.42	2121	2.18	2281	-0.04
1161	2.25	1321	1.68	2122	2.96	2282	2.44
1162	3.38	1322	1.71	2123	4.78	2283	1.79
1163	5.79	1323	4.07	2124	3.34	2284	2.64
1164	4.40	1324	3.30	2131	1.10		
		1331	-0.47				

```
                                              1
                                    123456789012345
```

FIGURE 5.2 Problem 4: Vocabulary Growth data--univariate form

```
                  1         2         3         4         5         6         7         8
         1234567890123456789012345678901234567890123456789012345678901234567890
      1. Title cards
PROBLEM 4  REPEATED MEASURES ANALYSIS OF LONGITUDINAL DATA
--UNIVARIATE MIXED MODEL
      2. Input Description card
      1   3   1                                       1
      3. Factor Identification card
SEX       2SUBJCT  36GRADE     4
      4. Comment cards

REPEATED MEASURES ANALYSIS THROUGH UNIVARIATE MIXED MODEL. DATA FROM
BOCK, R.D. MULTIVARIATE STATISTICAL METHODS IN BEHAVIORAL RESEARCH,
NEW YORK: MCGRAW-HILL, 1975, CHAPTER 7.

MALES AND FEMALES EACH TESTED IN GRADES 8,9,10,11. DEPENDENT VARIABLE IS
SCALED VOCABULARY SCORE.

TESTS FOR SEX DIFFERENCES, FOR GRADE DIFFERENCES, AND SEX-BY-GRADE INTERACTION.

TWO ERROR TERMS ARE REQUIRED FOR THE COMPLETE ANALYSIS. ONLY THE RESIDUAL
SUBJECTS-BY-GRADE INTERACTION IS USED AS THE ERROR TERM IN THIS RUN, SO THAT
THE PRINTED F-TEST FOR SEX IS NOT CORRECT. THE CORRECT F IS OBTAINED IN A SECOND
RUN OR BY HAND, DIVIDING MEAN SQUARE SEX/MEAN SQUARE SUBJECTS.
ORTHOGONAL POLYNOMIAL CONTRASTS ARE ESTIMATED OVER THE FOUR GRADE LEVELS.

FORMAT OF DATA CARDS:
    COL       CONTENTS
    1         SEX GROUP  1=MALE, 2=FEMALE
    2-3       SUBJECT NUMBER WITHIN SEX GROUP
              (1-36 FOR MALE, 1-28 FOR FEMALE)
    4         GRADE (1=8, 2=9, 3=10, 4=11)
    6-10      SCALED VOCABULARY SCORE  F5.2

      5. End-of-comments card
FINISH
      6. Variable Format card
(I1,I2,I1,1X,F5.2)
      9. Variable Label card
VOCABLRY
     10. Data
    DATA DECK  (DATA FORM 1)
        End of data

     12. Estimation Specification card
    70   8   1                     1               1
     13. Means key
1,3,1*3.
     15. Orthogonal Polynomials
GRADE
     16. Symbolic Contrast Vectors
D0,D0,D0,           CONSTANT                              CONST
D1,D0,D0,           SEX                                   SEX
D0,D0,P1,           LINEAR GRADE CONTRAST                 LINEAR
D0,D0,P2,           QUADRATIC GRADE CONTRAST              QUAD
D0,D0,P3,           CUBIC GRADE CONTRAST                  CUBIC
D1,D0,P1,           LINEAR GRADE X SEX INTERACTION        LINSEX
D1,D0,P2,           QUADRATIC GRADE X SEX INTERACTION     QUADSX
D1,D0,P3,           CUBIC GRADE X SEX INTERACTION         CUBSEX
I1,35D1,D0,         SUBJECTS IN GROUP 1 (MALE)            SUBJS
I2,27D1,D0,         SUBJECTS IN GROUP 2 (FEMALE)          SUBJS
     18. Analysis Selection card
    1
     21. Hypothesis Test card
1,1,3,3,62.
     18. Analysis Selection card
    1
     21. Hypothesis Test card
1,1,1,1,1,1,1,1.
     22. End-of-job card
                                                  STOP
                  1         2         3         4         5         6         7         8
         1234567890123456789012345678901234567890123456789012345678901234567890
```

FIGURE 5.3 Problem 4: MULTIVARIANCE control cards for mixed-model analysis

is only one observation in each of the 256 groups, each of the standard deviations is identically zero. Because of the 1 in column 60, optional intermediate computations will be printed throughout the problem run.

There are three factors of classification in the experimental design. Factor one is sex with two levels. The second factor is subjects, with 36 levels for the first sex group and 28 levels for the second sex group. The maximum of these two numbers is inserted as the number of levels for the subjects factor on the Factor Identification card. No other provision is necessary for the 8 fewer subjects in the second sex group. The third factor is grade, with four levels. Note the factors are named in the same order as that in which the identifying information is punched on the data cards. This order also establishes the order to be assumed for combined means. Note also that in Phase I, no special indication is necessary that subjects comprise a nested factor; for purposes of input, the setup may be treated as a three-way crossed design.

The Comments are terminated with a "FINISH" card. The Variable Format card contains three integer fields (I format) to read the subclass identifying information on the data cards. The measured variables, the vocabulary score, are read in F format. A Variable Label card is entered naming the vocabulary variable. Then the data cards themselves are entered. The data are terminated by one blank observation, which for this study is a single blank card.

The Phase II control cards differ in several ways from those of earlier examples. In particular, parameters must be adjusted to conform to the analysis-of-variance table (Table 5.1) and to the F ratios that must be constructed according to (35a) through (35c). The primary consideration at this stage is the choice on the analysis-of-variance error term. The MULTIVARIANCE program allows only a single error term per problem run. Therefore, a mixed-model analysis with two or more error terms either requires two or more separate runs of the program, or else some hand computations following the runs.

There is no within-cell variation in the present example, since there is only one subject per subclass. In any case, the within-cell mean square is not the appropriate denominator mean square for any of the important effects in the design. Instead, the 62-degree-of-freedom subjects-within-sex-groups effect is the error term for one F statistic, while the 186-degree-of-freedom subject-by-grade interaction is the error term for the other two fixed effects in the model. The Estimation Specification card is punched so that the latter, or residual, mean square will be employed as the error term in the problem run.

The residual sum of squares may be obtained directly in the MULTIVARIANCE program. To include all of the fixed effects plus the 62 subjects effects in the model, the rank of model for significance testing is set at 70. Column 12 of the Estimation Specification Card defines the error term for the run. This is set to "1", so that all residual variation is pooled to obtain the error sum of squares. The program will subtract the sum of squares for the first 70 effects from the total sum of squared scores. This is the interaction we are seeking, for there are no additional sources of variation remaining. Further, we write only 70 symbolic effect codes, instead of all 256.

Every test of significance will be conducted with the same error term however. The mean squares for sex, grade, and sex-by-grade interaction, as well as subjects-within-sex-groups, will be divided by the residual subjects-by-grade mean square. The F statistics for the grade and sex-by-grade interaction effects will be correct, while that for sex will not. In the process of conducting these tests, however, the program will also print the sex and subjects-within-sex-group mean squares. The simple ratio of these two values may be taken by hand to obtain the F ratio for sex (35a). This is the procedure followed in the present example.

It is also possible to have the program conduct the correct test of sex effect in a second run. This does not save time here. However, if there was more than one score per subject at each grade level, we would need the computer to conduct the multivariate test of sex differences. For the second run, all of the input cards to the program are left unchanged except the Estimation Specification card. The rank of the model for significance testing remains at 70, and the first 70 effects in the model are coded as in the first run. However, column 12 is set to "2", indicating a "special effects" error term. This means that some of the last effects *coded* in the model are to be used as the error term for significance tests. In particular, we would like the sum of squares for the last 62 effects coded to be used as the error term for the additional test. This number, 62, is entered in columns 13-16 of the Estimation Specification card. In this run, all of the fixed-effect mean squares will be divided by the subjects-in-sex-group mean square to obtain the test statistics. Only the test statistic for sex will be correct. In fact, the

Hypothesis Test card may also be altered so that the unnecessary tests of the grade and sex-by-grade effects are not conducted. Since this simple univariate example does not require much hand computation, the second run is not made.

So that all the fixed effects in the model and their standard errors will be estimated, the rank of the model for estimation is set to 8. The "1" in column 28 of the Estimation Specification card indicates that there is one factor in the sampling design for which orthogonal polynomial contrasts are required; this is the grade factor for which we wish to test linear, quadratic, and cubic trends in vocabulary growth.

Column 44 of the Estimation Specification card is set to "1" so that the observed means will be combined across the 256 groups to provide useful "row and column means." The Means Key which follows indicates that means are required for each level of the first (sex) factor, each level of the third (grade) factor, and each combination of sex and grade. We have no particular need for the mean score for each subject in each group.

The card following the Means Key names the factor for which orthogonal polynomial weights are required. The program constructs the matrix of weights before inspecting the effect codes which follow. There are 70 Symbolic Contrast Vector codes. Each code contains three sections, separated by commas. The first part of the code refers to the first factor (sex) on the Factor Identification card. The second part of the code corresponds to the subjects effect, and the third to the grade effect.

The constant term in the model, which is the first effect in Table 5.1, is the constant across all subjects in all groups. It is coded D0,D0,D0, as for a three-way crossed design. The code to indicate α_1 for the sex effect has D1, for the portion of the code corresponding to sex (i.e., the left hand portion) and D0's as space holders for the subjects and grade effects. Neither subject variation nor grade differences is involved in the contrast between sex groups.

The next three effects in Table 5.1 are the grade effects. In order to test linear, quadratic, and cubic grade effects, the codes P1, P2, and P3, appear in the grade (i.e., right hand) portion of three contrast cards. D0's are included in the first two positions as space holders; neither sex differences nor subject variation is involved in the trends over grade levels. Thus, the three cards for the orthogonal polynomial effects over grade levels are punched (the comments and labels on the right are optional):

D0 , D0 , P1 ,	L I NEAR GRADE CONTRAST	L I NEAR
D0 , D0 , P2 ,	QUADRAT I C GRADE CONTRAST	QUAD
D0 , D0 , P3 ,	CUB I C GRADE CONTRAST	CUB I C

The next three effects in the model are the sex-by-grade interactions. These are coded as every possible combination of the D1, sex code and the three polynomial grade codes. A space holder is put in the middle (subjects) portion of each code, because subject variation is not involved in the sex-by-grade interaction. For example, the first sex-by-grade interaction effect code is D1,D0,P1,. A test of this effect indicates whether *differences* between the sex-group means lie on a straight line across grade levels. The second sex-by-grade interaction code is D1,D0,P2,. A test of this effect indicates whether differences between sex groups lie on a parabolic curve, or deviate in a regular fashion from the straight line of the linear effect. The third sex-by-grade interaction code is D1,D0,P3,. This effect indicates whether the differences between male and female means form an irregular pattern over grade levels.

The next 62 effects are differences (variation) among subjects within particular sex groups. First we estimate variation among the 36 subjects in the first sex group (male). An additional letter code (I) is used in the Symbolic Contrast Vectors to restrict the effect to a particular level of one or more design factors. To obtain variation among subjects in sex group 1, we insert the code I1, in the sex (i.e., left hand) portion of each effect code. For example, to estimate $b_1^{(1)}$, the first subject effect in the male group, the complete effect code is I1,D1,D0,. I1, restricts the effect to the first sex group; D1, indicates that the first subject effect is to be obtained;

D0, is inserted as a space holder because there is no grade effect involved in differences among subjects. To obtain, then, 35 subject effects among the 36 males, the Symbolic Contrast Vectors are punched:

```
I 1 , D1 , D0 ,
I 1 , D2 , D0 ,
I 1 , D3 , D0 ,
        .
        .
        .
I 1 , D35 , D0 ,
```

Fortunately the MULTIVARIANCE program does not require punching all 35 of these cards. The codes may be indicated simultaneously on a single card reading:

```
I 1 , 35D1 , D0 ,      SUBJECTS IN GROUP 1 (MALE)              SUBJS
```

This card indicates that the initial I1, and the final D0, are to remain constant, while 35 successive subject codes are to be generated, beginning with D1,.

To estimate subject effects within sex group 2 (female), the sex portion of each card is coded I2,. The 27 subject effects among 28 girls are punched:

```
I 2 , D1 , D0 ,
I 2 , D2 , D0 ,
I 2 , D3 , D0 ,
        .
        .
        .
I 2 , D27 , D0 ,
```

All 27 effects may be coded on a single Symbolic Contrast Vector Card reading:

```
I 1 , 27D1 , D0 ,      SUBJECTS IN GROUP 2 (FEMALE)            SUBJS
```

The remaining input cards are for Phase III, the analysis phase of the program. The Analysis Selection card indicates that there is one criterion measure. The Hypothesis Test card indicates that tests are to be conducted of the first effect coded (the constant), the next one effect (sex), the next three effects simultaneously (grade), the next three effects simultaneously (sex × grade), and the final 62 effects simultaneously. Although a test of the last 62 effects is not of particular interest, the mean square for subjects in sex groups will be computed and printed.

A second pass through the analysis phase again has one criterion measure. The Hypothesis Test card indicates that there is to be a one-degree-of-freedom test of the constant, and a one-degree-of-freedom test of the sex effect. There are then three 1's on the Hypothesis Test card, instead of a "3". This indicates that there is to be a one-degree-of-freedom test of the first grade effect, a one-degree-of-freedom test of the second grade effect, and one test of the final grade effect. These are the three orthogonal polynomial contrasts, and this partition allows us to test each separately. The three-degree-of-freedom test from the first pass through Phase III will indicate whether there are any differences among grade levels; the partition to separate polynomials will determine the nature of those differences. Likewise, one-degree-of-freedom tests are coded for each of the sex-by-grade interactions. These will indicate the increasing or decreasing trend of differences between sex groups over age.

5.5 OUTPUT AND INTERPRETATION

PHASE I.   The input data are summarized in Figures 5.4-1 through 5.4-7. All of the subclass frequencies are one except for the final eight subjects in sex group. The program treats the latter as empty groups, and reduces all results to the 256 groups with observations. With a single observation per group, the 256 means are exactly the raw input data.

The observed combined means in Figure 5.4-3 give some indication of the effects in the data. Females have slightly higher vocabulary scores than males, and there is a clear tendency for scaled vocabulary scores to increase from grade eight to grade eleven. The "1*3" on the Means Key has produced the final table of means for each combination of sex and grade. The increase from grade eight to grade nine seems to be larger for females than for males, while girls increase less from grades nine to ten and from ten to eleven. This may be reflected in a significant interaction of sex and grade level.

PHASE II.   The input parameters for Phase II are listed beginning in Figure 5.4-4. The entire set of 70 Symbolic Contrast Vectors is listed. Note that the two symbolic codes I1,35D1,D0, and I2,27D1,D0, have been interpreted as the entire set of 62 explicitly written codes.

The residual mean square, with 186 degrees of freedom, is .818. This is the mean square used in the denominator of all F ratios computed within the problem run.

The estimated fixed effects are listed in both the raw and standard deviation units; their standard errors follow. We see that sex-group 1 is estimated to be about .06 points below the mean of all subjects on the vocabulary score. The standard error for this effect is not correct, since it is based on the residual variance. The standard error of the sex effect must be recomputed using the subjects-in-sex-group variance instead. This may be done by hand or by a second computer run.

The standard errors for the six estimated polynomial effects are all correct however. Using a critical t value of 1.96, we would judge that all polynomial effects in grade are significant. The strongest trend in the data is for a straight line representing the four means, with both general and erratic deviations from the straight line. The negative sign on the quadratic estimate reflects the *de*celerating trend in vocabulary growth. There is some suggestion of a quadratic grade-by-sex interaction. That is, differences between the sexes appear to increase at early grades and then decrease later. However, the overall tests, which also depend on the order of effects, are necessary for decisions about significance.

PHASE III.   The results of the overall tests of significance are listed in Figure 5.4-6. Reading this table from the last effect backwards, we first encounter the results for subjects within sex groups. The mean square of 14.0768 is the correct value, with 62 degrees of freedom. The F statistic is the ratio of this mean square to the residual mean square of .818. It is not a test of any hypothesis of concern in this study, and may be ignored.

The sex-by-grade interaction is of interest however. The mean square of .9324 has been correctly divided by the residual mean square to yield the F statistic of 1.14. This does not exceed the .05 critical value, with 3 and 186 degrees of freedom, and H_0 is accepted. This statistic gives an overall test of all interaction between sex and grade levels—that is, a test of equality of sex differences across all four grades. The interaction is not significant, and may be omitted from the model. However, specific portions of the interaction may appear significant when particular trends are tested.

The lack of interaction tells us also that we may interpret the grade or sex main effects without confounding. Any sex-mean differences or grade differences that are found are consistent across levels of the other factor.

Having found the interaction nonsignificant, we may proceed with the test of grade differences. The mean square among grades of 64.78 has been correctly divided by the residual mean square to yield the F statistic of 79.19.[2] This exceeds the .01 value with 3 and 186 degrees of freedom, as expected. However, it is of more

---

[2] Note that the mean square of 64.7795 has three degrees of freedom, so that the sum of squares for the grade effect is
$64.78 \times 3 = 194.3385$.

- -

PROBLEM 4 - REPEATED MEASURES ANALYSIS OF LONGITUDINAL DATA - UNIVARIATE MIXED MODEL

- -

PAGE   1

REPEATED MEASURES ANALYSIS THROUGH UNIVARIATE MIXED MODEL. DATA FROM
BOCK, R.D. MULTIVARIATE STATISTICAL METHODS IN BEHAVIORAL RESEARCH,
NEW YORK: MCGRAW HILL, 1975, CHAPTER 7.

MALES AND FEMALES EACH TESTED IN GRADES 8,9,10,11. DEPENDENT VARIABLE IS
SCALED VOCABULARY SCORE.

TESTS FOR SEX DIFFERENCES, FOR GRADE DIFFERENCES, AND SEX-BY-GRADE INTERACTION.

TWO ERROR TERMS ARE REQUIRED FOR THE COMPLETE ANALYSIS. ONLY THE RESIDUAL
SUBJECTS-BY-GRADE INTERACTION IS USED AS THE ERROR TERM IN THIS RUN, SO THAT
THE PRINTED F-TEST FOR SEX IS NOT CORRECT. THE CORRECT F IS OBTAINED IN A SECOND
RUN OR BY HAND, DIVIDING MEAN SQUARE SEX/MEAN SQUARE SUBJECTS.
ORTHOGONAL POLYNOMIAL CONTRASTS ARE ESTIMATED OVER THE FOUR GRADE LEVELS.

FORMAT OF DATA CARDS:
```
COL       CONTENTS
  1       SEX GROUP   1=MALE, 2=FEMALE
2-3       SUBJECT NUMBER WITHIN SEX GROUP
          (1-36 FOR MALE, 1-28 FOR FEMALE)
  4       GRADE (1=8, 2=9, 3=10, 4=11)
6-10      SCALED VOCABULARY SCORE F5.2
```

                          INPUT PARAMETERS
                          ================

PAGE   2

NUMBER OF VARIABLES IN INPUT VECTORS=   1

NUMBER OF FACTORS IN DESIGN=   3

```
NUMBER OF LEVELS OF FACTOR 1 (SEX    ) =         2
NUMBER OF LEVELS OF FACTOR 2 (SUBJCT ) =        36
NUMBER OF LEVELS OF FACTOR 3 (GRADE  ) =         4
```

INPUT IS FROM CARDS. DATA OPTION 1

MINIMAL PAGE SPACING WILL BE USED

COMPUTATION OF ST.DEV'S AND COVARIANCE MATRIX FOR EACH GROUP SUPPRESSED

*****NUMBER OF VARIABLE FORMAT CARDS NOT SPECIFIED. ASSUMED TO BE 1.

FORMAT OF DATA
   (I1,I2,I1,1X,F5.2)

FIRST OBSERVATION
SUBJECT   1 , CELL   1 1 1
                            1.7500

                   CELL IDENTIFICATION AND FREQUENCIES

PAGE   3

CELL	FACTOR LEVELS			N		CELL	SEX	SUBJCT	GRADE	N
	SEX	SUBJCT	GRADE							
1	1	1	1	1		49	1	13	1	1
2	1	1	2	1		50	1	13	2	1
3	1	1	3	1		51	1	13	3	1
4	1	1	4	1		52	1	13	4	1
5	1	2	1	1		53	1	14	1	1
6	1	2	2	1		54	1	14	2	1
7	1	2	3	1		55	1	14	3	1
8	1	2	4	1		56	1	14	4	1
9	1	3	1	1		57	1	15	1	1
10	1	3	2	1		58	1	15	2	1
11	1	3	3	1		59	1	15	3	1
12	1	3	4	1		60	1	15	4	1
13	1	4	1	1		61	1	16	1	1
14	1	4	2	1		62	1	16	2	1
15	1	4	3	1		63	1	16	3	1
16	1	4	4	1		64	1	16	4	1
17	1	5	1	1		65	1	17	1	1
18	1	5	2	1		66	1	17	2	1
19	1	5	3	1		67	1	17	3	1
20	1	5	4	1		68	1	17	4	1
21	1	6	1	1		69	1	18	1	1
22	1	6	2	1		70	1	18	2	1
23	1	6	3	1		71	1	18	3	1
24	1	6	4	1		72	1	18	4	1
25	1	7	1	1		73	1	19	1	1
26	1	7	2	1		74	1	19	2	1
27	1	7	3	1		75	1	19	3	1
28	1	7	4	1		76	1	19	4	1
29	1	8	1	1		77	1	20	1	1
30	1	8	2	1		78	1	20	2	1
31	1	8	3	1		79	1	20	3	1
32	1	8	4	1		80	1	20	4	1
33	1	9	1	1		81	1	21	1	1
34	1	9	2	1		82	1	21	2	1
35	1	9	3	1		83	1	21	3	1
36	1	9	4	1		84	1	21	4	1
37	1	10	1	1		85	1	22	1	1
38	1	10	2	1		86	1	22	2	1
39	1	10	3	1		87	1	22	3	1
40	1	10	4	1		88	1	22	4	1
41	1	11	1	1		89	1	23	1	1
42	1	11	2	1		90	1	23	2	1
43	1	11	3	1		91	1	23	3	1
44	1	11	4	1		92	1	23	4	1
45	1	12	1	1		93	1	24	1	1
46	1	12	2	1		94	1	24	2	1
47	1	12	3	1		95	1	24	3	1
48	1	12	4	1		96	1	24	4	1

FIGURE 5.4-1 Problem 4: Phase I output

97	1	25	1	1
98	1	25	2	1
99	1	25	3	1
100	1	25	4	1
101	1	26	1	1
102	1	26	2	1
103	1	26	3	1
104	1	26	4	1
105	1	27	1	1
106	1	27	2	1
107	1	27	3	1
108	1	27	4	1
109	1	28	1	1
110	1	28	2	1
111	1	28	3	1
112	1	28	4	1
113	1	29	1	1
114	1	29	2	1
115	1	29	3	1
116	1	29	4	1
117	1	30	1	1
118	1	30	2	1
119	1	30	3	1
120	1	30	4	1
121	1	31	1	1
122	1	31	2	1
123	1	31	3	1
124	1	31	4	1
125	1	32	1	1
126	1	32	2	1
127	1	32	3	1
128	1	32	4	1
129	1	33	1	1
130	1	33	2	1
131	1	33	3	1
132	1	33	4	1
133	1	34	1	1
134	1	34	2	1
135	1	34	3	1
136	1	34	4	1
137	1	35	1	1
138	1	35	2	1
139	1	35	3	1
140	1	35	4	1
141	1	36	1	1
142	1	36	2	1
143	1	36	3	1
144	1	36	4	1
145	2	1	1	1
146	2	1	2	1
147	2	1	3	1
148	2	1	4	1
149	2	2	1	1
150	2	2	2	1
151	2	2	3	1
152	2	2	4	1
153	2	3	1	1
154	2	3	2	1
155	2	3	3	1
156	2	3	4	1
157	2	4	1	1
158	2	4	2	1
159	2	4	3	1
160	2	4	4	1
161	2	5	1	1
162	2	5	2	1
163	2	5	3	1
164	2	5	4	1
165	2	6	1	1
166	2	6	2	1
167	2	6	3	1
168	2	6	4	1
169	2	7	1	1
170	2	7	2	1
171	2	7	3	1
172	2	7	4	1
173	2	8	1	1
174	2	8	2	1
175	2	8	3	1
176	2	8	4	1
177	2	9	1	1
178	2	9	2	1
179	2	9	3	1
180	2	9	4	1
181	2	10	1	1
182	2	10	2	1
183	2	10	3	1
184	2	10	4	1
185	2	11	1	1
186	2	11	2	1
187	2	11	3	1
188	2	11	4	1
189	2	12	1	1
190	2	12	2	1
191	2	12	3	1
192	2	12	4	1

193	2	13	1	1
194	2	13	2	1
195	2	13	3	1
196	2	13	4	1
197	2	14	1	1
198	2	14	2	1
199	2	14	3	1
200	2	14	4	1
201	2	15	1	1
202	2	15	2	1
203	2	15	3	1
204	2	15	4	1
205	2	16	1	1
206	2	16	2	1
207	2	16	3	1
208	2	16	4	1
209	2	17	1	1
210	2	17	2	1
211	2	17	3	1
212	2	17	4	1
213	2	18	1	1
214	2	18	2	1
215	2	18	3	1
216	2	18	4	1
217	2	19	1	1
218	2	19	2	1
219	2	19	3	1
220	2	19	4	1
221	2	20	1	1
222	2	20	2	1
223	2	20	3	1
224	2	20	4	1
225	2	21	1	1
226	2	21	2	1
227	2	21	3	1
228	2	21	4	1
229	2	22	1	1
230	2	22	2	1
231	2	22	3	1
232	2	22	4	1
233	2	23	1	1
234	2	23	2	1
235	2	23	3	1
236	2	23	4	1
237	2	24	1	1
238	2	24	2	1
239	2	24	3	1
240	2	24	4	1
241	2	25	1	1
242	2	25	2	1
243	2	25	3	1
244	2	25	4	1
245	2	26	1	1
246	2	26	2	1
247	2	26	3	1
248	2	26	4	1
249	2	27	1	1
250	2	27	2	1
251	2	27	3	1
252	2	27	4	1
253	2	28	1	1
254	2	28	2	1
255	2	28	3	1
256	2	28	4	1
EMPTY	2	29	1	0
EMPTY	2	29	2	0
EMPTY	2	29	3	0
EMPTY	2	29	4	0
EMPTY	2	30	1	0
EMPTY	2	30	2	0
EMPTY	2	30	3	0
EMPTY	2	30	4	0
EMPTY	2	31	1	0
EMPTY	2	31	2	0
EMPTY	2	31	3	0
EMPTY	2	31	4	0
EMPTY	2	32	1	0
EMPTY	2	32	2	0
EMPTY	2	32	3	0
EMPTY	2	32	4	0
EMPTY	2	33	1	0
EMPTY	2	33	2	0
EMPTY	2	33	3	0
EMPTY	2	33	4	0
EMPTY	2	34	1	0
EMPTY	2	34	2	0
EMPTY	2	34	3	0
EMPTY	2	34	4	0
EMPTY	2	35	1	0
EMPTY	2	35	2	0
EMPTY	2	35	3	0
EMPTY	2	35	4	0
EMPTY	2	36	1	0
EMPTY	2	36	2	0
EMPTY	2	36	3	0
EMPTY	2	36	4	0

TOTAL N=   256.

32 NULL SUBCLASS(ES).

FIGURE 5.4-2   Problem 4:   Phase I output (continued)

OBSERVED CELL MEANS --- ROWS ARE CELLS-COLUMNS ARE VARIABLES
----

	1 VOCABLR		1 VOCABLR		1 VOCABLR		1 VOCABLR		1 VOCABLR
1	1.75000	51	4.46000	101	1.35000	151	9.36000	201	-1.27000
2	2.60000	52	4.71000	102	4.63000	152	7.72000	202	1.26000
3	3.76000	53	3.30000	103	3.54000	153	0.87000	203	0.71000
4	3.68000	54	6.10000	104	5.24000	154	3.36000	204	2.68000
5	0.90000	55	7.19000	105	-0.56000	155	2.58000	205	2.81000
6	2.47000	56	7.46000	106	-0.36000	156	1.73000	206	5.19000
7	2.44000	57	2.75000	107	1.14000	157	-0.09000	207	6.33000
8	3.43000	58	2.53000	108	1.34000	158	2.29000	208	5.93000
9	0.80000	59	4.28000	109	0.26000	159	3.08000	209	2.62000
10	0.93000	60	5.93000	110	0.08000	160	3.35000	210	3.54000
11	0.40000	61	2.25000	111	1.17000	161	3.24000	211	4.86000
12	2.27000	62	3.38000	112	2.15000	162	4.78000	212	5.80000
13	2.42000	63	5.79000	113	1.22000	163	3.52000	213	0.11000
14	4.15000	64	4.40000	114	1.41000	164	4.84000	214	2.25000
15	4.56000	65	2.08000	115	4.66000	165	1.03000	215	1.56000
16	4.21000	66	1.74000	116	2.62000	166	2.10000	216	3.92000
17	-1.31000	67	4.12000	117	-1.43000	167	3.88000	217	0.61000
18	-1.31000	68	3.62000	118	0.80000	168	2.81000	218	1.14000
19	-0.66000	69	0.14000	119	-0.03000	169	3.58000	219	1.35000
20	-2.22000	70	0.01000	120	1.04000	170	4.67000	220	0.53000
21	-1.56000	71	1.48000	121	-1.17000	171	3.83000	221	-2.19000
22	1.67000	72	2.78000	122	1.66000	172	5.19000	222	-0.42000
23	0.18000	73	0.13000	123	2.11000	173	1.41000	223	1.54000
24	2.33000	74	3.19000	124	1.42000	174	1.75000	224	1.16000
25	1.09000	75	0.60000	125	1.68000	175	3.70000	225	1.55000
26	1.50000	76	3.14000	126	1.71000	176	3.77000	226	2.42000
27	0.52000	77	2.19000	127	4.07000	177	-0.65000	227	1.11000
28	2.33000	78	2.65000	128	3.30000	178	-0.11000	228	2.18000
29	-1.92000	79	3.27000	129	-0.47000	179	2.40000	229	-0.04000
30	1.03000	80	2.73000	130	0.93000	180	3.53000	230	0.50000
31	0.50000	81	-0.64000	131	1.30000	181	1.52000	231	2.60000
32	3.04000	82	-1.31000	132	0.76000	182	3.04000	232	2.61000
33	-1.61000	83	-0.37000	133	2.18000	183	2.74000	233	3.10000
34	0.29000	84	4.09000	134	6.42000	184	2.63000	234	2.00000
35	0.73000	85	2.02000	135	4.64000	185	0.57000	235	3.92000
36	3.24000	86	3.45000	136	4.82000	186	2.71000	236	3.91000
37	2.47000	87	5.32000	137	4.21000	187	1.90000	237	-0.29000
38	3.64000	88	6.01000	138	7.08000	188	2.41000	238	2.62000
39	2.87000	89	2.05000	139	6.00000	189	2.18000	239	1.60000
40	5.38000	90	1.80000	140	5.65000	190	2.96000	240	1.86000
41	-0.95000	91	3.91000	141	8.26000	191	4.78000	241	2.28000
42	0.41000	92	2.49000	142	9.55000	192	3.34000	242	3.39000
43	0.21000	93	1.48000	143	10.24000	193	1.10000	243	4.91000
44	1.82000	94	0.47000	144	10.58000	194	2.65000	244	3.89000
45	1.66000	95	3.63000	145	1.24000	195	1.72000	245	2.57000
46	2.74000	96	3.88000	146	4.90000	196	2.96000	246	5.78000
47	2.40000	97	1.97000	147	2.42000	197	0.15000	247	5.12000
48	2.17000	98	2.54000	148	2.54000	198	2.69000	248	4.98000
49	2.07000	99	3.26000	149	5.94000	199	2.69000	249	-2.19000
50	4.92000	100	5.62000	150	6.56000	200	3.50000	250	0.71000
								251	1.56000
								252	2.31000
								253	-0.04000
								254	2.44000
								255	1.79000
								256	2.64000

OBSERVED COMBINED MEANS
===============================

- -

FACTORS   1 (SEX   )

   LEVEL   1
   N =   144.

      MEANS   VOCABLRY= 2.484

   LEVEL   2
   N =   112.

      MEANS   VOCABLRY= 2.600

- -

FACTORS   3 (GRADE   )

   LEVEL   1
   N =   64.

      MEANS   VOCABLRY= 1.137

   LEVEL   2
   N =   64.

      MEANS   VOCABLRY= 2.542

   LEVEL   3
   N =   64.

      MEANS   VOCABLRY= 2.988

   LEVEL   4
   N =   64.

      MEANS   VOCABLRY= 3.472

FACTORS   1 (SEX   )   3 (GRADE   )

   LEVEL   1   1
   N =   36.

      MEANS   VOCABLRY= 1.141

   LEVEL   1   2
   N =   36.

      MEANS   VOCABLRY= 2.375

   LEVEL   1   3
   N =   36.

      MEANS   VOCABLRY= 2.880

   LEVEL   1   4
   N =   36.

      MEANS   VOCABLRY= 3.541

   LEVEL   2   1
   N =   28.

      MEANS   VOCABLRY= 1.133

   LEVEL   2   2
   N =   28.

      MEANS   VOCABLRY= 2.756

   LEVEL   2   3
   N =   28.

      MEANS   VOCABLRY= 3.127

   LEVEL   2   4
   N =   28.

      MEANS   VOCABLRY= 3.383

FIGURE 5.4-3 Problem 4: Phase I output (continued)

ESTIMATION PARAMETERS
=====================

RANK OF THE BASIS = RANK OF MODEL FOR SIGNIFICANCE TESTING =   70
RANK OF THE MODEL TO BE ESTIMATED IS   8
ERROR TERM TO BE USED IS (RESIDUAL)
NUMBER OF FACTORS WITH ORTHOGONAL POLYNOMIALS IS 1
ORTHOGONAL POLYNOMIAL CONTRASTS FOR FACTOR (GRADE   )

SYMBOLIC CONTRAST VECTORS
==========================

(1)			
(2)	D0,D0,D0,	CONSTANT	CONST
(3)	D1,D0,D0,	SEX	SEX
(4)	D0,D0,P1,	LINEAR GRADE CONTRAST	LINEAR
(5)	D0,D0,P2,	QUADRATIC GRADE CONTRAST	QUAD
(6)	D0,D0,P3,	CUBIC GRADE CONTRAST	CUBIC
(7)	D1,D0,P1,	LINEAR GRADE X SEX INTERACTION	LINSEX
(8)	D1,D0,P2,	QUADRATIC GRADE X SEX INTERACTION	QUADSX
(9)	D1,D0,P3,	CUBIC GRADE X SEX INTERACTION	CUBSEX
(10)	I1,D 1,D0,	SUBJECTS IN GROUP 1 (MALE)	SUBJS
(11)	I1,D 2,D0,	SUBJECTS IN GROUP 1 (MALE)	SUBJS
(12)	I1,D 3,D0,	SUBJECTS IN GROUP 1 (MALE)	SUBJS
(13)	I1,D 4,D0,	SUBJECTS IN GROUP 1 (MALE)	SUBJS
(14)	I1,D 5,D0,	SUBJECTS IN GROUP 1 (MALE)	SUBJS
(15)	I1,D 6,D0,	SUBJECTS IN GROUP 1 (MALE)	SUBJS
(16)	I1,D 7,D0,	SUBJECTS IN GROUP 1 (MALE)	SUBJS
(17)	I1,D 8,D0,	SUBJECTS IN GROUP 1 (MALE)	SUBJS
(18)	I1,D 9,D0,	SUBJECTS IN GROUP 1 (MALE)	SUBJS
(19)	I1,D 10,D0,	SUBJECTS IN GROUP 1 (MALE)	SUBJS
(20)	I1,D 11,D0,	SUBJECTS IN GROUP 1 (MALE)	SUBJS
(21)	I1,D 12,D0,	SUBJECTS IN GROUP 1 (MALE)	SUBJS
(22)	I1,D 13,D0,	SUBJECTS IN GROUP 1 (MALE)	SUBJS
(23)	I1,D 14,D0,	SUBJECTS IN GROUP 1 (MALE)	SUBJS
(24)	I1,D 15,D0,	SUBJECTS IN GROUP 1 (MALE)	SUBJS
(25)	I1,D 16,D0,	SUBJECTS IN GROUP 1 (MALE)	SUBJS
(26)	I1,D 17,D0,	SUBJECTS IN GROUP 1 (MALE)	SUBJS
(27)	I1,D 18,D0,	SUBJECTS IN GROUP 1 (MALE)	SUBJS
(28)	I1,D 19,D0,	SUBJECTS IN GROUP 1 (MALE)	SUBJS
(29)	I1,D 20,D0,	SUBJECTS IN GROUP 1 (MALE)	SUBJS
(30)	I1,D 21,D0,	SUBJECTS IN GROUP 1 (MALE)	SUBJS
(31)	I1,D 22,D0,	SUBJECTS IN GROUP 1 (MALE)	SUBJS
(32)	I1,D 23,D0,	SUBJECTS IN GROUP 1 (MALE)	SUBJS
(33)	I1,D 24,D0,	SUBJECTS IN GROUP 1 (MALE)	SUBJS
(34)	I1,D 25,D0,	SUBJECTS IN GROUP 1 (MALE)	SUBJS
(35)	I1,D 26,D0,	SUBJECTS IN GROUP 1 (MALE)	SUBJS
(36)	I1,D 27,D0,	SUBJECTS IN GROUP 1 (MALE)	SUBJS
(37)	I1,D 28,D0,	SUBJECTS IN GROUP 1 (MALE)	SUBJS
	I1,D 29,D0,	SUBJECTS IN GROUP 1 (MALE)	SUBJS

FIGURE 5.4-4 Problem 4: Phase II output

(39)	I1,D 30,D0,	SUBJECTS IN GROUP 1 (MALE)	SUBJS
(40)	I1,D 31,D0,	SUBJECTS IN GROUP 1 (MALE)	SUBJS
(41)	I1,D 32,D0,	SUBJECTS IN GROUP 1 (MALE)	SUBJS
(42)	I1,D 33,D0,	SUBJECTS IN GROUP 1 (MALE)	SUBJS
(43)	I1,D 34,D0,	SUBJECTS IN GROUP 1 (MALE)	SUBJS
(44)	I1,D 35,D0,	SUBJECTS IN GROUP 1 (MALE)	SUBJS
(45)	I2,D 1,D0,	SUBJECTS IN GROUP 2 (FEMALE)	SUBJS
(46)	I2,D 2,D0,	SUBJECTS IN GROUP 2 (FEMALE)	SUBJS
(47)	I2,D 3,D0,	SUBJECTS IN GROUP 2 (FEMALE)	SUBJS
(48)	I2,D 4,D0,	SUBJECTS IN GROUP 2 (FEMALE)	SUBJS
(49)	I2,D 5,D0,	SUBJECTS IN GROUP 2 (FEMALE)	SUBJS
(50)	I2,D 6,D0,	SUBJECTS IN GROUP 2 (FEMALE)	SUBJS
(51)	I2,D 7,D0,	SUBJECTS IN GROUP 2 (FEMALE)	SUBJS
(52)	I2,D 8,D0,	SUBJECTS IN GROUP 2 (FEMALE)	SUBJS
(53)	I2,D 9,D0,	SUBJECTS IN GROUP 2 (FEMALE)	SUBJS
(54)	I2,D 10,D0,	SUBJECTS IN GROUP 2 (FEMALE)	SUBJS
(55)	I2,D 11,D0,	SUBJECTS IN GROUP 2 (FEMALE)	SUBJS
(56)	I2,D 12,D0,	SUBJECTS IN GROUP 2 (FEMALE)	SUBJS
(57)	I2,D 13,D0,	SUBJECTS IN GROUP 2 (FEMALE)	SUBJS
(58)	I2,D 14,D0,	SUBJECTS IN GROUP 2 (FEMALE)	SUBJS
(59)	I2,D 15,D0,	SUBJECTS IN GROUP 2 (FEMALE)	SUBJS
(60)	I2,D 16,D0,	SUBJECTS IN GROUP 2 (FEMALE)	SUBJS
(61)	I2,D 17,D0,	SUBJECTS IN GROUP 2 (FEMALE)	SUBJS
(62)	I2,D 18,D0,	SUBJECTS IN GROUP 2 (FEMALE)	SUBJS
(63)	I2,D 19,D0,	SUBJECTS IN GROUP 2 (FEMALE)	SUBJS
(64)	I2,D 20,D0,	SUBJECTS IN GROUP 2 (FEMALE)	SUBJS
(65)	I2,D 21,D0,	SUBJECTS IN GROUP 2 (FEMALE)	SUBJS
(66)	I2,D 22,D0,	SUBJECTS IN GROUP 2 (FEMALE)	SUBJS
(67)	I2,D 23,D0,	SUBJECTS IN GROUP 2 (FEMALE)	SUBJS
(68)	I2,D 24,D0,	SUBJECTS IN GROUP 2 (FEMALE)	SUBJS
(69)	I2,D 25,D0,	SUBJECTS IN GROUP 2 (FEMALE)	SUBJS
(70)	I2,D 26,D0,	SUBJECTS IN GROUP 2 (FEMALE)	SUBJS
	I2,D 27,D0,	SUBJECTS IN GROUP 2 (FEMALE)	SUBJS

| VARIABLE | VARIANCE (ERROR MEAN SQUARES) | STANDARD DEVIATION |
| 1 VOCABLRY | 0.817981 | 0.9044 |

D.F.=   186.

ERROR TERM FOR ANALYSIS OF VARIANCE (RESIDUAL)

LEAST SQUARE ESTIMATES OF EFFECTS -- EFFECTS X VARIABLES

```
                    1
                 VOCABLRY
1   CONST        2.541915
2   SEX         -0.057817
3   LINEAR       1.657636
4   QUAD        -0.485417
5   CUBIC        0.225949
6   LINSEX       0.065316
7   QUADSX       0.198333
8   CUBSEX      -0.028244
```

FIGURE 5.4-5 Problem 4: Phase II output (continued)

ESTIMATES OF EFFECTS IN STANDARD DEVIATION UNITS-EFF X VARS
----

		1 VOCABLRY
1	CONST	2.810537
2	SEX	-0.063927
3	LINEAR	1.832811
4	QUAD	-0.536714
5	CUBIC	0.249827
6	LINSEX	0.072219
7	QUADSX	0.219293
8	CUBSEX	-0.031228

STANDARD ERRORS OF LEAST-SQUARES ESTIMATES--EFFECTS BY VARS
----

		1 VOCABLRY
1	CONST	0.056973
2	SEX	0.056973
3	LINEAR	0.113947
4	QUAD	0.113947
5	CUBIC	0.113947
6	LINSEX	0.113947
7	QUADSX	0.113947
8	CUBSEX	0.113947

LEAST-SQUARES ESTIMATES AS T-STATISTICS - EFFECTS X VARS
----

		1 VOCABLRY
1	CONST	44.61589
2	SEX	-1.01482
3	LINEAR	14.54748
4	QUAD	-4.26004
5	CUBIC	1.98294
6	LINSEX	0.57322
7	QUADSX	1.74058
8	CUBSEX	-0.24787

DEGREES OF FREEDOM =   186.

ANALYSIS OF VARIANCE

====================
====================

PAGE   7

1 DEPENDENT VARIABLE(S)

1 VOCABLRY

HYPOTHESIS   1   1 DEGREE(S) OF FREEDOM
==

PAGE   8

D0,D0,D0,   CONSTANT   CONST
- -

UNIVARIATE ANALYSIS OF VARIANCE FOR (VOCABLRY)

HYPOTHESIS MEAN SQUARE=   1644.7080   F= 2010.6917   WITH   1. AND   186. DEGREES OF FREEDOM   P LESS THAN 0.0001
. . . .

HYPOTHESIS   2   1 DEGREE(S) OF FREEDOM
==

D1,D0,D0,   SEX   SEX
- -

UNIVARIATE ANALYSIS OF VARIANCE FOR (VOCABLRY)

HYPOTHESIS MEAN SQUARE=   0.8424   F=   .0598   WITH   1. AND   62. DEGREES OF FREEDOM   P LESS THAN
. . . . (= .8424 / 14.0768) . . . .

HYPOTHESIS   3   3 DEGREE(S) OF FREEDOM
==

D0,D0,P1,   LINEAR GRADE CONTRAST   LINEAR
D0,D0,P2,   QUADRATIC GRADE CONTRAST   QUAD
D0,D0,P3,   CUBIC GRADE CONTRAST   CUBIC
- -

UNIVARIATE ANALYSIS OF VARIANCE FOR (VOCABLRY)

HYPOTHESIS MEAN SQUARE=   64.7795   F=   79.1943   WITH   3. AND   186. DEGREES OF FREEDOM   P LESS THAN 0.0001
. . . .

HYPOTHESIS   4   3 DEGREE(S) OF FREEDOM
==

D1,D0,P1,   LINEAR GRADE X SEX INTERACTION   LINSEX
D1,D0,P2,   QUADRATIC GRADE X SEX INTERACTION   QUADSX
D1,D0,P3,   CUBIC GRADE X SEX INTERACTION   CUBSEX
- -

UNIVARIATE ANALYSIS OF VARIANCE FOR (VOCABLRY)

HYPOTHESIS MEAN SQUARE=   0.9324   F=   1.1399   WITH   3. AND   186. DEGREES OF FREEDOM   P LESS THAN 0.3342
. . . .

FIGURE 5.4-6 Problem 4: Phase II output (concluded) and Phase III output

```
                       HYPOTHESIS   5      62 DEGREE(S) OF FREEDOM
                       =============================================
 I1,D  1,D0,                          SUBJECTS IN GROUP 1 (MALE)                      SUBJS
 I1,D  2,D0,                          SUBJECTS IN GROUP 1 (MALE)                      SUBJS
 I1,D  3,D0,                          SUBJECTS IN GROUP 1 (MALE)                      SUBJS
 I1,D  4,D0,                          SUBJECTS IN GROUP 1 (MALE)                      SUBJS
 I1,D  5,D0,                          SUBJECTS IN GROUP 1 (MALE)                      SUBJS
 I1,D  6,D0,                          SUBJECTS IN GROUP 1 (MALE)                      SUBJS
 I1,D  7,D0,                          SUBJECTS IN GROUP 1 (MALE)                      SUBJS
 I1,D  8,D0,                          SUBJECTS IN GROUP 1 (MALE)                      SUBJS
 I1,D  9,D0,                          SUBJECTS IN GROUP 1 (MALE)                      SUBJS
 I1,D 10,D0,                          SUBJECTS IN GROUP 1 (MALE)                      SUBJS
 I1,D 11,D0,                          SUBJECTS IN GROUP 1 (MALE)                      SUBJS
 I1,D 12,D0,                          SUBJECTS IN GROUP 1 (MALE)                      SUBJS
 I1,D 13,D0,                          SUBJECTS IN GROUP 1 (MALE)                      SUBJS
 I1,D 14,D0,                          SUBJECTS IN GROUP 1 (MALE)                      SUBJS
 I1,D 15,D0,                          SUBJECTS IN GROUP 1 (MALE)                      SUBJS
 I1,D 16,D0,                          SUBJECTS IN GROUP 1 (MALE)                      SUBJS
 I1,D 17,D0,                          SUBJECTS IN GROUP 1 (MALE)                      SUBJS
 I1,D 18,D0,                          SUBJECTS IN GROUP 1 (MALE)                      SUBJS
 I1,D 19,D0,                          SUBJECTS IN GROUP 1 (MALE)                      SUBJS
 I1,D 20,D0,                          SUBJECTS IN GROUP 1 (MALE)                      SUBJS
 I1,D 21,D0,                          SUBJECTS IN GROUP 1 (MALE)                      SUBJS
 I1,D 22,D0,                          SUBJECTS IN GROUP 1 (MALE)                      SUBJS
 I1,D 23,D0,                          SUBJECTS IN GROUP 1 (MALE)                      SUBJS
 I1,D 24,D0,                          SUBJECTS IN GROUP 1 (MALE)                      SUBJS
 I1,D 25,D0,                          SUBJECTS IN GROUP 1 (MALE)                      SUBJS
 I1,D 26,D0,                          SUBJECTS IN GROUP 1 (MALE)                      SUBJS
 I1,D 27,D0,                          SUBJECTS IN GROUP 1 (MALE)                      SUBJS
 I1,D 28,D0,                          SUBJECTS IN GROUP 1 (MALE)                      SUBJS
 I1,D 29,D0,                          SUBJECTS IN GROUP 1 (MALE)                      SUBJS
 I1,D 30,D0,                          SUBJECTS IN GROUP 1 (MALE)                      SUBJS
 I1,D 31,D0,                          SUBJECTS IN GROUP 1 (MALE)                      SUBJS
 I1,D 32,D0,                          SUBJECTS IN GROUP 1 (MALE)                      SUBJS
 I1,D 33,D0,                          SUBJECTS IN GROUP 1 (MALE)                      SUBJS
 I1,D 34,D0,                          SUBJECTS IN GROUP 1 (MALE)                      SUBJS
 I1,D 35,D0,                          SUBJECTS IN GROUP 1 (MALE)                      SUBJS
 I2,D  1,D0,                          SUBJECTS IN GROUP 2 (FEMALE)                    SUBJS
 I2,D  2,D0,                          SUBJECTS IN GROUP 2 (FEMALE)                    SUBJS
 I2,D  3,D0,                          SUBJECTS IN GROUP 2 (FEMALE)                    SUBJS
 I2,D  4,D0,                          SUBJECTS IN GROUP 2 (FEMALE)                    SUBJS
 I2,D  5,D0,                          SUBJECTS IN GROUP 2 (FEMALE)                    SUBJS
 I2,D  6,D0,                          SUBJECTS IN GROUP 2 (FEMALE)                    SUBJS
 I2,D  7,D0,                          SUBJECTS IN GROUP 2 (FEMALE)                    SUBJS
 I2,D  8,D0,                          SUBJECTS IN GROUP 2 (FEMALE)                    SUBJS
 I2,D  9,D0,                          SUBJECTS IN GROUP 2 (FEMALE)                    SUBJS
 I2,D 10,D0,                          SUBJECTS IN GROUP 2 (FEMALE)                    SUBJS
 I2,D 11,D0,                          SUBJECTS IN GROUP 2 (FEMALE)                    SUBJS
 I2,D 12,D0,                          SUBJECTS IN GROUP 2 (FEMALE)                    SUBJS
 I2,D 13,D0,                          SUBJECTS IN GROUP 2 (FEMALE)                    SUBJS
 I2,D 14,D0,                          SUBJECTS IN GROUP 2 (FEMALE)                    SUBJS
 I2,D 15,D0,                          SUBJECTS IN GROUP 2 (FEMALE)                    SUBJS
 I2,D 16,D0,                          SUBJECTS IN GROUP 2 (FEMALE)                    SUBJS
 I2,D 17,D0,                          SUBJECTS IN GROUP 2 (FEMALE)                    SUBJS
 I2,D 18,D0,                          SUBJECTS IN GROUP 2 (FEMALE)                    SUBJS
 I2,D 19,D0,                          SUBJECTS IN GROUP 2 (FEMALE)                    SUBJS
 I2,D 20,D0,                          SUBJECTS IN GROUP 2 (FEMALE)                    SUBJS
 I2,D 21,D0,                          SUBJECTS IN GROUP 2 (FEMALE)                    SUBJS
 I2,D 22,D0,                          SUBJECTS IN GROUP 2 (FEMALE)                    SUBJS
 I2,D 23,D0,                          SUBJECTS IN GROUP 2 (FEMALE)                    SUBJS
 I2,D 24,D0,                          SUBJECTS IN GROUP 2 (FEMALE)                    SUBJS
 I2,D 25,D0,                          SUBJECTS IN GROUP 2 (FEMALE)                    SUBJS
 I2,D 26,D0,                          SUBJECTS IN GROUP 2 (FEMALE)                    SUBJS
 I2,D 27,D0,                          SUBJECTS IN GROUP 2 (FEMALE)                    SUBJS
 - - - - - - - - - - - - - - - - - - - - - - - - - - - - - - - - - - - - - - - - - - -
                    UNIVARIATE ANALYSIS OF VARIANCE FOR (VOCABLRY)
 HYPOTHESIS MEAN SQUARE=      14.0768    F=    17.2092   WITH  62. AND   186. DEGREES OF FREEDOM    P LESS THAN 0.0001
```

Figure 5.4-7 Problem 4: Phase III output (continued)

interest to determine the nature of the growth curve over time than to discover that children have larger vocabularies as they mature.

The F statistic for the difference between sex groups in vocabulary scores is not correct, for the denominator is the subjects-by-grade interaction, or the 186-degree-of-freedom residual. The mean square for sex of .8424 is correct however. The mean square for subjects within sex groups, in Figure 5.4-7, is 14.0768. The ratio of these two, $F = .0598$, is the correct test statistic for the sex effect. This value does not exceed the critical F value with 1 and 62 degrees of freedom. We conclude that there is no significant difference between sex groups in mean vocabulary score.[3]

[3] Sex may be validly tested without reordering even though grade differences are significant. This is because there are equal numbers of observations at all grade levels, so that grade and sex effects are orthogonal.

Figure 5.4-8 results from the second Analysis Selection and Hypothesis Test cards. Here the first eight fixed effects are tested individually for tests of the separate polynomial trends.

While the overall test indicates that there is no interaction, the tests of the separate interaction polynomials (in Figure 5.4-8) may add some further information. Bock (1975) hypothesized a more rapid deceleration in vocabulary growth for girls than boys. There is some evidence of this in the data. Boys' scores increase about .5 points from grade 9 to 10 and .7 from 10 to 11. Girls' scores from grade 9 to 10 increase by only .4 points, and then by .3 from grade 10 to 11. While no F statistic is significant, a *one-tail* test of the sex-by-quadratic-grade interaction would exceed the .05 critical value. This trend, though weak, may be worthy of further investigation.

The three 1's on the Hypothesis Test Card corresponding to the three grade-effect codes produce the linear, quadratic, and cubic grade tests separately. The tests are read from the last toward the first—cubic effect is tested as a deviation from the linear and quadratic curves, and the quadratic effect is the deviation from a straight line connecting the means. This is, at each stage the additional complexity is tested, above and beyond differences that may be described by simpler curves.

The result for the cubic grade effect is marginal, but we may decide that it is not significant at the .05 level. ($p < .0507$ is not $p < .0500$.)

The F statistic for the quadratic grade effect of 16.60 is significant at the .01 level, with 1 and 186 degrees of freedom. Since a significant effect is obtained, testing stops at this point. Both the linear and quadratic grade effects are necessary to the model. This can be seen in Figure 5.5. The linear effect is reflected in the fact that the means increase monotonically from grade eight to grade eleven. The quadratic effect is seen in the decreasing acceleration of vocabulary scores as the children grow older. If there is no interaction, this trend is essentially the same for both sex groups.

The sum of squares for the three-degree-of-freedom age effect in the first pass with Phase III of the program is 194.3385. The mean squares for the three separate polynomials are equal to the sums of squares, since each has one degree of freedom. Summing the three mean squares, we have $177.5931 + 13.5792 + 3.1661 = 194.3385$. That is, these tests reflect an exact partition of the sum of squares for grades in a particular order. Variation has been attributed to curves of different complexity in order to decide if a subset of them explains the growth over time. In rejecting the null hypothesis for the linear effect, we conclude that the contrast given by (38) is nonzero in the population. By rejecting the null hypothesis for the quadratic effect, we conclude that a similar contrast, for the second set of weights in (37), is also nonzero.

Orthogonal polynomial weights are employed in this study because of the ordered nature of the grade effect. In other repeated-measures studies, simple differences, main effects, and interactions in the repeated measures are of interest. The form of the analysis is identical, although the specific design and contrasts may vary in complexity.

To summarize data from a study such as this, or for reporting the results, a graph like Figure 5.5 is invaluable. An accompanying table should give the means and standard deviations for both sex groups at all grade levels, as well as the intercorrelations among scores for the four grades. The analysis-of-variance results may be summarized in a table like Table 5.2; the order of elimination of effects should be indicated. However, before reporting the results, the researcher should examine the assumptions of the univariate model to decide whether a multivariate analysis, such as described in the next chapter, is necessary instead.

ANALYSIS OF VARIANCE
=====================
=====================

1 DEPENDENT VARIABLE(S)

1 VOCABLRY

HYPOTHESIS   1   1 DEGREE(S) OF FREEDOM
==

D0,D0,D0,   CONSTANT   CONST

- -

UNIVARIATE ANALYSIS OF VARIANCE FOR (VOCABLRY)

HYPOTHESIS MEAN SQUARE=   1644.7080   F=   2010.6917   WITH   1. AND   186. DEGREES OF FREEDOM   P LESS THAN 0.0001
• •

HYPOTHESIS   2   1 DEGREE(S) OF FREEDOM
==

D1,D0,D0,   SEX   SEX

- -

UNIVARIATE ANALYSIS OF VARIANCE FOR (VOCABLRY)

HYPOTHESIS MEAN SQUARE=   0.8424   F=   1.0299   WITH   1. AND   186. DEGREES OF FREEDOM   P LESS THAN 0.3114
• •

HYPOTHESIS   3   1 DEGREE(S) OF FREEDOM
==

D0,D0,P1,   LINEAR GRADE CONTRAST   LINEAR

- -

UNIVARIATE ANALYSIS OF VARIANCE FOR (VOCABLRY)

HYPOTHESIS MEAN SQUARE=   177.5931   F=   217.1115   WITH   1. AND   186. DEGREES OF FREEDOM   P LESS THAN 0.0001
• •

HYPOTHESIS   4   1 DEGREE(S) OF FREEDOM
==

D0,D0,P2,   QUADRATIC GRADE CONTRAST   QUAD

- -

UNIVARIATE ANALYSIS OF VARIANCE FOR (VOCABLRY)

HYPOTHESIS MEAN SQUARE=   13.5792   F=   16.6009   WITH   1. AND   186. DEGREES OF FREEDOM   P LESS THAN 0.0001
• •

HYPOTHESIS   5   1 DEGREE(S) OF FREEDOM
==

D0,D0,P3,   CUBIC GRADE CONTRAST   CUBIC

- -

UNIVARIATE ANALYSIS OF VARIANCE FOR (VOCABLRY)

HYPOTHESIS MEAN SQUARE=   3.1661   F=   3.8706   WITH   1. AND   186. DEGREES OF FREEDOM   P LESS THAN 0.0507
• •

HYPOTHESIS   6   1 DEGREE(S) OF FREEDOM
==

D1,D0,P1,   LINEAR GRADE X SEX INTERACTION   LINSEX

- -

UNIVARIATE ANALYSIS OF VARIANCE FOR (VOCABLRY)

HYPOTHESIS MEAN SQUARE=   0.2688   F=   0.3286   WITH   1. AND   186. DEGREES OF FREEDOM   P LESS THAN 0.5673
• •

HYPOTHESIS   7   1 DEGREE(S) OF FREEDOM
==

D1,D0,P2,   QUADRATIC GRADE X SEX INTERACTION QUADSX

- -

UNIVARIATE ANALYSIS OF VARIANCE FOR (VOCABLRY)

HYPOTHESIS MEAN SQUARE=   2.4782   F=   3.0296   WITH   1. AND   186. DEGREES OF FREEDOM   P LESS THAN 0.0834
• •

HYPOTHESIS   8   1 DEGREE(S) OF FREEDOM
==

D1,D0,P3,   CUBIC GRADE X SEX INTERACTION   CUBSEX

- -

UNIVARIATE ANALYSIS OF VARIANCE FOR (VOCABLRY)

HYPOTHESIS MEAN SQUARE=   0.0503   F=   0.0614   WITH   1. AND   186. DEGREES OF FREEDOM   P LESS THAN 0.8046
• •

CORE USED FOR DATA= 2147 LOCATIONS OUT OF 3072 AVAILABLE

Figure 5.4-8 Problem 4: Phase III output (concluded)

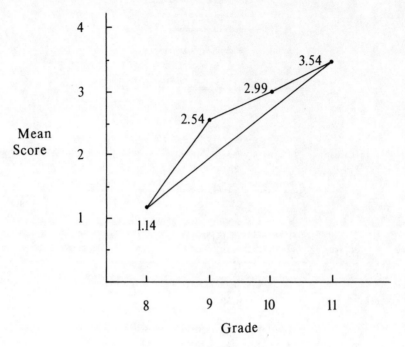

FIGURE 5.5   Average Vocabulary Growth

Table 5.2   Univariate Analysis of Variance for Sex × Grade Longitudinal Study

Source of Variation	Degrees of Freedom	Mean Square	F	Error Term
Fixed effects:				
Constant	1	—	—	—
Sex, eliminating constant	1	.842	.06	MS_S
Grade, eliminating constant and sex	3	64.780	**79.19	MS_R
Linear	1	177.593	**217.11	MS_R
Quadratic	1	13.579	**16.60	MS_R
Cubic	1	3.166	3.87	MS_R
Sex × grade, eliminating constant, sex, and grade	3	.932	1.14	MS_R
Random effects:				
Subjects in sex groups, eliminating fixed effects	62	$MS_S = 14.077$		
Residual, eliminating all else	186	$MS_R = .818$		
Total	256			

**$p < .01$

6

GROWTH IN VOCABULARY:
MULTIVARIATE ANALYSIS OF REPEATED MEASURES DATA

In education, repeated measures data typically arise from longitudinal studies and pretest-posttest experiments. In psychological and medical research, they arise when the same individuals are measured with various drugs, or under different experimental conditions, or at different times. All of these data have a common characteristic: differences among the *measures* (that is, among the outcomes for different times or conditions) are themselves of scientific interest.

Following Lindquist (1953), psychologists have frequently employed "within-and-between-subject" analyses for repeated measures data by treating the measures as a classification factor in the analysis-of-variance design. Subject differences are treated as random effects nested within experimental or naturally occurring groups and crossed with the measures (within-subject) factors. Chapter 5 presented an example of this type of analysis based on a longitudinal study of vocabulary growth. There were two groups of subjects, male and female, and the measures of vocabulary were taken at four points in time corresponding to grade levels eight, nine, ten, and eleven.

Two properties of the vocabulary study should be noted. First, both the classification of subjects and the repeated measures dimension (grade level) are natural and are not experimentally manipulated. Thus, we were not able to infer that "boyness" or "girlness" or age *caused* the vocabulary score to attain a certain level. We *are* able to say, however, that there are significant differences in mean vocabulary knowledge for pupils at different age levels, but not for pupils of different sex groups, since sex differences were not significant. This information is of interest in itself. In addition, we were able to determine that growth in vocabulary scores follows a quadratic curve, as depicted in Figure 5.5.

Second, the classification of subjects (i.e., sex) and of measures (i.e., time) both have a simple structure; sex has only two levels, and the measures differ only on a single dimension. In some studies, both dimensions may have more factors and/or levels. For example, in three different schools we might measure the amount of time each student spends in independent study both in and out of school when he has a male teacher, and again with a female teacher. In that case the between-groups dimension would have three levels, while the within-subject dimension would have two factors, each with two levels. The analysis of these more complicated designs is essentially the same as presented for the vocabulary study. The coded effects for both dimensions would become more complex, reflecting the three levels of grade, the 2×2 crossed nature of the within-subject factors, as well as the interaction of within- and between-subject dimensions.

6.1 MULTIVARIATE APPROACH

In contrast to the univariate analysis, the multivariate analysis of repeated measures data begins with different assumptions about the outcome measures and imposes different requirements. The basic principle is that the multiple measures are not considered as a factor in the sampling design, but as multiple, intercorrelated responses from the same subjects. In the longitudinal vocabulary study, for example, the 36 male and 28 female subjects were measured on a scaled vocabulary score at four successive time points. From the multivariate point of view, there is a total of 64 observations, each having *four dependent variables*. These outcomes are four random variables, and may have *any* arbitrary pattern of intercorrelations and *any* variances. This is the typical case in multivariate models.

In an experimental study, on the other hand, where each subject is administered two drugs, each at two dosage levels, we may still assume that each subject has four intercorrelated outcome measures, namely, his response measures for drug 1 dosage 1, drug 1 dosage 2, drug 2 dosage 1, and drug 2 dosage 2.[1] The subjects may be further classified into groups according to, say, the severity of the disease. Still, each subject in each severity group is considered to have four intercorrelated outcome scores.

The classification of subjects (between-subject dimensions), or the dimension which distinguishes one measure from another (within-subject dimensions), may be still more complex. But common to all these designs is the interest in not only comparing one group of subjects with another, but also one measure with another. Thus, when the measures are treated as multiple dependent variables, some of the effects of interest reside in differences among the outcome variables.

6.1.1 The Vocabulary Growth Study

In the vocabulary study each subject had four response measures, viz., a score at each grade level. The purpose of the study was to determine differences, or trends, across the growth measures or, multivariate-wise, across the dependent variables. Similarly, in a drug study in which two drugs are administered to each patient at each of two dosage levels, interest is in the different response levels between drugs, the difference between dosages, and the interaction of the two.[2] Again, from a multivariate point of view, these are differences among the dependent variables.

For this reason, we say that repeated measures data have a *design on the dependent variables*. Conversely, the factors which distinguish one unique group of subjects from other groups constitute the *sampling design*.

For the multivariate analysis of repeated measures, the basic problem definition is set up only for the sampling design. That is, the design is treated as a crossed or nested arrangement, depending only on the nature of the classification of populations sampled. In the vocabulary study, the sampling design has only one factor, sex, with two levels. In the drug study, the design again has only one factor, severity, with two (or more) levels.

All responses of each subject in each group are then treated as multiple variables. Tests of the differences among dependent variables are conducted by transforming the original variables into contrasts of interest. For example, in the longitudinal vocabulary study, we wish to test three fixed effects, viz., sex, grade, and sex-by-grade interaction. The problem is set up as a one-way design with two levels in which each subject has four scores. To test the overall sex effect, we may create a new score as the sum of the four time measures for each student. Let the original four measures be represented by y_1 through y_4, where

$$y_1 = \text{Grade eight vocabulary score}$$

$$y_2 = \text{Grade nine vocabulary score}$$

---

[1] Or in the study-time research, there may be measures of study time in school or out, when the student has a male or female teacher, etc.

[2] Or in the study-time research, interest is in time differences between locations (in school-out), between teacher-sex responses, and the interaction of location and teacher-sex.

y_3 = Grade ten vocabulary score

y_4 = Grade eleven vocabulary score

Then we may create a new score, y_1^*, by (39a).

$$y_1^* = y_1 + y_2 + y_3 + y_4 \tag{39a}$$

It is then a simple matter to conduct a test of differences between sex-group means on variable y_1^*.

In testing grade differences, we are interested in three orthogonal contrasts across grade levels. These contrasts are given by equations (37) and (38) in Chapter 5. We may use the three sets of weights to form three contrasts among the time means; i.e., we create three new dependent variables, y_2^*, y_3^*, and y_4^*. These are:

$$y_2^* = -3y_1 - y_2 + y_3 + 3y_4 \tag{39b}$$

$$y_3^* = y_1 - y_2 - y_3 + y_4 \tag{39c}$$

$$y_4^* = -y_1 + 3y_2 - 3y_3 + y_4 \tag{39d}$$

Thus, means of all subjects on y_2^* will be significantly different from zero if there is a linear trend across grade levels. The mean of all subjects on y_3^* will be significantly different from zero if there is a quadratic trend in the data. The mean of all subjects on y_4^* will be significantly different from zero if there is a cubic trend in vocabulary growth over grade levels.

The MULTIVARIANCE program may be used to test these effects as follows: the design is described as a one-factor, two-level problem (males and females). Each subject has four input scores, y_1 through y_4. These measures are transformed to the new variables, y_1^* through y_4^*, at the input phase. The sources of variation and degrees of freedom are listed in Table 6.1. There is only a constant term $\underset{\sim}{\mu}$ and an $\underset{\sim}{\alpha}$ term for sex in the model.

Table 6.1   Effect Table for Multivariate Analysis of the Transformed Growth Data

Source of Variation	d.f.	Symbolic Code	Effects y_1^*	y_2^*	y_3^*	y_4^*
Constant	1	D0,	Grand Mean	Grade		
$\underset{\sim}{\mu}$				Linear	Quadratic	Cubic
Sex	1	D1,	Sex	Sex × Grade		
$\underset{\sim}{\alpha}$				Linear	Quadratic	Cubic
Among means	2					
Within groups	$N-2$		Subjects	Subject × Grade		
				Linear	Quadratic	Cubic
Total	N					

Using the usual MULTIVARIANCE coding, the symbolic code D0 refers to the constant term and the code D1 to sex. Each term accounts for one degree of freedom.

Let us consider the three major hypotheses. The hypothesis about sex differences is:

$$H_0(1): \quad [\mu_{y_1^*}]_{\text{MALE}} = [\mu_{y_1^*}]_{\text{FEMALE}} \tag{40}$$

This is a hypothesis that the means for the two sex groups are equal on the total of all time measures. Thus, we run the MULTIVARIANCE program and select just y_1^* as the criterion variable. The mean square for the sex difference on y_1^* will be divided by mean square within groups on y_1^* to obtain a correct test statistic.

We note that the mean square within groups on y_1^* is the variance of subjects' scores, within sex groups, on total vocabulary. In univariate terminology, this is exactly the subjects-within-sex-groups variance. Therefore, by selecting y_1^* as the dependent variable, we obtain exactly the correct univariate F ratio for sex in (35a).

The hypothesis of no time effect may be represented as in (41).

$$H_0(2): \quad \begin{bmatrix} \mu_{y_2^*} \\ \mu_{y_3^*} \\ \mu_{y_4^*} \end{bmatrix} = \begin{bmatrix} 0 \\ 0 \\ 0 \end{bmatrix} \tag{41}$$

This asserts that the means for all subjects for the three time differences are simultaneously zero. Returning to Table 6.1, we see how a test of this hypothesis may be obtained. Variables y_2^*, y_3^*, and y_4^* are selected as simultaneous criterion measures. In this case, a test is obtained of the constant term as well as of the sex effect. The first of these, the multivariate test of the constant term, is exactly the test we require. Furthermore, the MULTIVARIANCE program provides a univariate test statistic for each of the separate criterion measures. It yields an F statistic for the linear effect, one for the quadratic effect, and another for the cubic effect.

Consider the error term for this test. We have designated the design as a one-factor, two-level design, and replications within groups are used as the source of error variation. Variation among subjects within sex groups on y_2^*, y_3^*, and y_4^* is computed, as well as covariation among these measures. Variation among subjects on y_2^* alone is exactly the interaction of subjects and the linear age effect from the univariate analysis. Likewise, variation among subjects on criterion measures y_3^* and y_4^* provides the mean squares for subjects-by-quadratic grade effects and subjects-by-cubic grade, respectively. That is, each univariate F statistic is computed with exactly the correct numerator and denominator mean squares from the univariate analysis.

It is likely, however, that scores on y_2^*, y_3^*, and y_4^* are intercorrelated. The original y measures are intercorrelated, as are the linear combinations of them. This means that the univariate test statistics that are provided here or in the univariate mixed-model analysis (Chapter 5) are not independent of one another. Thus, the multivariate test statistic is the only valid measure of overall differences among age levels.

The *step-down* results may be inspected for y_2^*, y_3^*, and y_4^* separately. These provide tests of the linear effect, the quadratic effect eliminating the linear effect, and of the cubic effect, eliminating both the linear and quadratic effects. The step-down results, like the overall test statistic, are valid under general multivariate assumptions. They may be used to decide whether a simple or complex model describes variation among grade-level means.

The third hypothesis of concern is that for interaction represented in (42).

$$H_0(3): \begin{bmatrix} \mu_{y_2^*} \\ \mu_{y_3^*} \\ \mu_{y_4^*} \end{bmatrix}_{MALE} = \begin{bmatrix} \mu_{y_2^*} \\ \mu_{y_3^*} \\ \mu_{y_4^*} \end{bmatrix}_{FEMALE} \qquad (42)$$

The hypothesis asserts that the differences across grade levels are equal for the two sex groups. This is identical with the hypothesis of interaction in the univariate model. In the multivariate approach, the test of $H_0(3)$ is obtained at the same time as the test of $H_0(2)$. The results for D1, or sex differences, with y_2^* through y_4^* as dependent variables, yield the correct statistics.

The multivariate test of sex differences on the three time effects is a valid test of the sex-by-grade interaction. The univariate tests for the separate measures y_2^* through y_4^* yield information about the linear, quadratic, and cubic interaction, respectively, but are not independent. In their place, the step-down statistics should be used to test the degree of the curve describing the sex differences.

As is the case for the grade-level differences, the sex-by-grade interaction test is made with the correct error term. Variation within sex groups on the three difference scores are identical with subjects-by-linear, subject-by-quadratic, and subjects-by-cubic time effects from the univariate analysis. In addition, however, the multivariate analysis incorporates the covariances of the effects, which may be nonzero and must be included in test criteria.

To summarize then, the multivariate analysis of repeated measures separates sampling factors in the design from sampling factors which distinguish one measure from another and define a *design on the dependent variables*. Phase II of the MULTIVARIANCE program is set up only for the sampling factors, while the outcome measures for each subject appear as multiple criterion variables. These variables are transformed to new measures reflecting the research hypotheses. In this study, the new measures consist of a total score for testing sex-group differences and polynomial growth scores for testing grade differences and interactions of sex and grade.

For each transformed variable, variation among subjects within groups is computed by the program. For the total score, variation among subjects in sex groups is just "subjects" variation. For the scores that are differences among the original measures, variation within groups consists of subjects-by-measures interactions. Because variation across subjects within groups is computed for each of the transformed variables, the correct error mean square is *always* employed in tests of the main effects and interactions. In the multivariate analysis, it is neither necessary to write the expected mean squares to determine which error terms we used for which effect, nor is it necessary to have multiple computer runs or perform hand computations in order to obtain all of the correct results.

In addition to the univariate test statistics, the multivariate and step-down test criteria provide valid tests of overall mean differences and particular effects in the data, respectively. Because these statistics do not require that the transformed variables be uncorrelated with one another, the original measures may have any intercorrelations and variances.

Tests of significance are conducted by selectively choosing transformed measures in the analysis phase of the program and testing the appropriate between-group effects. Unlike most models where the constant term across groups is not of particular interest, in repeated measures analyses we often test the overall mean of differences among the criterion variables. This usually provides tests of the within-subjects main effects. Once the variables and hypotheses are indicated in the Phase III control cards, the appropriate error terms for the analysis-of-variance tests always follow.

6.1.2 A Hypothetical Example

Let us consider an additional hypothetical example. Assume that we have randomly sampled three groups of students from grades four, five, and six. Assume that we measure the amount of independent study time (in hours) spent by each child over some fixed period of weeks. Study time may be measured both in school and out of school, and we may be interested in comparing the average in- and out-of-school time. Furthermore, let us arrange to have each student taught by both a male teacher and a female teacher, with half of the sample taught by a male teacher in the first half of the term, and by a female teacher in the second half term; let the other half of the students be taught by male and female teachers in first and second half terms, but in the reverse order. Our hypotheses concern the differences in study time across grade levels in response to the teacher's sex, and differences between in-school and out-of-school study time. Also there may be interactions of the fixed effects—for example, male teachers may encourage more out-of-school study than female teachers.

The design may be diagrammed as in Figure 6.1. Each student at each grade level has four measures—study time in school and out of school, with a male and female teacher. We would set up the MULTIVARIANCE program by indicating a one-way three-group design, with four measures for each pupil (i.e., four dependent variables). In order to test main effects and interactions of the within-subject factors (teacher's sex, in-school-out), we form four new variables from the original four measures. They are:

$$y_1^* = y_{11} + y_{12} + y_{21} + y_{22}$$

$$y_2^* = \frac{y_{11} + y_{12}}{2} - y_{..}$$

$$y_3^* = \frac{y_{11} + y_{21}}{2} - y_{..}$$

$$y_4^* = (y_{11} - y_{12}) - (y_{21} - y_{22}) \tag{43}$$

The first new variable y_1^*, which is the sum of the four response measures, allows us to test mean differences among the three grade levels on total study time.

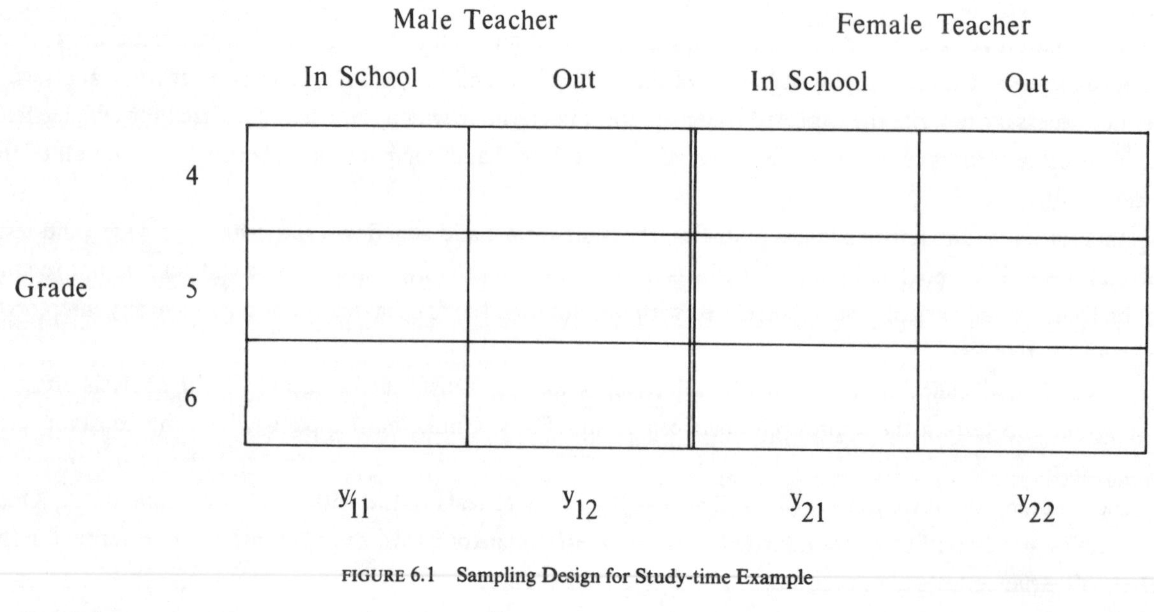

FIGURE 6.1   Sampling Design for Study-time Example

The second new variable y_2^* is the difference between the mean of the two scores that the subject obtains with the male teacher and the mean of all four scores $(y_{..})$. A test that the grand mean of y_2^* is zero is equivalent to testing the teacher sex effect. The test of differences on y_2^* across three grade levels is precisely the test of the teacher-sex-by-grade interaction.

The third new variable y_3^* is the average of each subject's study time in school, minus the average of all of his study time. Testing that the grand mean of y_3^* equals zero is equivalent to testing that the mean study times in and out of school are equal. Testing mean differences among grade levels on y_3^* is identical to testing the interaction of grade and in-school-out-of-school differences.

The final variable y_4^* constructed from original measures is an interaction variable of teacher sex and in school-out of school. This interaction is the difference between the in-school and out-of-school discrepancies for the two teacher sexes. If the amount by which study time in school exceeds study time out of school is the same for both teacher sexes, we say that the interaction is zero. Testing that the population mean for all subjects on y_4^* equals zero is the test of interaction between teacher sex and in-and-out-of-school study time. Thus, the test of grade differences on y_4^* is a test of the three-way interaction of grade, teacher sex, and in-school-out-of-school study time.

It is likely that the new variables y_1^* through y_4^* will have nonzero intercorrelations. This is true because the original outcomes y_{11}, y_{12}, y_{21}, and y_{22} are all correlated, as is typical of scores from the same individuals. Intercorrelations of the y^* variables will also be nonzero if the assumptions for a mixed model analysis do not hold. It is for this reason that multivariate test criteria, which allow for arbitrary intercorrelations of the dependent variables, must in general be employed in this type of study.

The tests of significance require two Phase III steps of the program. In the first step, variables y_2^*, y_3^*, and y_4^* are selected for analysis. The grand mean across all grades is tested (D0,). The first step-down F ratio (for variable y_2^*) will indicate whether there is a significant difference in means for the two teacher sexes. The second step-down test statistic (for y_3^*) will indicate whether there are any in-school-out-of-school differences, eliminating teacher sex. The final step-down test statistic (for y_4^*) will indicate whether there is any interaction of teacher sex and in-school-out-of-school differences, eliminating both main effects.

As a second analysis, all four variables y_1^* through y_4^* are selected in order to test the differences (D1, and D2,).[3] Again the step-down statistics yield the valid results: the first statistic (for y_1^*) indicates whether there is any significant difference among grade levels in total study time; the second step-down F statistic (for y_2^*) indicates whether there is any grade-by-teacher-sex interaction, eliminating the grade main effect; the third step-down F statistic (for y_3^*) indicates whether there is any grade by in-school-out-of-school interaction, eliminating grade and grade-by-teacher-sex; the final step-down statistic (for y_4^*) indicates whether there is any three-way grade by teacher-sex by in-school-out-of-school interaction, eliminating all other effects. The step-down results allow for the intercorrelations of the various outcomes.

The new variables that are formed in this analysis correspond to the main effects and interaction of teacher sex in-school-out-of-school. If we had coded these effects using MULTIVARIANCE coding conventions, we might treat teacher sex as the first factor, and in-school vs. out-of-school as the second factor for the *design on the dependent variables*. Then the symbolic contrast codes that represent the linear combinations of the means y_1^* through y_4^* are given in Table 6.2. y_1^*, or the grand mean, would be coded D0,D0,. y_2^* is coded D1,D0, for the teacher-sex effect, and so on. The MULTIVARIANCE program allows the user to write these codes for the within-subject factors and not to involve himself with the actual construction of the weight vectors or transformations of (43).

---

[3] The Hypothesis Test Card may read "-1,2." The "-1" indicates that the constant is not to be tested. The "2" indicates the simultaneous test of the two degrees grades of freedom.

108

Table 6.2   Symbolic Effect Codes for the Hypothetical Study-Time Example

Variable	Symbolic Code	Effect
y_1^*	D0,D0,	Constant
y_2^*	D1,D0,	Teacher sex
y_3^*	D0,D1,	In-school, out-of-school
y_4^*	D1,D1,	Sex $\times$ in-school, out-of-school

6.2   TRANSFORMING THE DATA

There are three ways in which MULTIVARIANCE allows the input variables to be transformed for repeated-measures analysis. The first occurs external to the program. The transformed scores may be computed ahead of time and punched on the cards, or prepared on a separate data file by an external program such as SPSS (see Mattsson, 1975). The transformed variables are then read as raw data. At the same time, the untransformed variables may also be input to the program so that means and summary statistics may be obtained for the individual measures if required.

The transformed variables may also be obtained by means of general data transformations. These are presented in the MULTIVARIANCE *User's Guide* on pages 39 to 41. While these transformations allow the greatest versatility in altering the original scores, a long list of transformations may be necessary to create the new scores for repeated-measures analysis. These transformations operate on the scores for each subject as they are entered into the program. Since the transformations necessary for the repeated-measures analysis are linear, this procedure is inefficient. The mean and variance-covariance matrix computed from the original measures may be transformed instead, reducing the number of operations considerably.

An efficient way to transform the data is through a linear "transformation matrix," as described on pages 49-52 of the *User's Guide*. Each *row* of the transformation matrix defines one new variable, and the transformation matrix may have any number of rows; i.e., any number of linear transformations may be constructed from the original input data. If the transformation matrix results in more variables than originally read by the program, or fewer, the resulting number must be punched in columns 29-32 of the Input Description card. The variable labels that are entered in the problem run are applied to the transformed variables, not to those read from the original data cards.

Let us construct a transformation matrix for the four-grade-level longitudinal study. We wish to create the variables defined by (39a) through (39d). Since the transformation matrix works by replacement—i.e., the transformed variables replace the original set—we should also create four variables that are identically the four individual time-point scores. That is, by retaining the original measures y_1 through y_4 in the data set, we shall be able to obtain means and standard deviations on these variables as well as their intercorrelations.[4] We would indicate to the program that there are to be eight variables after the transformation matrix is applied (punch "8" in column 32 of Input Description card). Of these, the first four will be the original y scores and variables five through eight will be transformed y^* measures.

To maintain the original four scores, we construct the first rows of the transformed matrix from the numbers 1 and 0. For example, the row (1 0 0 0) defines the transformation $y_1^* = 1y_1 + 0y_2 + 0y_3 + 0y_4$. This is the first row of the array in (44).

[4]Alternatively, the summary data for the original four measures could be obtained in a separate computer run in which the scores are not transformed.

$$
\begin{array}{c}
1. \\
2. \\
3. \\
4. \\
5. \\
6. \\
7. \\
8.
\end{array}
\begin{bmatrix}
1 & 0 & 0 & 0 \\
0 & 1 & 0 & 0 \\
0 & 0 & 1 & 0 \\
0 & 0 & 0 & 1 \\
1 & 1 & 1 & 1 \\
-3 & -1 & 1 & 3 \\
1 & -1 & -1 & 1 \\
-1 & 3 & -3 & 1
\end{bmatrix}
\begin{array}{c}
y_1 \\
y_2 \\
y_3 \\
y_4 \\
y_1^* \\
y_2^* \\
y_3^* \\
y_4^*
\end{array}
\qquad (44)
$$

To create a second variable that is identically the grade nine (y_2) score, we add a row to the transformation matrix which has "1" in the y_2 position and zeros elsewhere. Likewise rows three and four are added to the transformation matrix to maintain scores y_3 and y_4 among those of the transformed set.

To obtain the sum of the four y scores, or y_1^*, we add row five to the transformation matrix which has "1" in all positions. This defines the linear combination $y_1^* = 1y_1 + 1y_2 + 1y_3 + 1y_4$. To create y_2^* we enter the linear orthogonal polynomial weights as an additional row in the matrix; this defines the combination $y_2^* = -3y_1 - 1y_2 + 1y_3 + 3y_4$. Similarly, the quadratic and cubic polynomial weights are added as the final rows of the transformation matrix, to create variables y_3^* and y_4^*, respectively.

Once means, variances, and covariances of the original four variables are computed, the transformation matrix is applied to obtain the means, variances, and covariances of the new variables. The means and variances that are printed in Phase I of the program will be the results for all eight of the transformed variables.

When there is a design on the dependent variables, it is not necessary to write the weights for the transformation matrix for the repeated-measures analysis. The program allows the transformation matrix to be generated automatically from the same symbolic effect codes as used for the sampling design. This permits the design on the dependent variables to be expressed in terms of effects and degrees of freedom in exactly the same way as the between-subjects effects.

The matrix of weights in (44), for example, may be constructed as follows: to indicate that a transformation matrix is to be generated from Symbolic Contrast Vectors, the number "2" is entered in column 28 of the Input Description card. At the point in the data deck where the transformation matrix would be entered, a card is inserted with the number of factors (1) in the design on the dependent variables; a second card follows naming the factor (Grade) and giving the number of levels (4). Then the eight symbolic effect codes are inserted, each on a separate card.

For example, the code for the first four rows of the matrix are I1, I2, I3, and I4,. I1, indicates the first row of an identity matrix, or that the effects to be estimated should be restricted to only the first variable. Similarly, I2, I3, and I4, represent the second, third, and fourth rows of an identity matrix, respectively.

To generate the four sets of weights for the y^* variables, exactly the same symbolic codes are used as in the univariate analysis of Chapter 5. These are P0, for the constant term, and P1, P2, and P3, for the linear, quadratic, and cubic effects, respectively. Punching each of these codes on a separate card is sufficient to cause the program to generate the matrix given by (44). (Although in this case, the program must also be told that orthogonal weights are to be employed.)

In the study-time example, there are two within-subject factors, and the transformations to be made are somewhat more complex. But if we again adopt the conventions that we use for coding the design factors, all is simple. We may create the four transformed variables of (43) as follows. We first enter a card giving the number of factors in the design on the dependent variables (2); we enter second a card which names the factors (Teacher-sex and In-out) and gives the levels of each (2 and 2). The transformed variables y_1^* through y_4^* are constructed by inserting the symbolic codes listed in Table 6.2. This causes the computer to generate rows of the transformation matrix so that the constant, teacher-sex, in-school-out, and interaction effects may be tested.

If we wish also to maintain the original four measures in the study-time example, the one-zero rows for the transformation matrix are generated by the codes:

$$\begin{array}{ll} \text{I1,I1,} & y_1 \\ \text{I1,I2,} & y_2 \\ \text{I2,I1,} & y_3 \\ \text{I2,I2,} & y_4 \end{array}$$

In every case, it is necessary that the researcher note the order in which he has generated the transformed variables so that he may correctly select them for tests of significance. In the matrix given by (44), for example, the resulting variables within the computer run are numbered 1 through 8, with variables 1 through 4 the original measures and 5 through 8 the transformed measures. Note that there is no particular order in which these variables need to be constructed.

o.3 EXTRACTING THE UNIVARIATE RESULTS

Any univariate results obtained in the course of the multivariate run (for example, the sex effect in the longitudinal study) will agree with those from the univariate mixed-model analysis. The step-down tests and the joint multivariate tests, however, will generally differ from the results of the univariate analysis.

It is always possible, however, to retrieve the complete univariate mixed-model analysis from the multivariate printout. This is desirable when the assumptions of the mixed-model analysis are met. Because the multivariate analysis requires less core and takes less computer time than the univariate analysis, it is best to use the former even when the univariate results are required. The multivariate analysis requires only that the means of the groups, rather than the scores of individual subjects, be stored, usually with a great saving in core memory.

The condition necessary for retrieving the univariate mixed-model results from the multivariate problem run is that the matrix of weights for the transformed variables be *orthonormal*. This property of the matrix does not affect any of the test statistics, but enables us to reproduce exactly the univariate mean squares.[5] The MULTIVARIANCE program has an option to orthonormalize automatically the rows of the transformation matrix. If we wish to obtain the univariate mean squares in the multivariate run, we need only punch "3" in column 28 of the Input Description card. The additional requirement is that the rows of the matrix for the transformed variables have as many leading rows as the original number of input variables.

To reproduce the univariate results for the longitudinal vocabulary growth study, for example, we would interchange rows 5 through 8 with rows 1 through 4 of the transformation matrix (44). This may be done by inserting the symbolic codes, P0, through P3, ahead of those for I1, through I4,. Since there are originally four variables read from the data cards, the leading four rows of the matrix will be orthonormalized when option "3" is coded. We are then able to average the mean squares for the linear, quadratic, and cubic effects to obtain the mean square for "grades" in the univariate analysis. We may also average the mean squares within groups for these variables to obtain the mean square for subjects-by-grades. The ratio of these two averages is the univariate mixed-model F statistic given by (35b). We must, however, remember that these are valid estimates of the variances only if the transformed measures are uncorrelated, i.e., if the mixed-model assumptions are met.

In the example, it is not necessary to orthonormalize the transformation matrix and thus not necessary that the transformed variables appear first. The univariate mixed-model results are obtainable from the multivariate run, nevertheless, because orthogonal polynomials, unlike other effects that may be defined, are always

---

[5] Since the test statistics remain unchanged, a mathematical description of "orthonormal" is irrelevant to most researchers.

generated by the program as an orthonormal matrix. The fact that they are placed last in (44) does not alter this property.

It is also *not necessary* to orthonormalize the transformation matrix in order to conduct the *multivariate* analysis of the repeated-measures data. The weight vectors that we have already defined, although not having the property of orthonormality, are easier to understand and give valid test statistics under the nonrestrictive multivariate model.

6.4 ASSUMPTIONS OF THE MULTIVARIATE MODEL

In the univariate mixed-model analysis, the repeated-measures dimensions are treated as additional design factors. This is valid only if, first, the variances of the measures at each time point, or under each experimental condition, are homogeneous and, second, if the correlations between measures at different time points, or under different experimental conditions, are equal. These assumptions are stated algebraically in (36a) and (36b).

In the multivariate analysis, on the other hand, the separate measures are considered as multiple criterion variables, and they may have unequal variances and a general pattern of covariances or correlations. The variances of the measures at different times or under different experimental conditions are estimated from the data and utilized in the analysis. Similarly, the pattern of correlations is estimated from the data and incorporated in computing the multivariate test statistics.

Because the variances of the original measures may differ, and the correlations may not all be equal, the transformed variables are, in general, intercorrelated even when the transformations are orthogonal (e.g., orthogonal polynomials). The presence of nonzero correlations among the transformed variables indicates that the mixed-model assumptions are not met, and that it will be necessary to use multivariate test criteria (the general F test or the step-down results) to test for the main effects and interactions of within-subjects factors.

The multivariate approach to the analysis of repeated-measures data is not only less restrictive, but usually more realistic. Especially in longitudinal data, we expect that the correlations will not be uniform. A clear example is given in Finn (1969) where boys and girls were each measured on "standing height" at three days of age, one year, two years, three years, four years, and five years of age. (The three-days measure was "recumbent length".) The correlations between each height measure and the five-year measure are .30, .66, .75, .80, and .89, respectively. As might be expected, close time points have high correlations while those more distant have lower correlations. Further, the standard deviations of the height measure increase monotonically from birth to age five, with the last time point having more than double the standard deviation of the first time point.

In experimental data, there is often no reason to assume that the correlations among the observations will have any simple pattern. In ambiguous cases a test of significance can be applied to the correlation matrix to see if the pattern of compound symmetry can be assumed in the population. The test is given in Harris (1963). If the pattern can be assumed, the univariate solution should be used. Otherwise, the multivariate solution is necessary.

6.5 THE MULTIVARIANCE RUN OF THE VOCABULARY DATA

6.5.1 Format of the Data

The data deck for the multivariate analysis of the vocabulary scores is listed in Figure 6.2. There are 64 data cards in all, one for each subject of the study. Each data card is punched according to the following format:

Columns	Variables
1	Sex, 1 = male, 2 = female
2-3	Subject number
6-10	Scaled vocabulary score grade eight
11-15	Scaled vocabulary score grade nine
16-20	Scaled vocabulary score grade ten
21-25	Scaled vocabulary score grade eleven

The only identification number on these cards is the sex code in column 1. The subject number is not used in the analysis. Unlike the data deck for the univariate run, there is no grade-level code on the cards, because the scores for all four grade levels for each subject are punched following one another. Each is in F5.2 format.

6.5.2 MULTIVARIANCE Setup

The input for the MULTIVARIANCE run, exclusive of the data, is listed in Figure 6.3. The cards for Phase I are somewhat more complex than for the other problem runs. The raw data are read in, classified only by the small number of levels of the sampling factor, but must be transformed to the mean differences necessary for testing the within-subjects effects.

Following the two Title cards, the Input Description card indicates that there are four variables. These are the original four repeated measurements for each subject. There is one factor in the sampling design, viz., sex. Data Form 1 can be used since there is a sex code (1 or 2) in the leading columns of each data card. Since the program will count the cards and place them in the appropriate sex group, they need not be sorted beforehand. There is one Variable Format card.

The information in columns 28 to 32 of the Input Description card pertains to the transformation of the four input variables into eight new variables. The new variables are defined by eight linear combinations of the original measures, given by the rows of the matrix in (44). The first four linear functions maintain the original four y measures. The final four linear functions define orthogonal polynomial contrasts over the grade levels. The matrix is applied to the means and the variance-covariance matrix of the four original variables in order to produce the means and variance-covariance matrix for the resulting transformed measures.

The "2" in column 28 of the Input Description card indicates that a transformation matrix will be used in the problem run; the matrix is supplied in later input cards. If a "1" is inserted in column 28, the rows of the transformation matrix are punched on individual cards and entered at a later point. The "2" indicates that the rows will be generated internally from Symbolic Contrast Vectors in the data deck. The "8" in column 32 indicates that there are eight variables resulting from the transformation.

An option on the Input Description card requests optional printed output where intermediate computations are available.

The Factor Identification card names and gives the number of levels of the sampling factor (sex). The factors in the design on the repeated measures are named at a later point. The Variable Formats card follows the

```
              1         2         3         4         5         6         7         8
     1234567890123456789012345678901234567890123456789012345678901234567890123456789 0

 1 1    1.75 2.60 3.76 3.68
 1 2    0.90 2.47 2.44 3.43
 1 3    0.80 0.93 0.40 2.27
 1 4    2.42 4.15 4.56 4.21
 1 5   -1.31-1.31-0.66-2.22
 1 6   -1.56 1.67 0.18 2.33
 1 7    1.09 1.50 0.52 2.33
 1 8   -1.92 1.03 0.50 3.04
 1 9   -1.61 0.29 0.73 3.24
 110    2.47 3.64 2.87 5.38
 111   -0.95 0.41 0.21 1.82
 112    1.66 2.74 2.40 2.17
 113    2.07 4.92 4.46 4.71
 114    3.30 6.10 7.19 7.46
 115    2.75 2.53 4.28 5.93
 116    2.25 3.38 5.79 4.40
 117    2.08 1.74 4.12 3.62
 118    0.14 0.01 1.48 2.78
 119    0.13 3.19 0.60 3.14
 120    2.19 2.65 3.27 2.73
 121   -0.64-1.31-0.37 4.09
 122    2.02 3.45 5.32 6.01
 123    2.05 1.80 3.91 2.49
 124    1.48 0.47 3.63 3.88
 125    1.97 2.54 3.26 5.62
 126    1.35 4.63 3.54 5.24
 127   -0.56-0.36 1.14 1.34
 128    0.26 0.08 1.17 2.15
 129    1.22 1.41 4.66 2.62
 130   -1.43 0.80-0.03 1.04
 131   -1.17 1.66 2.11 1.42
 132    1.68 1.71 4.07 3.30
 133   -0.47 0.93 1.30 0.76
 134    2.18 6.42 4.64 4.82
 135    4.21 7.08 6.00 5.65
 136    8.26 9.5510.2410.58
 2 1    1.24 4.90 2.42 2.54
 2 2    5.94 6.56 9.36 7.72
 2 3    0.87 3.36 2.58 1.73
 2 4   -0.09 2.29 3.08 3.35
 2 5    3.24 4.78 3.52 4.84
 2 6    1.03 2.10 3.88 2.81
 2 7    3.58 4.67 3.83 5.19
 2 8    1.41 1.75 3.70 3.77
 2 9   -0.65-0.11 2.40 3.53
 210    1.52 3.04 2.74 2.63
 211    0.57 2.71 1.90 2.41
 212    2.18 2.96 4.78 3.34
 213    1.10 2.65 1.72 2.96
 214    0.15 2.69 2.69 3.50
 215   -1.27 1.26 0.71 2.68
 216    2.81 5.19 6.33 5.93
 217    2.62 3.54 4.86 5.80
 218    0.11 2.25 1.56 3.92
 219    0.61 1.14 1.35 0.53
 220   -2.19-0.42 1.54 1.16
 221    1.55 2.42 1.11 2.18
 222   -0.04 0.50 2.60 2.61
 223    3.10 2.00 3.92 3.91
 224   -0.29 2.62 1.60 1.86
 225    2.28 3.39 4.91 3.89
 226    2.57 5.78 5.12 4.98
 227   -2.19 0.71 1.56 2.31
 228   -0.04 2.44 1.79 2.64

              1         2         3         4         5         6         7         8
     1234567890123456789012345678901234567890123456789012345678901234567890123456789 0
```

FIGURE 6.2 Problem 5: Vocabulary Growth data--multivariate form

```
            1         2         3         4         5         6         7         8
   12345678901234567890123456789012345678901234567890123456789012345678901234567890
```

        1. Title cards
PROBLEM 5 - REPEATED MEASURES ANALYSIS OF LONGITUDINAL DATA
- MULTIVARIATE ANALYSIS
        2. Input Description card
     4   1   1   1   2   8   1
        3. Factor Identification card
SEX   2
        4. Comment cards
REPEATED MEASURES ANALYSIS THROUGH MULTIVARIATE PROCEDURES. DATA FROM
BOCK, R.D.,MULTIVARIATE STATISTICAL METHODS IN BEHAVIORAL RESEARCH
NEW YORK: MCGRAW-HILL,1975, CHAPTER 7.

MALES AND FEMALES EACH TESTED IN GRADES 8,9,10,11. OUTCOME MEASURE IS A SCALED
VOCABULARY SCORE.

TESTS FOR SEX DIFFERENCES,FOR GRADE DIFFERENCES, AND SEX-BY-GRADE INTERACTION.

ORTHOGONAL POLYNOMIAL CONTRASTS ARE ESTIMATED OVER THE FOUR GRADE LEVELS.
THE GRADE EFFECT IS INDICATED BY MEASURES ON FOUR DEPENDENT VARIABLES FOR EACH
SUBJECT. THE DESIGN IS SET UP FOR ONLY THE SEX FACTOR. CONTRASTS OVER TIME ARE
CONSTRUCTED THROUGH A TRANSFORMATION MATRIX APPLIED TO THE FOUR TIME-POINT
SCORES.

FORMAT OF DATA CARDS:

     COL   CONTENTS
      1   SEX 1 = MALE, 2 = FEMALE
     2-3   SUBJECT NUMBER
                 (UNUSED IN THE MULTIVARIATE ANALYSIS)
     6-10   SCALED VOCABULARY SCORE GRADE 8
    11-15   SCALED VOCABULARY SCORE GRADE 9
    16-20   SCALED VOCABULARY SCORE GRADE 10
    21-25   SCALED VOCABULARY SCORE GRADE 11
        5. End-of-comments card
FINISH
        6. Variable Format card
(I1,4X,4F5.2)
        9. Variable Label card
GRADE   8GRADE   9GRADE 10GRADE 11CONSTANTLINEAR GQUAD G   CUBIC G
        10. Data
    DATA DECK   (DATA FORM 1)
        End of data

        11. Transformation Matrix
        (A)
    1   1
        (B)
GRADE   4
        (C)
GRADE
(D)
I1,   GRADE 8
I2,   GRADE9
2I3,   ETC
P0,   CONST.

P1,   LINEAR
P2,   QUADRIC
P3,   CUBIC
        12. Estimation Specification card
     2   2
        16. Symbolic Contrast Vectors
D0, GRMEAN
D1, SEX   ALPHA1
        18. Analysis Selection card
    1   1
        19. Variable Select key
5.
        21. Hypothesis Test card
-1,1.
        18. Analysis Select card
    3   1
        19. Variable Select key
6,7,8.
        21. Hypothesis Test card
1,1.
        22. End-of-job card
                                                            STOP
```
            1         2         3         4         5         6         7         8
   12345678901234567890123456789012345678901234567890123456789012345678901234567890
```

FIGURE 6.3   Problem 5:   MULTIVARIANCE control cards for repeated measures analysis

Comments and End-of-comment cards. The I1 field is for reading the sex code, and the four floating-point fields are for reading the subject's scores at the four grade levels.

The Variable Labels card names the variables after transformations. There are eight labels corresponding to the eight resulting measures, viz., the four original vocabulary scores, the sum of the four scores, and the three polynomial effects in time. The labels are followed by the data and one blank data card.

Information for constructing the transformation matrix follows the data. The first cards describe the design on the repeated measures. There is one factor in the design (grade level). The "1" in column 12 of the Design card indicates that orthogonal polynomials are to be used in constructing the transformation matrix. The following card gives the names and number of levels of the within-subject factors (exactly as the Factor Identification card earlier in the deck does for between-subject factors). The number of levels (four in this case) determine how many columns there are in the transformation matrix. The number of *rows* in the transformation matrix is the "number of variables after transformation matrix" on the Input Description card.

Because the program constructs the matrix of the orthogonal polynomials prior to placing them in the transformation matrix, the following card names the factor for which orthogonal polynomials are used. The factor has four levels, and so the program constructs the 3×4 matrix of polynomial weights. The matrix is orthonormalized and only orthonormal weights appear in the transformation matrix. These are proportional to the weights presented in (44).

The Symbolic Contrast Vectors, from which the program constructs the transformation matrix, appear next. The first rows of the matrix are four rows of an identity matrix coded I1, I2, I3, and I4,. The "repeat code" may be used on these cards; all four may be represented on one card as 4I1, or else they may be coded, as in the data deck, I1, I2, and 2I3,. Although the saving in punching is small, the code 2I3, represents effect codes I3, and I4, completing the identity matrix.

The following codes represent the orthogonal polynomial weight vectors. The zero effect, or grand mean, is proportional to the simple sum of all the original measures. Since we are using P or polynomial contrasts for remaining rows of the matrix, the constant code is represented as P0,. As in the univariate analysis, the three polynomial effect codes are P1, P2, and P3, for linear, quadratic, and cubic effects, respectively. The effect codes cause the eight rows of the transformation matrix to be constructed. The weights in the matrix are then applied to the original four measures to produce the eight transformed variables.

The estimation phase pertains to only the sex factor. The rank of the model for significance testing is two, comprising one degree of freedom for the constant or grand mean, and one degree of freedom for the difference between the sexes. These effects are listed in Table 6.1, and the Symbolic Contrast Vectors are D0, and D1, respectively. The grand mean and sex difference will be estimated for all eight transformed variables. Specific variables may be selected in subsets for tests of the within- and between-subjects fixed effects.

Cards numbered 18, 19, and 21 comprise one pass through the analysis phase of the program, with the first set of analysis cards testing the difference between the two sex groups. There is a single dependent variable for the test—the sum of the original four measures. A "1" is punched in column 12 of the Analysis Selection card to indicate that a key follows for selecting the measure from the set of eight. The Variable Select Key indicates that this is the fifth variable, or the sum score y_1^*. The Hypothesis Test card indicates that a test of the constant term over all subjects may be bypassed, and a test will be conducted of the one-degree-of-freedom difference between the two sexes.

The second set of analysis cards enables us to test the hypotheses given by (41) and (42). The three dependent variables are the three polynomial contrasts among the grade means. A "1" is punched in column 12 of the Analysis Selection Card to indicate that a key follows to select the three measures from the total set of eight. The Variable Select Key determines that these are the sixth, seventh, and eighth variables, or transformed scores y_2^*, y_3^*, and y_4^*. The Hypothesis Test card indicates that a one-degree-of-freedom test of the constant term is to be conducted, as well as a one-degree-of-freedom test of the difference between the sex groups.

The test that the constant term is zero for all three variables is a simultaneous test that all three polynomial functions in grade are null. This is the test of the grade main effect, given by (41). The step-down tests of this effect will assess individual terms of the polynomial function. The test of the sex differences on the three variables simultaneously is the test of interaction of sex and grade levels specified by hypothesis (42). Again, individual step-down statistics will indicate the polynomial complexity of the sex differences over age levels.

6.6 OUTPUT AND INTERPRETATION

PHASE I.   The results of the input phase of the MULTIVARIANCE run are listed in Figures 6.4-1 and 2. All of the input parameters are listed, as are the four vocabulary scores for the first male subject. The data are transformed to the linear combinations given by (44). The matrix is generated internally from coded Symbolic Vectors. The codes are listed in Figure 6.4-1, where it can be seen that the card punched with the code 2I3, was interpreted as two cards, I3, and I4,.

The transformation matrix which is generated is listed at the bottom of the figure. This matrix agrees with (44), except that the final three (polynomial) vectors have been *normalized*. That is, the elements of each row have been divided by the square root of the sum of squared values. For the quadratic trend, for example, the weight vector is $(1, -1, -1, 1)$. The sum of squares of these elements is $4 \times 1^2 = 4$, and its square root is 2. Thus, each of the elements in the vector is divided by two in the normalized form, and the resulting vector is $(.5, -.5, -.5, .5)$.

The matrix of sum of squared scores and sums of cross-products is followed by the means of the eight measures for both sex groups. The first columns of means show the trend for vocabulary scores to increase across grade levels. In addition, this table contains the means for boys and girls separately for the sum of the four grade-level scores, and for the three weighted polynomial functions.

PHASE II.   The output from the estimation phase of MULTIVARIANCE is listed in Figures 6.4-2 and 3. Between-group effects are coded for the sex factor. The matrices of variances and covariances of the eight variables are computed separately for boys and for girls and are pooled in the same manner as the matrices for separate sexes in the regression example (equation 9 of Chapter 2).

The pooled within-group variance-covariance matrix, or error variance-covariance matrix, is given in Figure 6.4-2. The diagonal elements of this matrix are the common within-group variances for the eight transformed measures. For example, the variances of the vocabulary score at the four grade levels are 3.626, 4.380, 4.764, and 3.761, respectively.

The variances among subjects within sex groups are also given for the four y^* variables. For example, the variance among subjects for total vocabulary score is 56.307. This is proportional to the mean square for subjects within sex groups from the univariate mixed-model analysis.

The variances among subjects within sex groups on the polynomial transformations, y_2^*, y_3^*, and y_4^*, are .809, .669, and .976, respectively. These are the univariate mean squares for the subjects-by-linear-grade interaction, subjects-by-quadratic-grade interaction, and subjects-by-cubic-grade interaction, respectively. They are not computed separately in the univariate analysis, but the average of these numbers, or .818, is exactly the subjects-by-grade interaction mean square in the univariate analysis, and has 186 degrees of freedom.

In contrast, each of the mean squares is estimated separately in the multivariate run, and each has 62 degrees of freedom. The nonzero covariances of the three terms indicate that they are not independent, due to the intercorrelations among the original four observed scores. Therefore, they should not be averaged to obtain results for the univariate analysis. The program uses the covariances in conducting the multivariate tests.

The variances and covariances are more easily interpreted in correlation form. In the pooled within-group correlation matrix at the top of Figure 6.4-3, we may inspect the correlations among the four grade measures. Correlations among the vocabulary measures range from a low value of .76 to a high of .87; the data do not exhibit the simplex pattern with distant time points having lower correlations than those closer together. Instead, all of the correlations among the vocabulary scores appear generally homogeneous.

- -

PROBLEM 5 - REPEATED MEASURES ANALYSIS OF LONGITUDINAL DATA - MULTIVARIATE ANALYSIS

- -

REPEATED MEASURES ANALYSIS THROUGH MULTIVARIATE PROCEDURES. DATA FROM
R.D.BOCK,MULTIVARIATE STATISTICAL METHODS IN BEHAVIORAL RESEARCH   CHAPTER 7
NEW YORK: MCGRAW HILL, 1975, CHAPTER 7.

MALES AND FEMALES EACH TESTED IN GRADES 8,9,10,11. OUTCOME MEASURE IS A SCALED
VOCABULARY SCORE.

TESTS FOR SEX DIFFERENCES,FOR GRADE DIFFERENCES, AND SEX-BY-GRADE INTERACTION.

ORTHOGONAL POLYNOMIAL CONTRASTS ARE ESTIMATED OVER THE FOUR GRADE LEVELS.
THE GRADE EFFECT IS INDICATED BY MEASURES ON FOUR DEPENDENT VARIABLES FOR EACH
SUBJECT. THE DESIGN IS SET UP FOR ONLY THE SEX FACTOR. CONTRASTS OVER TIME ARE
CONSTRUCTED THROUGH A TRANSFORMATION MATRIX APPLIED TO THE FOUR TIME-POINT
SCORES.

FORMAT OF DATA CARDS:

COL	CONTENTS
1	SEX 1 = MALE, 2 = FEMALE
2-3	SUBJECT NUMBER
	(UNUSED IN THE MULTIVARIATE ANALYSIS)
6-10	SCALED VOCABULARY SCORE GRADE 8
11-15	SCALED VOCABULARY SCORE GRADE 9
16-20	SCALED VOCABULARY SCORE GRADE 10
21-25	SCALED VOCABULARY SCORE GRADE 11

INPUT PARAMETERS
================

NUMBER OF VARIABLES IN INPUT VECTORS=   4

NUMBER OF FACTORS IN DESIGN=   1

  NUMBER OF LEVELS OF FACTOR 1 (SEX   ) =   2

NUMBER OF VARIABLES AFTER TRANSFORMATION MATRIX= 8

TRANSFORMATION MATRIX BEING GENERATED BY SYMBOLIC CONTRAST VECTORS

INPUT IS FROM CARDS. DATA OPTION 1

MINIMAL PAGE SPACING WILL BE USED

ADDITIONAL OUTPUT WILL BE PRINTED

COMPUTATION OF COVARIANCE MATRIX FOR EACH GROUP
IMPOSSIBLE DUE TO FORM OF DATA INPUT

FORMAT OF DATA
   (I1,4X,4F5.2)

FIRST OBSERVATION
SUBJECT   1 , CELL   1

        1.7500   2.6000   3.7600   3.6800

DESIGN AND SYMBOLIC CONTRAST VECTORS FOR TRANSFORMATION MATRIX
===

NUMBER OF FACTORS IN DESIGN=   1

  NUMBER OF LEVELS OF FACTOR 1 (GRADE   ) =   4

ORTHOGONAL POLYNOMIAL CONTRASTS FOR FACTOR (GRADE   )

- -

    I1,   GRADE 8

    I2,   GRADE9

    I 3,   ETC

    I 4,   ETC

    P0,   CONST.

    P1,   LINEAR

    P2,   QUADRIC

    P3,   CUBIC

TRANSFORMATION MATRIX --- NEW X OLD VARIABLES

	1	2	3	4
1 GRADE 8	1.000000	0.0	0.0	0.0
2 GRADE 9	0.0	1.000000	0.0	0.0
3 GRADE 10	0.0	0.0	1.000000	0.0
4 GRADE 11	0.0	0.0	0.0	1.000000
5 CONSTANT	0.500000	0.500000	0.500000	0.500000
6 LINEAR G	-0.670820	-0.223607	0.223607	0.670820
7 QUAD G	0.500000	-0.500000	-0.500000	0.500000
8 CUBIC G	-0.223607	0.670820	-0.670820	0.223607

FIGURE 6.4-1 Problem 5: Phase I output

118

CELL IDENTIFICATION AND FREQUENCIES

```
CELL    FACTOR LEVELS    N

              SEX
     1         1         36
     2         2         28
```

TOTAL N=   64.

TOTAL SUM OF CROSS-PRODUCTS
----

	1 GRADE 8	2 GRADE 9	3 GRADE 10	4 GRADE 11	5 CONSTANT	6 LINEAR G	7 QUAD G	8 CUBIC G
1 GRADE 8	307.565							
2 GRADE 9	385.979	687.311						
3 GRADE 10	441.185	709.618	867.830					
4 GRADE 11	432.427	756.199	877.418	1004.885				
5 CONSTANT	783.578	1269.554	1448.026	1535.464	2518.311			
6 LINEAR G	96.104	253.339	328.011	411.122	544.288	228.018		
7 QUAD G	-43.586	-127.376	-129.422	-98.152	-199.268	-37.062	57.530	
8 CUBIC G	-9.113	67.820	-8.587	46.689	48.404	20.348	-10.829	63.733

OBSERVED CELL MEANS --- ROWS ARE CELLS-COLUMNS ARE VARIABLES
----

	1 GRADE 8	2 GRADE 9	3 GRADE 10	4 GRADE 11	5 CONSTANT	6 LINEAR G	7 QUAD G	8 CUBIC G
1	1.140556	2.375000	2.880278	3.540556	4.968194	1.722952	-0.287083	0.197706
2	1.132857	2.756071	3.127143	3.382857	5.199464	1.592320	-0.683750	0.254193

ESTIMATION PARAMETERS
=====================

RANK OF THE BASIS = RANK OF MODEL FOR SIGNIFICANCE TESTING =   2

RANK OF THE MODEL TO BE ESTIMATED IS   2

ERROR TERM TO BE USED IS (WITHIN CELLS)

VARIANCE-COVARIANCE FACTORS AND CORRELATIONS AMONG ESTIMATES WILL BE PRINTED

SYMBOLIC CONTRAST VECTORS
=========================

```
( 1)
        D0,                                              GRMEAN
( 2)
        D1,         ALPHA1                               SEX
```

ERROR SUM OF CROSS-PRODUCTS
----

	1 GRADE 8	2 GRADE 9	3 GRADE 10	4 GRADE 11	5 CONSTANT	6 LINEAR G	7 QUAD G	8 CUBIC G
1 GRADE 8	224.7996							
2 GRADE 9	201.0393	271.5630						
3 GRADE 10	223.7281	222.0330	295.3611					
4 GRADE 11	179.7475	192.4260	214.0950	233.1818				
5 CONSTANT	414.6572	443.5307	477.6086	409.7251	872.7608			
6 LINEAR G	-25.1485	-16.8532	9.9346	40.6902	4.3115	50.1558		
7 QUAD G	-10.1102	-50.0653	-39.7855	3.2041	-48.3785	11.2302	41.4724	
8 CUBIC G	-25.2941	31.2997	-51.3440	-2.5877	-23.9630	-3.2478	-3.9188	60.5163

ERROR VARIANCE -COVARIANCE MATRIX
----

	1 GRADE 8	2 GRADE 9	3 GRADE 10	4 GRADE 11	5 CONSTANT	6 LINEAR G	7 QUAD G	8 CUBIC G
1 GRADE 8	3.62580							
2 GRADE 9	3.24257	4.38005						
3 GRADE 10	3.60852	3.58118	4.76389					
4 GRADE 11	2.89915	3.10365	3.45315	3.76100				
5 CONSTANT	6.68802	7.15372	7.70336	6.60847	14.07679			
6 LINEAR G	-0.40562	-0.27183	0.16023	0.65629	0.06954	0.80897		
7 QUAD G	-0.16307	-0.80751	-0.64170	0.05168	-0.78030	0.18113	0.66891	
8 CUBIC G	-0.40797	0.50483	-0.82813	-0.04174	-0.38650	-0.05238	-0.06321	0.97607

FIGURE 6.4-2 Problem 5: Phase I output (continued)

ERROR CORRELATION MATRIX
----

		1 GRADE 8	2 GRADE 9	3 GRADE 10	4 GRADE 11	5 CONSTANT	6 LINEAR G	7 QUAD G	8 CUBIC G
1	GRADE 8	1.000000							
2	GRADE 9	0.813669	1.000000						
3	GRADE 10	0.868253	0.783981	1.000000					
4	GRADE 11	0.785087	0.764683	0.815798	1.000000				
5	CONSTANT	0.936147	0.911047	0.940693	0.908234	1.000000			
6	LINEAR G	-0.236839	-0.144406	0.081623	0.376254	0.020607	1.000000		
7	QUAD G	-0.104709	-0.471762	-0.359475	0.032582	-0.254288	0.246233	1.000000	
8	CUBIC G	-0.216863	0.244157	-0.384040	-0.021784	-0.104270	-0.058951	-0.078223	1.000000

	VARIABLE	VARIANCE (ERROR MEAN SQUARES)	STANDARD DEVIATION
1	GRADE 8	3.625799	1.9042
2	GRADE 9	4.380048	2.0929
3	GRADE 10	4.763888	2.1826
4	GRADE 11	3.760996	1.9393
5	CONSTANT	14.076787	3.7519
6	LINEAR G	0.808965	0.8994
7	QUAD G	0.668909	0.8179
8	CUBIC G	0.976070	0.9880

D.F.=   62.

ERROR TERM FOR ANALYSIS OF VARIANCE (WITHIN CELLS)

LEAST SQUARE ESTIMATES OF EFFECTS -- EFFECTS X VARIABLES
----

		1 GRADE 8	2 GRADE 9	3 GRADE 10	4 GRADE 11	5 CONSTANT	6 LINEAR G	7 QUAD G	8 CUBIC G
1	GRMEAN	1.136706	2.565536	3.003710	3.461706	5.083829	1.657636	-0.485417	0.225949
2	SEX	0.003849	-0.190536	-0.123433	0.078849	-0.115635	0.065316	0.198333	-0.028244

ESTIMATES OF EFFECTS IN STANDARD DEVIATION UNITS-EFF X VARS
----

		1 GRADE 8	2 GRADE 9	3 GRADE 10	4 GRADE 11	5 CONSTANT	6 LINEAR G	7 QUAD G	8 CUBIC G
1	GRMEAN	0.596962	1.225854	1.376186	1.785002	1.355000	1.842996	-0.593514	0.228702
2	SEX	0.002021	-0.091041	-0.056552	0.040658	-0.030820	0.072620	0.242500	-0.028588

STANDARD ERRORS OF LEAST-SQUARES ESTIMATES--EFFECTS BY VARS
----

		1 GRADE 8	2 GRADE 9	3 GRADE 10	4 GRADE 11	5 CONSTANT	6 LINEAR G	7 QUAD G	8 CUBIC G
1	GRMEAN	0.239901	0.263675	0.274986	0.244332	0.472696	0.113317	0.103042	0.124472
2	SEX	0.239901	0.263675	0.274986	0.244332	0.472696	0.113317	0.103042	0.124472

LEAST-SQUARES ESTIMATES AS T-STATISTICS - EFFECTS X VARS
----

		1 GRADE 8	2 GRADE 9	3 GRADE 10	4 GRADE 11	5 CONSTANT	6 LINEAR G	7 QUAD G	8 CUBIC G
1	GRMEAN	4.73824	9.72991	10.92314	14.16802	10.75498	14.62833	-4.71087	1.81527
2	SEX	0.01604	-0.72262	-0.44887	0.32271	-0.24463	0.57640	1.92479	-0.22691

DEGREES OF FREEDOM =   62.

VARIANCE-COVARIANCE FACTORS OF ESTIMATES
----

		1 GRMEAN	2 SEX
1	GRMEAN	1.587302D-02	
2	SEX	-1.984127D-03	1.587302D-02

INTERCORRELATIONS AMONG THE ESTIMATES
----

		1 GRMEAN	2 SEX
1	GRMEAN	1.000000	
2	SEX	-0.125000	1.000000

FIGURE 6.4-3 Problem 5: Phase II output (concluded)

In fact, they may meet the assumption of the univariate mixed-model analysis. If this is the case, the univariate model should be employed and may be extracted from the multivariate run. According to Bloom (1964), the correlation of vocabulary scores with adult vocabulary increases as the child ages, but the age range from thirteen to sixteen years in this study may be too small to show an increasing pattern.

The variances or error mean squares are extracted from the diagonal of the error variance-covariance matrix and are listed along with the standard deviations in Figure 6.4-3. The standard deviations for the four grade levels do not increase monotonically, as we should expect for younger children, but are relatively homogeneous and indicate again that the assumptions of the univariate mixed-model may be met.

The estimate of the constant term for all subjects, and the deviation effect for the first sex group, are given in the table of "Least-squares Estimates of Effects" in both raw score form and in standard deviation units. A table of standard errors of the estimates follows. They may be used in constructing confidence intervals and testing the significance of individual elements. Confidence bounds may also be constructed on *sets* of effects, using Scheffé or Roy procedures discussed in most multivariate analysis texts (see Bock, 1975, pp. 227, 266).

The effects of greatest interest pertain to the four transformed variables. The first row contains the grand mean across all subjects on each of the measured variables. The grand mean of the sum score, y_1^*, is of little interest. The grand means of y_2^* through y_4^*, however, are the estimated polynomials across grade levels. The multivariance test of significance of these three terms (1.66, −.49, .23) is a test of significance for the grade effect.

The second row estimates the difference between the mean of males and the mean of all subjects for each variable. The estimate of the sex effect for the sum of the vocabulary scores is −.23 points, indicating that the overall mean is higher. A test of significance of only this term reveals whether there are differences between sex means on vocabulary scores. The remaining terms are differences between the male mean and the overall mean on the three polynomials in age. A multivariate test of these terms indicates whether there is a significant interaction of sex and age.

Among the optional printed output are the matrices of variance-covariance factors of the estimates, and intercorrelations among the estimates. These indicate the extent to which the simple one-way design is nonorthogonal due to unequal cell frequencies. In particular, there is a correlation of −.125 between the constant term and the sex difference. This indicates only that we should test for the sex main effect and for interactions of sex and grade, eliminating the grand mean.

PHASE III.　The output produced from Phase III of the multivariate analysis is listed in Figures 6.4-4 and 6.4-5. For the first pass through Phase III, variable 5, or the total vocabulary score, is selected as the only criterion measure. As there is no particular interest in testing the grand mean on this variable, the test is bypassed. The one-degree-of-freedom test is made of the difference between sex groups. The resulting statistic is $F = .0598$. This is not significant at any reasonable probability level; $H_0(1)$ of (40) is accepted.

Since this result is a simple univariate test of sex differences, eliminating the grand mean, the F statistic of .06 agrees exactly with that obtained from the univariate mixed-model solution. This F statistic is a ratio of mean square sex to mean square subjects, or 3.37/56.31. The two mean squares are proportional to the mean squares from the univariate mixed-model analysis. They are not identical in value only because the vector of weights in the transformation matrix for y_1^* is not normalized.[6] This is not necessary to obtain the correct test statistic.

For the second pass through the analysis phase of the program, the three polynomials in age are chosen as criterion measures. In other designs the scale of the measures is arbitrary, and we have no interest in testing the constant over all subjects. In this instance, we have a specific hypothesis that the constant, or the overall mean of the growth measures, is zero. We indicate a test of the grand mean effect by the first "1" on the Hypothesis Test

---

[6] Elements of the normalized vectors would all be .5, and y_1^* would be one half the sum of the four vocabulary scores instead of the simple sum.

ANALYSIS OF VARIANCE
====================
====================

1 DEPENDENT VARIABLE(S)

5 CONSTANT

LOG-DETERMINANT ERROR SUM OF CROSS-PRODUCTS = 0.67716615D+01

HYPOTHESIS   1   1 DEGREE(S) OF FREEDOM
===

D0,   GRMEAN

- -

TESTS OF HYPOTHESIS BEING SKIPPED

* *

HYPOTHESIS   2   1 DEGREE(S) OF FREEDOM
===

D1,   ALPHA1   SEX

- -

UNIVARIATE ANALYSIS OF VARIANCE FOR (CONSTANT)

HYPOTHESIS MEAN SQUARE=   0.8424   F=   0.0598   WITH   1. AND   62. DEGREES OF FREEDOM   P LESS THAN 0.8076

* *

ANALYSIS OF VARIANCE
====================
====================

3 DEPENDENT VARIABLE(S)

6 LINEAR G
7 QUAD G
8 CUBIC G

LOG-DETERMINANT ERROR SUM OF CROSS-PRODUCTS = 0.11672703D+02

HYPOTHESIS   1   1 DEGREE(S) OF FREEDOM
===

D0,   GRMEAN

- -

LOG-DETERMINANT SCP HYPOTHESES + SCP ERROR, ADJUSTED FOR ANY COVARIATES, = 0.13422870E+02

F-RATIO FOR MULTIVARIATE TEST OF EQUALITY OF MEAN VECTORS=   95.1113

D.F.=   3. AND   60.0000   P LESS THAN 0.0001

(LIKELIHOOD RATIO = 0.17374480E+00   LOG = -0.17501678E+01)

VARIABLE	HYPOTHESIS MEAN SQ	UNIVARIATE F	P LESS THAN	STEP DOWN F	P LESS THAN
1 LINEAR G	177.5931	219.5312	0.0001	219.5312	0.0001
				STEP-DOWN MEAN SQUARES =(177.5931/	0.8090)
2 QUAD G	13.5792	20.3006	0.0001	15.3356	0.0003
				STEP-DOWN MEAN SQUARES =(9.7942/	0.6387)
3 CUBIC G	3.1661	3.2437	0.0766	0.7725	0.3830
				STEP-DOWN MEAN SQUARES =(0.7731/	1.0007)

DEGREES OF FREEDOM FOR HYPOTHESIS=   1
DEGREES OF FREEDOM FOR ERROR=   62.

HYPOTHESIS MEAN PRODUCTS, ADJUSTED FOR ANY COVARIATES
----

	1 LINEAR G	2 QUAD G	3 CUBIC G
1 LINEAR G	177.5931		
2 QUAD G	-49.1078	13.5792	
3 CUBIC G	23.7124	-6.5569	3.1661

FIGURE 6.4-4 Problem 5: Phase III output

122

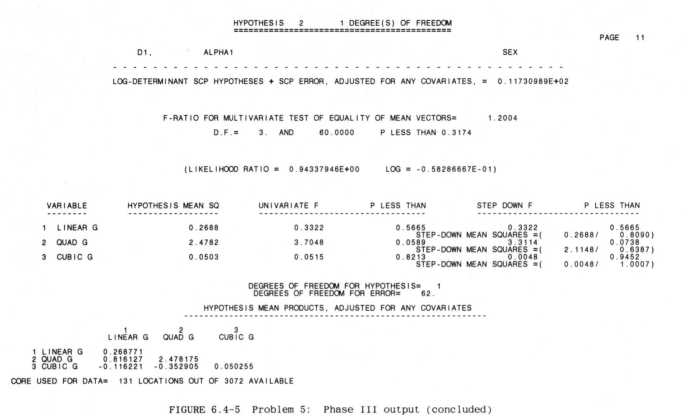

HYPOTHESIS   2   1 DEGREE(S) OF FREEDOM
==
PAGE   11

          D1,   ALPHA1   SEX
- -
      LOG-DETERMINANT SCP HYPOTHESES + SCP ERROR, ADJUSTED FOR ANY COVARIATES, = 0.11730989E+02

          F-RATIO FOR MULTIVARIATE TEST OF EQUALITY OF MEAN VECTORS=   1.2004
                  D.F.=   3. AND   60.0000   P LESS THAN 0.3174

              (LIKELIHOOD RATIO = 0.94337946E+00   LOG = -0.58286667E-01)

   VARIABLE   HYPOTHESIS MEAN SQ   UNIVARIATE F   P LESS THAN   STEP DOWN F   P LESS THAN
   --------   ------------------   ------------   ----------   ------------   -----------
 1 LINEAR G   0.2688   0.3322   0.5665   0.3322   0.5665
                                                                     STEP-DOWN MEAN SQUARES =(0.2688/   0.8090)
 2 QUAD G   2.4782   3.7048   0.0589   3.3114   0.0738
                                                                     STEP-DOWN MEAN SQUARES =(2.1148/   0.6387)
 3 CUBIC G   0.0503   0.0515   0.8213   0.0048   0.9452
                                                                     STEP-DOWN MEAN SQUARES =(0.0048/   1.0007)
              DEGREES OF FREEDOM FOR HYPOTHESIS=   1
              DEGREES OF FREEDOM FOR ERROR=   62.
          HYPOTHESIS MEAN PRODUCTS, ADJUSTED FOR ANY COVARIATES
          ----

              1   2   3
           LINEAR G   QUAD G   CUBIC G

 1 LINEAR G   0.268771
 2 QUAD G   0.816127   2.478175
 3 CUBIC G   -0.116221 -0.352905   0.050255
CORE USED FOR DATA= 131 LOCATIONS OUT OF 3072 AVAILABLE

FIGURE 6.4-5   Problem 5: Phase III output (concluded)

card. The card also has a second "1" to indicate that the test of sex difference is to be conducted. This result is given in Figure 6.4-5.

6.6.1 Sex-by-grade Interaction

A test of sex differences on the polynomials in time is a test of the sex-by-grade interaction. When the polynomial variables are chosen as criterion measures, the interactions of those variables with subjects within groups are automatically selected as the error terms. The multivariate test of the sex-by-grade interaction is not significant. The F value of 1.20 has 3 and 60 degrees of freedom, and does not exceed the .05 critical value.

If we wish to test for the complexity of the interaction by increasing degrees, we should employ the step-down results. The last step-down test statistic ($F = .005$ with 1, 60 d.f.) is not significant. Thus we turn to the one preceding it. The second step-down statistic ($F = 3.31$ with 1, 61 d.f.) indicates that there is no sex-by-quadratic-grade effect.[7] The first step-down statistic for the interaction of sex and a linear grade effect is also not significant. From either multivariate procedure, there is no sex-by-grade interaction in the data; $H_0(3)$ of (42) is accepted.

If the assumptions of the univariate mixed-model analysis are not met, then one of the multivariate test procedures must be employed. If the variances of the original measures are equal, and the correlations among the original four measures are equal, then we may employ the univariate mixed-model solution. The results for the univariate mixed-model analysis are obtained from the printout as follows: the univariate mean square for sex-by-grade interaction, with three degrees of freedom, is .932 from the results given in Chapter 5. It is obtained in the present run by averaging the three specific mean squares for sex-by-grade. That is,

[7] Had we chosen to make a one-tail test, this statistic would be significant at the .05 level. This is suggested in Chapter 5, following a hypothesized directional sex-by-grade interaction.

$$(.269 + 2.478 + .050)/3 = .932$$

The result has $1 + 1 + 1 = 3$ degrees of freedom.

Similarly, the mean square from the univariate mixed-model analysis for subjects-by-grade interaction is .818. This is exactly the average of the three grade-by-subject-within-sex group mean squares from the multivariate results in Figure 6.4-3. That is,

$$(.809 + .669 + .976)/3 = .818$$

The result has $62 + 62 + 62 = 186$ degrees of freedom. The ratio of the two results .932/.818 is exactly the univariate F ratio for sex by occasions, or 1.14. This test statistic is valid provided the assumptions of the univariate mixed model are met. When they are not, the multivariate results should be interpreted directly.

6.6.2 Grade Levels

Having found interaction not significant, we interpret the preceding test of differences among grade levels (Figure 6.4-4). The multivariate test of all three transformed variables yields $F = 95.1$, with 3 and 60 degrees of freedom; this is significant at the .01 level. Since our main interest is in testing for specific curves describing the growth trends, we inspect the step-down results.

The third step-down F statistic, corresponding to the cubic effect in time, is not significant. We therefore inspect the second step-down statistic and find the F value of 15.34, which is significant at the .01 level. We conclude that a quadratic function is necessary to describe vocabulary growth.

The results of the univariate mixed-model analysis can also be obtained from the multivariate run. In particular, the univariate mean square for the grade effect (see Chapter 5) is 64.78. This is exactly the average of the three univariate mean squares obtained here for the separate polynomial contrasts:

$$(177.59 + 13.58 + 3.17)/3 = 64.78$$

Similarly, the univariate mean square for the subjects-by-grade effect is the average of the three separate within-group mean squares, or .818. (The same value is used for the test of the sex-by-grade interaction.) The univariate F statistic is $64.78/.818 = 79.19$.

The results of the multivariate analysis may be summarized as in Table 6.3. Again it is important to indicate which effects have been eliminated when conducting each statistical test. The vertical lines are used for this purpose when inserted between the y^* titles. For example, $y_3^* | y_2^*$ indicates a test of y_3^*, eliminating all variation due to y_2^*.

In this study the results of the univariate and multivariate analyses are largely consistent with one another. In particular, we conclude that the same quadratic trend is significant in vocabulary growth. Also, there may be a sex-by-quadratic-grade interaction due to girls' scores decelerating more rapidly than boys'. In these data the assumption of the univariate mixed model is well met. In other instances the results of the two analyses may differ in important ways.

Table 6.3   Multivariate Analysis of Variance for Longitudinal Vocabulary Data

Source of Variation	d.f.	y_1^*	Step-down tests		
			y_2^*	$y_3^* \mid y_2^*$	$y_4^* \mid y_2^*, y_3^*$
Constant	1	—	**219.53	**15.34	.77
Sex, eliminating constant	1	.06	.33	3.31	.00
Within-group mean square	62	56.31	.81	.67	.98
Total	64				

**$p < .01$

$y_1^* =$ Total vocabulary score $y_3^* =$ Quadratic grade
$y_2^* =$ Linear grade $y_4^* =$ Cubic grade

6.7 SUMMARY

Whenever subjects have been measured on the same scale at more than one point in time, or under varying experimental conditions, the multiple scores should be treated as simultaneous criterion measures in a multivariate model. The sampling design is separated from the design on the dependent variables. Main effects and interactions in both designs are coded symbolically.

Main effects and interactions in the design on the dependent variables take the form of contrasts among the original variables. Tests of significance are conducted by selecting the correct contrast variables from the set of measured outcomes, and testing specific between-group sources of variation.

If the original measured scores are intercorrelated to different extents, or have different variances, then the transformed variables will also have nonzero intercorrelations. In this case only the multivariate statistics (i.e., the overall multivariate test or the step-down results) will give valid test results. If, on the other hand, the original measures have equal variances and homogeneous intercorrelations, then the univariate mixed-model solution should be employed.

The univariate results may be obtained from the multivariate program run by averaging mean squares between and within groups and taking the appropriate ratio of the averages. Thus, even if the univariate analysis is required, the multivariate computer setup is smaller and should be used.

In the present data there is one between-group dimension, sex, and one within-subjects dimension, grade. The differences over time take the form of polynomial effects, and the vectors that transform the original variables were orthonormal when constructed. In other cases, to reproduce the univariate mixed-model solution from the multivariate problem run, the vectors must be orthonormalized by the MULTIVARIANCE program. If this is to be done, it must be indicated by the user early in the input deck. However, this feature is only useful for obtaining the univariate mean squares. The test statistics and all multivariate results will be correct in any case.

The analysis of this same problem is presented in Chapter 7 of Bock (1975). The numerical results presented in both this and the preceding chapter differ slightly from Bock's results. This occurs because the data in Bock's Table 7.1-4 are rounded from five-figure data used in his calculations (Bock, personal communication).

The researcher about to analyze repeated-measures data in a multivariate manner should do the following:

1. List the effects in the sampling design (main effects and interactions).
2. List the effects in the design on the dependent variables (main effects and interactions).
3. Punch the data cards so that each subject has his scores on one card, in a consistent order. All scores for the same subject should be on the card (of course, more than one card may be used per subject if necessary).
4. Set up Phase I of the MULTIVARIANCE program for only the sampling design.
5. Code the symbolic effects for the design on the dependent variables. Request that the MULTIVARIANCE program generate a transformation matrix, and include these codes for defining the rows of the matrix. (Remember to note which variables in the transformed set result from which codes.)
6. Code the symbolic effects for the sampling design. It is useful to make a table such as Table 6.1, listing all of the effects in both designs.
7. Cause the program to test each hypothesis by a selection of transformed measures, and by obtaining tests of the appropriate sampling-design effects. By the nature of the multivariate model, the correct error term always appears for each hypothesis.

Finally, if the researcher requires the mean squares for the univariate mixed-model analysis, he should average the terms from the MULTIVARIANCE printout, as in the example.

Several current and useful discussions, comparing the univariate and multivariate analysis of repeated-measures data, are listed in the references (Davidson, 1972; McCall and Applebaum, 1973; Poor, 1973). Chapter 7 of Bock (1975) contains an extensive description with many examples.

7

ADDITIONAL TOPICS

7.1 MORE ABOUT THE SYMBOLIC CONTRAST VECTORS

The symbolic codes which are entered into the MULTIVARIANCE program in Phase II represent the effects in an analysis-of-variance model. There are as many coded effects as degrees of freedom in the model. For example, in a one-way analysis-of-variance model with parameters μ and α_1 through α_5, we enter one symbolic code, D0, to symbolize μ, and four symbolic codes, D1, through D4, to represent α_1, α_2, α_3, and α_4. Once μ is estimated, there are only four degrees of freedom among the five group means, or four independent deviations from μ. α_5 may be estimated as minus the sum of the other four terms.

Each of the four codes, D1, through D4, causes a vector of weights to be generated within the program. The weights are actually *contrasts* among the subclass means. As an example, consider the one-way design with five groups, as diagrammed in Figure 7.1. Let the five subclass means be μ_1 through μ_5, respectively, and the overall population be μ, where

$$\mu = \sum \mu_j/5 = \mu_1/5 + \mu_2/5 + \mu_3/5 + \mu_4/5 + \mu_5/5 \qquad (45)$$

In terms of the subclass means, α_1 is the deviation $\mu_1 - \mu$ or

$$\begin{aligned} \alpha_1 &= \mu_1 - \mu \\ &= \mu_1 - (\mu_1/5 + \mu_2/5 + \mu_3/5 + \mu_4/5 + \mu_5/5) \\ &= 4\mu_1/5 - \mu_2/5 - \mu_3/5 - \mu_4/5 - \mu_5/5 \end{aligned} \qquad (46)$$

That is, α_1 is actually a contrast among the subclass means; it is a weighted linear combination of means, such that the sum of the weights is exactly zero. The code D1, denoting α_1 is interpreted by the program as representing the entire weight vector $(4/5, -1/5, -1/5, -1/5, -1/5)$.[1] In like manner, the codes D2,

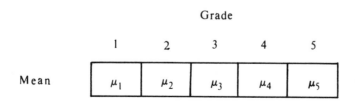

FIGURE 7.1   Sampling Diagram for One-factor Five-level Design

---

[1] It is for this reason that the codes are termed "Symbolic Contrast Vectors."

126

through D4, each reflect a different contrast vector, with the weight 4/5 applying to μ_2, μ_3, and μ_4, respectively.

The Symbolic Contrast Vectors determine the type of effects that are displayed in the matrix of "Least-squares Estimates of Effects." They are among the most useful interpretive results. Together with their standard errors, the least-squares estimates of μ and the contrasts give the direction, magnitude, and precision of between-group differences for each criterion variable. Tests of significance on individual effects may also be made from these estimates and standard errors.

Sometimes it is useful to have other effects displayed in the table instead of μ, the α's, β's, and so on. By preceding the code by a letter other than D, different contrasts may be estimated. For example, suppose that group 5 is a control group, while groups 1 through 4 in Figure 7.1 are different experimental conditions. Then we might like to estimate the contrast of every experimental condition with the control group. That is, we would be interested in estimates of the differences $\mu_1 - \mu_5$, $\mu_2 - \mu_5$, $\mu_3 - \mu_5$, and $\mu_4 - \mu_5$. The overall test of significance of between-group differences will remain the same, but the interpretive results we obtain will be more directly useful.

By replacing the letter D on the Symbolic Contrast Vectors with the letter C, *simple* contrasts may be obtained for this design. Simple contrasts are the comparisons of every group, except one, with the remaining group. If we code effects C1, C2, C3, and C4, we obtain the estimated differences listed in Table 7.1.

Each symbolic code in Table 7.1 represents the entire vector of weights given at the right of the table. The effect obtained by applying these weights to the five subclass means is given in the middle column. In this instance, the effects represent the estimated differences of each group mean with that of the fifth group.

When using the simple (C) contrasts, the grand mean or constant term is still deemed the "zero" effect, but it is represented as C0, rather than D0,. For the group contrasts, the convention adopted in the MULTI-VARIANCE program is that if $\mu - 1$ simple contrasts are coded for a μ-level factor, the level number *omitted* is the control level. In Table 7.1, contrast C5 was omitted, so that group 5 is assumed to be the common comparison group. If we were to code C1, C3, C4, and C5, omitting instead C2, then group 2 would be the common comparison group. The effects estimated from these codes would then be $\mu_1 - \mu_2$, $\mu_3 - \mu_2$, $\mu_4 - \mu_2$, and $\mu_5 - \mu_2$, respectively.

Another set of contrasts provided by the MULTIVARIANCE program are *Helmert* contrasts, with the code letter H. If we compare the five groups in Figure 7.1 by Helmert contrasts, then the constant term is coded H0, and the four remaining Symbolic Contrast Vectors are H1, H2, H3, and H4,.

The Helmert contrasts compare the first four groups with the average of means of all groups to their right. This is described in Table 7.2. H1, indicates that μ_1 is compared to the average of the other four group means. H2, indicates that μ_2 is to be compared to the average of groups 3, 4, and 5. H3, indicates that μ_3 is to be compared to the average of groups 4 and 5, while H4, indicates that μ_4 is to be compared with μ_5.

Table 7.1 Simple (C) Contrasts for One-way Five-level Design

Symbolic Contrast Vector	Contrast	Weights				
		μ_1	μ_2	μ_3	μ_4	μ_5
C1,	$\mu_1 - \mu_5$	1	0	0	0	−1
C2,	$\mu_2 - \mu_5$	0	1	0	0	−1
C3,	$\mu_3 - \mu_5$	0	0	1	0	−1
C4,	$\mu_4 - \mu_5$	0	0	0	1	−1

Table 7.2   Helmert (H) Contrasts for One-way, Five-level Design

Symbolic Contrast Vector	Contrast	Weights				
		μ_1	μ_2	μ_3	μ_4	μ_5
H1,	$\mu_1 - (\mu_2 + \mu_3 + \mu_4 + \mu_5)/4$	1	$-1/4$	$-1/4$	$-1/4$	$-1/4$
H2,	$\mu_2 - (\mu_3 + \mu_4 + \mu_5)/3$	0	1	$-1/3$	$-1/3$	$-1/3$
H3,	$\mu_3 - (\mu_4 + \mu_5)/2$	0	0	1	$-1/2$	$-1/2$
H4,	$\mu_4 - \mu_5$	0	0	0	1	-1

Helmert contrasts are particularly useful when there is some order inherent in the definition of the subgroups. For example, in a study of the personality characteristics of college student activists, Cryns and Finn (1973) defined three groups. The first consisted of non-active students, the second of somewhat-active students who would protest in a non-violent manner, and the third of those who would engage in violent confrontations with police and campus officials. Helmert contrasts were used to compare the personality characteristics of the non-active students with the mean of those in the active participation groups. The non-active group contained the fewest students, and the ways in which their personalities differed from the majority group was one question of interest. The other question in the study concerned the differences between the students who would, and who would not, participate in violent confrontations, and the second Helmert contrast was used to compare means for those two groups.

Helmert contrasts have the convenient property that the weight vectors are orthogonal. This can be seen by inspection of the right hand portion of Table 7.2. Thus, if a sampling design has equal numbers of subjects in the cells, Helmert contrasts may be used to keep the design completely orthogonal. This adds a degree of simplicity, because when contrasts are orthogonal and subclass frequencies are equal, the tests of significance do not depend on the order of the effects, and consideration of orders of eliminating effects is obviated.

It often happens that the contrasts provided by the MULTIVARIANCE program are not the ones required for a particular study. If so, the user may prepare and enter his own set of weight vectors for any factor of a sampling design. The weight vectors are written as in the right hand portions of Tables 7.1 and 7.2. Each vector is punched in F format on a single card, excluding the vector corresponding to the grand mean or constant term. The Symbolic Contrast Vector code used for these "arbitrary contrasts" is the letter L. For a five-level factor, as in Figure 5, where the user has entered his own weight vectors, the contrast codes are L0, and L1, through L4,. The contrasts do not need to be orthogonal, but they cannot be exact linear combinations of one another.

Two other letter codes are used in the examples in preceding chapters. The letter I signifies nested effects of contrasts within one level of the designated factor. The letter I causes the program to generate a column of an identity matrix in place of a contrast among means.

The letter P signifies orthogonal polynomials. P0, is the constant term, and P1, P2, P3, P4, etc., indicate that polynomials of increasing degree are to be fit to the subclass means. P1, tests for a linear trend; P2, tests for a quadratic trend orthogonal to the linear trends; P3, tests cubic trend orthogonal to linear and quadratic trend, and so on.

Orthogonal polynomial weights are only meaningful when there is a defined *metric* underlying the subgroup definition, as, for example, in the longitudinal study where four groups of subjects were measured at grade levels eight, nine, ten, and eleven, respectively. Without such a metric, it is not meaningful to ask whether means lie on a straight line, or on a curve of any degree of complexity. That is, without a quantitative spacing of levels of the independent variable, the groups may be at any distance from one another, and we could always separate them sufficiently so that any monotonic curve of means would fall, say, on a straight line.

While orthogonal polynomials assume that there is a defined underlying metric, the metric is not always evenly spaced. In that case, the orthogonal polynomial weights that are tabled in many statistics books cannot be used, because they always assume an equal-interval metric underlying group differences. It would be unrealistic to attempt to table orthogonal polynomials otherwise. The MULTIVARIANCE program, however, does not use tables of orthogonal polynomial weights. Instead, it generates the weights at run time for any metric. The program provides the user the option to punch and enter the scale underlying the group definitions. For example, we may measure improvement in clinical state after one day of medication, after two days, three days, one week, and one month. For this, the metric would have the numbers 1, 2, 3, 7, and 30. These numbers are read early in the run, and the program generates polynomials as functions of the uneven scale. The Symbolic Contrast Vectors are still written, however, as P0, through P4, for the constant, and linear through quadratic effect, respectively.

The discussion up to this point relates only to a single design factor (i.e., a one-way design). However, all of the same conventions may be used when the factor is one of several in a crossed or nested design. One factor may have simple contrasts, another Helmert, and another use the D codes. It is only necessary to keep the letter code on each part of the Symbolic Contrast Vector cards appropriate to that factor. That is, if we are using simple contrasts for the A factor in a three-way design, Helmert contrasts for the B factor, and deviation (D) contrasts for the C factor, each card would have three letter codes, C, H, and D, in that order. So, for example, the constant code would be C0,H0,D0,; the A main-effect code would be C1,H0,D0, and so on. Several examples are given in the MULTIVARIANCE *User's Guide*.

All of these coding conventions may also be used in a design on the dependent variables. In particular, the same conventions are employed for between-subject and within-subject effects in repeated-measures problems. The latter indicate the manner in which a transformation matrix is constructed.

7.2 ANALYSIS OF COVARIANCE

The linear model for predicting one or more criterion measures from one or more independent variables has a different form depending on the nature of the independent variables. If the predictor variables are *measured* scores, as in the Chapter 2 example, the model is termed the linear regression model. If the independent variables define separate *groups* of subjects, the linear model is that of analysis of variance. Finally, if both types of independent variables are in a single model, the model is termed an analysis-of-covariance model. The group-membership variables are termed factors, as in an analysis-of-variance design, and the measured independent variables are termed *covariates*.

Analysis-of-covariance designs, with one or more independent variables of either type, may be analyzed with the MULTIVARIANCE program. The analysis-of-variance part of the design is described to the program as in the examples of the preceding chapters. The dependent variables and the covariates are read into Phase I as measured variables. That is, the total number of measured variables (criteria plus covariates) is entered in columns 1-4 of the Input Description card. All of the summary data in Phase I are obtained without distinguishing between the two sets of measured scores. Similarly, in Phase II, the analysis-of-variance part of the design is described as in preceding chapters, and effects are estimated for both sets of scores.

The distinction between covariables and dependent variables is made in Phase III. In the first two fields of the Analysis Selection card, the user indicates the number of dependent variables and number of covariates. The covariates are ordered last, following the dependent variables; if not so ordered on the data cards, they may be reordered using the Variable Select Key. By indicating some number of covariates on the Analysis Selection card, the analysis of covariance is obtained automatically. Then at each stage in the analysis of variance, the effects of the covariates are eliminated. The degrees of freedom between groups on the Hypothesis Test card are indicated exactly as they would be for the analysis-of-variance model.

The estimation data from the analysis of covariance include all of the information obtained in a regression analysis. That is, the regression weights of the dependent variables on the covariates, and their standard errors, are obtained, and also the estimated means and mean differences, adjusted for covariates. The within-group correlation matrix and mean squares are also reduced by eliminating variation due to the covariates.

Three sets of significance tests result from the analysis of covariance. The first is the entire set of regression tests. These indicate whether there is any significant relationship between the dependent variables and the covariates after eliminating between-group differences. All of the features of the regression section of the program may be used in making these tests.

Second, if a "1" is inserted in column 40 of the Analysis Selection card, a test of regression parallelism is performed. This is a test that the regression weights of the dependent variables on the covariates are the same for all groups of subjects in the analysis-of-variance design. Parallel regression lines are a necessary assumption in analysis of covariance, because only one regression adjustment is made based on the common within-group variance-covariance matrix. The parallelism test indicates whether this is an appropriate adjustment for all groups of subjects.

The parallelism test may also be of interest in its own right however. For example, in comparing presentation of mathematics in a verbal mode or nonverbal mode, we might be interested in whether the regression of achievement on intelligence is different for the experimental and control groups. (We might expect a lower relationship between verbal intelligence and achievement if the nonverbal approach is effective.)

The third set of significance tests in the covariance analysis are the tests of mean differences, holding constant the covariates. That is, we test whether there are significant differences among subclass means after all possible variation has been attributed to the measured independent variables. We may test this hypothesis for one, or more than one, factor of classification, or for any interaction.

7.3 CANONICAL ANALYSIS

There are three canonical analyses performed by the MULTIVARIANCE program—principal components analysis, canonical correlation analysis, and discriminant function analysis. All are options in the analysis phase (Phase III) of the program, and all operate by finding linear combinations of the measured variables with certain optimal properties. If, for example, there are p criterion measures, $y_1, y_2, ..., y_p$, the canonical analysis attempts to find a new variable y^* defined as a linear combination of the original measures, as in (47):

$$y^* = a_1 y_1 + a_2 y_2 + ... + a_p y_p \qquad (47)$$

In the case of principal components, the weights a_j are obtained such that the variable y^* has maximum variance. A second y^* variable is then obtained such that the variable has maximal variance, subject to the restriction that the second variable is uncorrelated with the first. A third variable is obtained, and the weights are selected in such a way that the third y^* has maximal variance, and is uncorrelated with both of the first two, and so on.

In this manner, a maximal amount of variance in the original y measures is condensed into the smallest possible set of y^* measures. The analysis may be useful when it is necessary to reduce the number of variables, or to give some indication of how many important "factors" there are underlying the original p measures. The principal components analysis is obtained from the MULTIVARIANCE program by selecting the desired set of y measures in Phase III, and entering a "1" or "2" in column 20 of the Analysis Selection card.

The discriminant function analysis operates in a manner similar to the principal components analysis, but with a different criterion for selecting the weights. In discriminant analysis, the weights a_1 to a_p are selected so that y^* has maximum between-group variance, relative to variance within groups. Thus for any factor in the sampling design, weights a_j are selected so that the linear combination of the dependent variables has the maximum univariate F ratio of any linear combination possible. If there are more than two groups of observations, a second linear composite is also obtained, such that the second y^* variable also has the maximum F ratio across groups; however, it is subject to the additional restriction that it maximizes between-group variation on a dimension *orthogonal* to the first. If a third discriminant function is computed, it results in a third y^*, which has maximum between-group variation on a dimension orthogonal to the first two, and so on.

A multivariate test of between-group differences on *all possible y^** variables is identical to the multivariate test for the p original criterion measures. However, tests of significance may also be obtained for the first y^*, the second, and the third, separately. Thus, we may test whether significant differences among groups exist only on a single dimension, which is a linear combination of the original p measures, whether the groups differ on two dimensions, or many.

The test statistics obtained for the discriminant functions are different from those discussed in preceding chapters. The likelihood ratio statistic may be partitioned for separate y^* variables (i.e., discriminant functions), and other test criteria, such as Roy's largest root criterion or Hotelling's trace criterion, may be obtained. The largest root statistic is especially useful because it is sensitive to unidimensional departures from the null hypothesis. The discrimant analysis may be obtained in the MULTIVARIANCE program for each between-group hypothesis. The analysis of variance is run as usual, but, in addition, a "1" is punched in column 24 of the Analysis Selection card.

In the multivariate multiple regression model (i.e., multiple predictors, multiple criteria), the strength of association between the two sets of variables may be estimated through canonical correlation analysis. In this case, y^* variables are defined as linear combinations of the y measures, while x^* variables are defined as linear combinations of the x measures (the independent variables or predictors). That is,

$$x^* = b_1 x_1 + b_2 x_2 + ... + b_q x_q \tag{48}$$

The weights a_j and b_k are chosen so that the resulting linear combinations, y^* and x^*, have maximum correlation in the sample. A second y^* and x^* set of composites is obtained, such that the second composites also have as high a correlation as possible, subject to the restriction that the second y^* and x^* are uncorrelated with the first y^* and x^*, respectively. The canonical correlations are the maximal simple correlations of composites y^* and x^*. There are as many canonical correlations, defining as many unique composites of the variables, as the minimum of the number of variables in the two sets. If we have p outcome measures and q predictors, this is $\min(p,q)$.

A test of significance of all canonical correlations is equivalent to the test of overall association of the two sets of variables demonstrated in Chapter 2. However, approximate tests may also be conducted on individual canonical correlations. These determine whether the association between the two sets of measures is concentrated in a small number of linear functions of the original variables. If it is found, for example, that one linear combination of the y variables and one linear combination of the x variables produce the only significant canonical correlation, then the relationship between the two sets is confined to one dimension. However, this introduces a double complexity in interpretation, for the researcher must "explain" both of the linear composites. This complexity in interpretation frequently limits the practical applicability of canonical correlation analysis.

In a model with one criterion variable and one predictor, the measure of strength of association between the two variables is the simple correlation. When there is one criterion measure and many predictors, the multiple correlation indicates the strength of association. The multiple correlation is the correlation of the outcome measure with a "best" weighted linear composite of the predictors. Likewise, when there are multiple criteria and multiple predictors, the measure of strength of association is the canonical correlation. Unfortunately, a number of canonical correlations may be necessary to describe the association, and the interpretation of each is complex.

The canonical correlation analysis may be obtained from the MULTIVARIANCE program in either regression or covariance models. The appropriate criterion and predictor variables are selected in Phase III, and "1" is entered in column 32 of the Analysis Selection card.

REFERENCES

ANDERSON, T. W. *An introduction to multivariate statistical analysis*. New York: Wiley, 1958.

BETTMAN, J. R. Measuring individual's priorities for national goals: A methodology and empirical example. *Policy Sciences*, 1971, **2**, 373-390.

BLOOM, B. S. *Stability and change in human characteristics*. New York: Wiley, 1964.

BOCK, R. D. Programming univariate and multivariate analysis of variance. *Technometrics*, 1963, **5**, 95-117.

BOCK, R. D. *Multivariate statistical methods in behavioral research*. New York: McGraw-Hill, 1975.

BOCK, R. D. & HAGGARD, E. A. The use of multivariate analysis of variance in behavioral research. In D. Whitla (Ed.), *Handbook of measurement and assessment in the behavioral sciences*. Boston: Addison-Wesley, 1968, 100-142.

BROPHY, J. E. & GOOD, T. L. *Teacher-student relationships: Causes and consequences*. New York: Holt, Rinehart and Winston, 1974.

COLEMAN, J. S., et al. *Equality of educational opportunity*. Washington: U. S. Government Printing Office, 1966.

COMBER, L. C. & KEEVES, J. P. Science education in nineteen countries. *International Studies in Evaluation*. Stockholm: Almqvist & Wiksell, 1973.

CRYNS, A. G. & FINN, J. D. A multivariate analysis of some attitudinal and ideological correlates of student activism. *Sociology of Education*, 1973, **46**, 127-142.

DAVIDSON, M. L. Univariate versus multivariate tests in repeated-measures experiments. *Psychological Bulletin*, 1972, **77**, 446-452.

FINN, J. D. Multivariate analysis of repeated measures data. *Multivariate Behavioral Research*, 1969, **4**, 391-413.

FINN, J. D. Expectations and the educational environment. *Review of Educational Research*, 1972, **42**, 387-410.

FINN, J. D. *User's Guide. MULTIVARIANCE: Univariate and multivariate analysis of variance, covariance, and regression*. Chicago: National Educational Resources, 1976.

FINN, J.D. *A general model for statistical methods in behavioral research*. New York: Holt, Rinehart and Winston, 1974.

HARRIS, C. W. (Ed.). *Problems in measuring change*. Madison: University of Wisconsin Press, 1963.

HARRISON, F. I. Aspirations as related to school performance and socio-economic status. *Sociometry*, 1969, **32**, 70-79.

HUMMEL, T. J. & SLIGO, J. R. Empirical comparison of univariate and multivariate analysis of variance procedures. *Psychological Bulletin*, 1971, **76**, 49-57.

HUSEN, T., et al. *Svensk skola i internationell belysning I. Natur-orienterande amnen*. Stockholm: Almqvist & Wiksell, 1973.

JACKSON, P. W. *Life in classrooms*. New York: Holt, Rinehart and Winston, 1968.

JENCKS, C., et al. *Inequality: A reassessment of the effect of family and schooling in America*. New York: Basic Books, 1972.

LINDQUIST, E. F. *Design and analysis of experiments in psychology and education*. Boston: Houghton Mifflin Co., 1953.

MATTSSON, I. *Input for MULTIVARIANCE from SPSS (Statistical Package for Social Sciences)*. Chicago: National Educational Resources, 1974.

McCALL, R. B. & APPLEBAUM, M. I. Bias in the analysis of repeated-measures design: Some alternative approaches. *Child Development*, 1973, **44**, 401-415.

MORRISON, D. F. *Multivariate analysis*. New York: McGraw-Hill, 1967.

POOR, D. D. S. Analysis of variance for repeated measures designs: Two approaches. *Psychological Bulletin*, 1973, **80**, 204-209.

PURVES, A. C. Literature education in ten countries. *International Studies in Evaluation II*. Stockholm: Almqvist & Wiksell, 1973.

ROY, S. N. & BARGMANN, R. E. Tests of multiple independence and the associated confidence bounds. *Annals of Mathematical Statistics*, 1958, **29**, 491-503.

SNOW, R. E. Representative and quasi-representative designs for research on teaching. *Review of Educational Research*, 1974, **44**, 265-292.

TATSUOKA, M. M. *Multivarate analysis: Techniques for educational and psychological research*. New York: Wiley, 1971.

THORNDIKE, R. L. Reading comprehension education in fifteen countries. *International Studies in Evaluation III*. New York: Halstead Press, Wiley, 1973.

Index

136

138